America's Best

A NATIONAL COMMUNITY COOKBOOK

TO BENEFIT THE U.S. SKI TEAM

America's Best

A NATIONAL COMMUNITY COOKBOOK

TO BENEFIT THE U.S. SKI TEAM

WORKMAN PUBLISHING NEW YORK

Library of Congress Cataloging in Publication Data
Main entry under title:

America's best.

   "To benefit the U.S. Ski Team."
   Includes index.
   1. Cookery, American.   I. United States Ski Team.
TX715.A547   1983   641.5973   83-40037
ISBN 0-89480-593-2 (pbk.)

Cover photograph by Robert Grant
Illustrations by Susan Gaber
Book design by Paul Hanson

Workman Publishing Company, Inc.
1 West 39th Street
New York, N.Y. 10018

Manufactured in the United States of America
First printing September 1983

10   9   8   7   6   5   4   3   2   1

Acknowledgments

America's Best is not only a collection of some of the most outstanding recipes this country has to offer, but it represents the unity and the support of America's ski team by corporations and individuals across the nation.

We wish to thank the following U.S. Ski Team gold, silver, and bronze medal sponsors and team members for their enthusiasm and financial support, so vital to the success of this project.

GOLD MEDALISTS
The American Lamb Council
First National Bank of Englewood
Skiing magazine
The Snowmass Co.

SILVER MEDALISTS
C. L. Biederman Enterprises

BRONZE MEDALISTS
AIRCOA
Adolph Coors Co.
AMS Realstar
Bonne Bell, Inc.
Bosworth & Slivka, P.C.
Denver Orthopedic Clinic, P.C.
Robert P. Mack, M.D.
Steamboat Ski Corp.

SUPPORT TEAM MEMBERS
Athalon Products, Ltd.
Food for Thought, Ann Kennedy
Hesdorfer-Hesse Ltd.
High Country Printing
Swix Sport
Arthur Ellison, M.D.
George M. Hewson, M.D.
Grady L. Jeter, M.D., Inc.
Inez Aimee

Many thanks for the enthusiasm, direction, counsel, or other direct support to the following: Warren Sheridan; Richard Steckel; Candi Rogers; Nina Macheel; Glen Boat; Bea Reichel; Steve Knowlton; Hank Kashiwa; Peggy Lamm and Colorado Ski Country, U.S.A.; Kurt Johnston; Claudia Eisenberg; and Jacki Sorenson's Aerobic Dancing.

In addition to the above—and among the hundreds who have been a part of this project—special thanks go to the people all over America who shared their favorite recipes. Personal thanks go to Robert Mack and to Dick and Gay Steadman, who first heard of the cookbook idea and encouraged it; to the staff and board of trustees of the United States Ski Educational Foundation for their continued support and active involvement; to Art Bosworth, who provided invaluable counsel; and to the staff at Workman Publishing Company, Inc., who have helped with *America's Best*. Above it all, special thanks to Charlie Biederman, whose humor, counsel, creativity, and support made this all possible.

About This Book

RECIPE
CLASSIFICATIONS

 EASY

 MORE
DIFFICULT

 MOST
DIFFICULT

America's Best is a national community cookbook, perhaps the first of its kind. A nationwide effort has created this collection of favorite all-American recipes in the support of our cause: the U.S. Ski Team. The Ski Team is funded entirely through private and corporate contributions, and its great achievements in recent years validate its support by the American public.

America's Best is a collection of more than four hundred recipes selected from over four thousand submitted from across the country. The recipe contributions, while not necessarily original or ethnically authentic, are regional favorites old and new. Each recipe in the book has been enthusiastically endorsed by one of fourteen separate testing teams to represent the best of its kind. Every recipe has undergone rigorous testing to ensure outstanding results in any kitchen.

For the convenience of all cooks, the degree of difficulty of each recipe is indicated by the use of these designation marks: circle = easy; square = more difficult; diamond = most difficult. These classifications relate to the ease rather than the time of preparation.

Fresh ingredients are called for wherever possible so that each recipe can be enjoyed at its flavorful best. By using fresh, natural products, you can offer your guests and your family a true taste of *America's Best*.

The U.S. Ski Team Cookbook Committee

Cookbook Committee

PROJECT CHAIRMAN
Patty Mack
EDITOR-IN-CHIEF
Jaydee Boat
MANAGING EDITOR
Regina Biederman

SECTION CHAIRMEN
Appetizers: Sue Mason, Andrea Shannon
Soups: June Boswick
Brunch Specialties: Pat Cotsworth
Meats: Sharon Wilkinson
Fish and Poultry: Sally Clayton
Salads: Jerry Cunningham, Kris Ryall
Pasta: Mary Greco
Vegetables: Helen Powell
Breads: Becky Perry
Make-Ahead Favorites: Mimi Nelson, Nancy Wiedel
Desserts: Mary Bell
Index: Martha Smith

EDITORIAL ASSISTANTS
Nicholas Howe, Michele Hughes, Elizabeth Mack, Nancy Steller

REGIONAL COORDINATORS
Cathy Allen *(Maine)*, Kathy Allen *(Missouri)*, Diane Anderson *(Steamboat Springs, Colorado)*, Irene Block *(Pennsylvania)*, Jane Boland *(Massachusetts)*, Marie Bowes *(Steamboat Springs, Colorado)*, Angela Browne *(Kansas)*, Babs Ellison *(Massachusetts)*, Martha Feagin *(Wyoming)*, Linda Hardee *(Virginia)*, Sue Henning (Kansas), Wallis Hewson *(Arizona)*, Janice Hutchins *(Mississippi)*, Charlotte Kalinna *(Aspen, Colorado)*, Jeanne Kretzler *(Washington)*, Rosemary Larson *(Oregon)*, Puddy Leidholt *(Denver, Colorado)*, Alice Lewis *(Steamboat Springs, Colorado)*, Martha Madsen *(Aspen, Colorado)*, Jim McCaleb *(Massachusetts, Rhode Island, Connecticut)*, Anna McIntyre *(New Hampshire)*, Jeanne Myers *(Aspen, Colorado)*, Eloise Newdorp *(Washington, D.C.)*, Phyllis Saer *(Louisiana)*, Diann Scaravilli *(Ohio)*, Gay Steadman *(California)*, K. K. Sullivan *(Ohio)*, Gaye Tullos *(Texas)*

Contents

About This Book 7

First Course Appetizers 15
Hot Appetizers 18
Cold Appetizers 27
Dips 30
Pastry Appetizers 32
Miscellaneous 33

APPETIZERS
13

Hot Cream Soups 37
Cold Cream Soups 44
Main Dish Soups 47
Clear and Vegetable Soups 56
Seafood Soups 60

SOUPS
35

BRUNCH SPECIALTIES 63

Fruit Dishes 65
Eggs and Cheese Dishes 67
Pancakes, Waffles & French Toast 77
Meat Dishes 81
Other Specialties 82

SALADS 87

Main Dish Salads 89
Green Salads 94
Potato and Rice Salads 98
Vegetable Salads 101
Molded Salads 102
Salad Dressings 105

MEATS 109

Meat Sauces and Marinades 111
Beef Dishes 115
Veal Dishes 120
Pork Dishes 123
Lamb Dishes 129
Game Dishes 132

POULTRY
135

Chicken Breasts *137*
Cut-up Chicken *141*
Chicken Dishes *146*
Chicken Casseroles *149*
Game Bird Dishes *154*

SEAFOOD
157

Fish Dishes *159*
Shellfish Dishes *164*
Seafood Combinations *170*

PASTA
175

Homemade Pasta *177*
Pasta Sauces *178*
Pasta Salads *182*
Pasta with Seafood *186*
Pasta Casseroles *188*
Filled Pasta *193*
Unexpected Pasta Dishes *198*

VEGETABLES
199

Vegetables *201*
Vegetarian Main Dishes *220*

BREADS
223

Yeast Breads *225*

Quick Breads *232*

Coffee Cakes *237*

Biscuits and Muffins *241*

Variety Breads *245*

MAKE-AHEAD
FAVORITES
249

Sandwiches *251*

Salads *257*

Other Picnic Fare *260*

DESSERTS
267

Fruit Desserts *269*

Pies *273*

Ice Cream and Sherbets *275*

Cookies and Bars *278*

Pastry *283*

Tortes and Cakes *284*

Chilled Desserts *295*

Puddings *297*

Frozen Desserts *299*

Special Sweets *302*

APPENDIXES
305

Contributors *307*

Index *311*

Appetizers

San Francisco Egg Rolls

SECTION CHAIRMEN
Sue Mason
Andrea Shannon

TESTERS
Judy Anderson
Lark and Becky Anderson
Steve and Colleen Baker
Patty Barnard
Cindy Bershof
Chuck and Valerie Blood
Nonnie Bolton
Sharyn Bolton-Miazga
Don and Cindy Butterfield
Bill and Pat Cotsworth
Jean Easley
Steve and Judy Fallin
Stewart and Priscilla Fry
Bob and Kris Gary
Greg and Betty Gulich
Steve and Ann Hall
Karen Heimel
Jeanne Mastrandrea
Cozette Matthews
Sandy Ross McGuire
Frank and Judy Meeks
Liz Mehrtens
Marty Nemecek
Peg Olson
Ted and Lynn Paster
Donna Piehler
Betty Riddell
Jeannette Rieck
Dave and Helen Robinette
Tom and Mary Jo Rodeno
Jerry and Karen Schmidt
Dal Shannon
Dick and Arlene Spinelli
Dee Ann Spivak
Roxie Turk
Janet and Rick Weiner

SERVES 6 AS A FIRST COURSE

Shrimp and Avocado with Carnival Sauce

Cut pita loaves in half lengthwise, then into pie-shaped thirds. Toast the triangles and serve instead of crackers.

3 egg yolks, at room temperature
1½ teaspoons dry mustard
¼ cup wine vinegar or sherry wine vinegar
¼ cup Cognac
½ cup vegetable oil
½ cup light olive oil
2 tablespoons prepared horseradish
2 tablespoons minced celery
1 tablespoon chopped chives
1 tablespoon chopped fresh parsley
2 tablespoons minced shallot or green onion
2 tablespoons lemon juice
⅓ cup chili sauce
salt and freshly ground black pepper to taste
3 medium avocados
1 pound medium shrimp, cooked, shelled, and deveined

Place the egg yolks in a bowl with the dry mustard and vinegar. Whisk until well combined, at least 1 minute. Add the remaining ingredients, except the avocados and shrimp, and whisk to blend well. Set aside (can be made ahead several hours and refrigerated).

Peel and pit the avocados. Slice the avocados into ½-inch thick slices or make balls with a melon baller. Divide the avocado slices or balls among 6 small gratin dishes. Top with the shrimp. Whisk the sauce to reblend and pour over the shrimp. Serve cold.

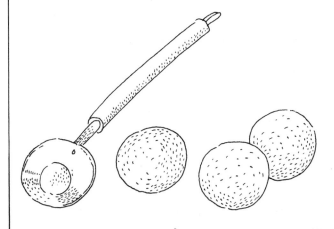

SERVES 8 AS A FIRST COURSE

Seattle Seafood Mélange

4 tablespoons butter
3 cloves garlic, minced
1 tablespoon chopped fresh parsley
¼ cup dry vermouth
3 tablespoons lemon juice
1 teaspoon salt
½ teaspoon freshly ground black pepper
½ pound whole mushrooms
1 pound medium-large shrimp, shelled and deveined
½ pound bay scallops

Melt the butter in a large stainless-steel skillet. Add the garlic, parsley, vermouth, lemon juice, salt, pepper, and mushrooms. Bring to a boil over high heat. Reduce the heat and simmer for 5 minutes, stirring frequently.

Add the shrimp and cook and stir for 2 minutes. Add the scallops and cook 2 minutes more, or until the scallops are white.

With a slotted spoon, remove the mushrooms, shrimp, and scallops to heated serving dishes and keep warm.

Over high heat, reduce the sauce in the skillet to ¾ cup. Divide the sauce evenly among the dishes and serve.

SERVES 6 AS A FIRST COURSE

Cheesy Mussels with Herbs

2 quarts scrubbed and soaked mussels (see page 166)
2 tablespoons minced chives
2 tablespoons minced fresh dill
2 tablespoons butter, melted
3 cups grated Gouda cheese (12 ounces)

Steam the mussels in water until open, about 2 minutes. Discard any that do not open.

Preheat the broiler.

Break off and discard the top shells from the mussels and arrange the mussels in the bottom shells in one layer in 6 gratin dishes.

In a small bowl, combine the chives, dill, and butter and spoon the mixture over the mussels.

Sprinkle the mussels with the cheese and broil about 4 inches from the heat for 5 minutes, or until the cheese is melted and golden.

The Olympic winter games of 1924, in Chamonix, the 1928 winter games, St. Moritz, Switzerland, and the 1932 winter games at Lake Placid, New York, were for men only, and consisted of Nordic events.

SERVES 6 TO 8 AS A FIRST COURSE

Mussels are enjoying a surge of popularity in America. They have for generations been known to Europeans as the "oyster of the poor" because of their quality and inexpensive price.

Mussels Verde

4 dozen mussels, scrubbed and soaked (see page 166)
¼ cup minced garlic
10 ounces fresh spinach, washed, trimmed, cooked, and drained
3 cups chopped fresh basil (do not use dried)
juice of 1 lemon
1 teaspoon dried dill weed
¼ cup minced fresh parsley
½ teaspoon salt
¾ to 1 cup mayonnaise

GARNISH:
roasted red peppers
parsley sprigs

Place the mussels in a large kettle with the garlic and 1 inch of water. Cover and bring to a boil, then cook about 2 minutes, or until the mussels open. Remove mussels with a slotted spoon and discard unopened mussels. Break off the empty shell and discard. Strain the cooking water through a fine sieve and save the garlic. Distribute the garlic evenly on the mussels. Place the mussels on a baking sheet and refrigerate.

In a food processor, purée the spinach, basil, lemon juice, dill, parsley, and salt. Add only enough mayonnaise to make a thick sauce.

At serving time, place a spoonful of sauce on each mussel. Serve garnished with peppers and parsley.

SERVES 6 AS A FIRST COURSE

Caviar-Stuffed New Potatoes

18 to 24 tiny, uniform new potatoes
¼ cup sour cream
2 tablespoons golden American caviar

Bake or steam the unpeeled potatoes until tender.

Remove a small scoop of potato flesh from the top of each potato, using the tip of a spoon.

Place a small dollop of sour cream in the indentation and garnish with caviar. Serve hot, 3 to 4 per person as a first course.

MAKES 2 DOZEN

Dim sum may be frozen, before or after baking. Bake uncooked dim sum at 400° F. for 20 minutes. Bake cooked dim sum at 400° F. for 10 minutes.

Pork Dim Sum

½ pound ground lean pork
2 tablespoons soy sauce
1 tablespoon cornstarch
1 tablespoon minced green onion
2 teaspoons dry sherry
½ teaspoon grated fresh ginger root
2 cups all-purpose flour
⅔ cup vegetable shortening
4 to 5 tablespoons ice water
1 egg
1 tablespoon water

Preheat the oven to 400° F.

In a medium bowl, stir together the ground pork, soy sauce, cornstarch, green onion, sherry, and ginger root.

In another bowl, combine the flour and shortening until crumbly. Sprinkle ice water over the mixture while tossing to blend well. Press the dough firmly into 2 balls with hands.

On a lightly floured surface, roll out one ball of dough to ¹⁄₁₆-inch thickness. Cut out circles with a 3-inch round cookie cutter. Knead scraps into remaining dough, then roll and cut as before.

Place about 1 heaping teaspoon of filling in the center of each circle. Fold over into a crescent shape and seal edges tightly with a fork. Place the crescents on an ungreased cookie sheet and pierce each with a fork. Repeat with the remaining ball of dough.

Beat the egg with water. Brush tops of the puffs with the egg mixture. Bake 20 minutes, or until lightly browned.

MAKES 45 EGG ROLLS

To shred, cut the food into strips about ¼ inch wide and 1 to 2 inches long.

San Francisco Egg Rolls

MARINADE FOR PORK AND CHICKEN:
1 teaspoon salt
1 tablespoon light soy sauce
1 teaspoon rice wine or dry sherry
1 teaspoon cornstarch

MARINADE FOR SHRIMP:
¼ teaspoon salt
¼ teaspoon pepper
¼ teaspoon cornstarch
¼ teaspoon rice wine or dry sherry

SAUCE:
2 teaspoons light soy sauce
1 cup water (½ cup if using Chinese cabbage)
3 tablespoons cornstarch
1 tablespoon oyster sauce

FILLING:
1½ pounds pork loin, chicken breast, raw shrimp, or a combination of these, shredded
4 tablespoons vegetable oil
1 green onion with top, shredded
4 black Chinese mushrooms, soaked until soft, then shredded
6 ounces bamboo shoots, shredded
1 pound Chinese cabbage or regular cabbage, shredded
2 stalks celery, shredded
1 pound bean sprouts
salt and freshly ground pepper to taste
2 tablespoons light soy sauce

45 egg roll skins
2 cups oil for deep frying

Combine the marinade and sauce ingredients, each in separate bowls. Blend well. Marinate the meat and/or shrimp for about 15 minutes.

Heat 2 tablespoons of the oil in a wok. Stir-fry the onion for a few seconds, then add the mushrooms, bamboo shoots, cabbage, celery, and bean sprouts. Cook 5 minutes, stirring. Cover the wok and let the vegetables steam for another 5 minutes. Add salt and pepper and light soy sauce. Set aside.

Wash the wok. Heat 2 tablespoons oil in the wok. Stir-fry the meat and shrimp for a few minutes until they change color. Add the cooked vegetables and cook for 5 minutes. Make a well in the center of the wok and add the sauce. Stir until thickened. Stir the sauce into the vegetables and meat. Cool in the refrigerator several hours or overnight.

Lay an egg roll skin out so that it is a diamond shape in front of you. Place about ¼ cup of the filling just below the center point. Bring the bottom corner up and around the filling. Brush the edges of the skin with water or a beaten egg. Bring the side corners to the center over the filling. Roll toward the top edge. Seal by pressing together.

Heat the 2 cups oil in a large skillet. Deep-fry the egg rolls, a few at a time, until a lightly golden brown, about 3 minutes. (Can be frozen after cooking. Reheat, frozen, at 425° F. for 20 minutes.)

The World Cup circuit began with an evening of talk in a Portillo, Chile, hotel room in 1966. Honore Bonnet, architect of the great French team of the 1960s, Serge Lang, a leading French ski journalist, and Bob Beattie, coach of the U.S. team, wanted an annual, season-long race circuit to augment the quadrennial Olympic and world championship format. That evening of talk led to the first World Cup season in 1967.

MAKES 24 PIECES

If gyoza skins are unavailable, use wonton wrappers cut into circles.

Pot Stickers

1 pound ground lean pork
1 large clove garlic, minced
½ to 1 carrot, peeled and shredded
1 egg
1 package gyoza skins
¼ cup vegetable oil

OPTIONAL:
1 egg, beaten
Scallion Sauce (recipe follows)

Mix the pork, garlic, carrot, and egg together in a bowl. Put approximately ½ teaspoon of the mixture in the middle of the gyoza skin and seal the edges by brushing water or beaten egg around the edges and pressing together.

Heat the oil in a large, covered skillet. Place pot stickers in the hot oil and cook for 2 to 3 minutes over medium heat. Add a few tablespoons of water, cover, and steam over low heat for 25 to 30 minutes, adding more water if necessary. The bottom of the pot stickers will be dark brown, the top dumpling-like.

Serve with hot Scallion Sauce for dipping.

SCALLION SAUCE:
3 to 4 green onions, chopped
3 to 4 cloves garlic, minced
5 tablespoons soy sauce
2 tablespoons vegetable oil
¼ cup granulated sugar
2 tablespoons dry sherry
⅛ teaspoon freshly ground black pepper

Combine all the ingredients in a small saucepan and simmer for 5 minutes. Serve warm.

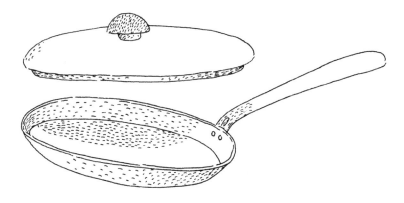

Atlantic City Puffs

MAKES 32 TRIANGLES

Fresh ginger root has a pungent, hot flavor and can be stored for weeks immersed in sherry in a covered glass container or ginger jar.

2 tablespoons olive oil
1 medium onion, minced
¼ pound ground beef round
3 cloves garlic, minced
2 teaspoons ground coriander
2 teaspoons chili powder
1 tablespoon grated fresh ginger root
½ teaspoon ground cumin
2 tart apples, peeled, cored, and chopped
½ cup water
1 teaspoon salt
1 pound frozen puff pastry
1 egg, beaten

Heat the oil in a skillet and add the onion, beef, garlic, coriander, chili powder, ginger root, and cumin. Sauté until the onion is tender and the beef is browned, about 10 minutes.

Stir in the apples, water, and salt. Reduce the heat and simmer until the apple is soft, about 20 minutes. Stir to mash the apple. Cool.

Preheat the oven to 400° F.

Use one piece of pastry at a time and roll out into a 12-inch square. Cut into 3-inch squares. Place a rounded teaspoonful of filling in the center of each square. Moisten the edges with water. Fold the squares diagonally in half to enclose the filling. Press to seal; press edges with the tines of a fork (can be frozen at this point).

Brush the tops of the puffs with beaten egg, pierce the tops with a fork, and bake on an ungreased cookie sheet for 15 minutes. Serve hot.

Oklahoma Chili Dip

MAKES 6 TO 7 CUPS

4 cups prepared chili with meat (see page 50)
½ pound processed American or Cheddar cheese, grated
1 cup prepared green chilies with tomatoes

OPTIONAL:
1 to 2 tablespoons chili powder

Combine all the ingredients in a large saucepan and heat, stirring, until the cheese is incorporated. Serve hot, with tortilla chips.

MAKES 40
WONTONS

Wontons Filled with Pork and Shrimp

3 cups plus 2 tablespoons peanut oil
½ pound freshly ground lean pork
1 clove garlic, minced
½ pound shrimp, shelled, deveined, and finely chopped
2 cups finely chopped bok choy
1 cup chopped fresh mushrooms
½ cup minced green onion
½ cup minced celery
½ cup chopped fresh or canned water chestnuts
2 tablespoons soy sauce
1 tablespoon dry sherry
½ teaspoon granulated sugar
2 teaspoons cornstarch dissolved in 1 tablespoon water
40 wonton skins
Plum Sauce (see page 34)

Heat a wok or skillet over high heat for 30 seconds. Pour in the 2 tablespoons oil, swirl it around, and add the pork and garlic. Stir-fry for 1 minute. Add the shrimp and stir-fry for 30 seconds. Add the vegetables. Stir-fry for 2 to 3 minutes more. Add the soy sauce, sherry, sugar, and cornstarch. Cook until thickened, then transfer to a bowl to cool.

Place 1½ teaspoons of the filling in the center of each wonton wrapper. With a finger dipped in water, moisten the edges of the wrapper. Bring one corner up over the filling to the opposite corner, but fold the wrapper at an angle so that two overlapping triangles are formed, with their points side by side and about ½ inch apart. Pull the two bottom corners of the folded triangle forward and below the folded edge so that they meet one another and slightly overlap. Moisten one end with a finger dipped in water and pinch the two ends firmly together. As each wonton is finished, place it on a plate and cover the wontons with a towel.

Heat 3 cups of peanut oil in a wok over high heat to 375° F.

Deep-fry the wontons, a few at a time and without crowding, for 2 minutes, or until golden. Transfer them to paper toweling to drain. Serve with Plum Sauce.

Fried wontons can be kept warm for 1 hour in a 250° F. oven, reheated for 5 minutes in a 450° F. oven, or heated frozen (without thawing) in a 350° F. oven for about 15 minutes.

**MAKES
2 LOAVES**

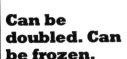

**Can be
doubled. Can
be frozen.**

Poppy Seed Bacon Bread

1 loaf French bread (not baguette)
½ cup butter
1 medium onion, minced
4 to 5 ounces mushrooms, minced
2 tablespoons poppy seeds
¼ cup prepared spicy brown mustard
¾ pound Swiss cheese, sliced
8 slices bacon, uncooked

Preheat the oven to 350° F.

Trim the crust from the top and sides of the loaf. Slice the loaf lengthwise to make 2 pieces. Cut each piece at ½-inch intervals almost to the bottom.

Melt the butter in a medium skillet and sauté the onions for 5 minutes over medium heat. Add the mushrooms and sauté 2 minutes more. Add the poppy seeds and mustard and stir to blend well.

Cut the cheese slices to fit the bread. Spread a heaping teaspoonful of the onion-mushroom mixture between the cuts in the bread. Place a cheese slice between the cuts in the bread. Lay the bacon on top of the bread in a criss-cross manner.

Bake on a baking sheet for 30 minutes, or until the bacon is crisp and the cheese is melted.

SERVES 12

Mexican Layered Dip

2 cans (16 ounces each) refried beans
2 cans (4 ounces each) chopped green chilies
3 medium tomatoes, peeled, seeded, chopped, and drained
1 cup chopped green onion
2 cups grated Cheddar cheese (8 ounces)

GARNISH:
1 cup guacamole
½ cup sour cream

Preheat the oven to 375° F.

On a large shallow ovenproof serving dish, layer the beans, green chilies, tomatoes, onion, and cheese. Bake for 20 minutes, or until the cheese is bubbly.

Top with dollops of guacamole and sour cream. Serve with tortilla chips.

SERVES 12

Double cream cheeses such as Camembert and Brie should not be served chilled. Let stand at room temperature until softened before serving.

Almond Brie

1 12-inch round of Brie, all paper wrap removed
⅓ cup confectioner's sugar, or as needed
⅓ cup sliced almonds, or as needed

Preheat the broiler to 450° F.

Place the cheese on a broiler rack. Spread the sugar evenly over the cheese with a spatula. Sprinkle the almonds on top of the sugar. (The amount of sugar and almonds needed will vary with the size of the cheese round.)

Place the cheese under the broiler just until the sugar melts and starts to bubble, about 1 to 1½ minutes.

Serve with plain, unseasoned crackers such as water biscuits, or with fresh apple or pear wedges.

MAKES 16 PIECES

Pepperoni Puff

1 sheet (8 ounces) frozen puff pastry, thawed
3 cups Monterey Jack hot pepper cheese (12 ounces)
4 to 6 ounces sliced pepperoni

Preheat the oven to 425° F.

Roll out the pastry into a 14-inch circle or rectangle and place on a pizza tray or cookie sheet. Pinch the pastry together around the edges to form a rim to hold in the cheese. Sprinkle the pastry thickly with the cheese. Arrange the pepperoni slices over all.

Bake for 12 to 15 minutes, or until the crust is light brown and the cheese is bubbly. Cool for 5 minutes before cutting into wedges.

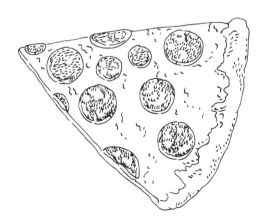

MAKES 30

Crab Rangoon

2 packages (8 ounces each) cream cheese, softened
3 tablespoons milk
4 tablespoons freshly grated Parmesan cheese
¼ teaspoon garlic powder
½ pound crabmeat
1 pound wonton skins
vegetable oil

Beat the cream cheese and milk together until creamy. Add the cheese, garlic powder, and crabmeat.

Put ¾ teaspoon of the mixture in the center of a wonton skin. Put enough water on fingers to moisten the corners of the wonton skin. Pinch them together to form a triangle. Repeat until all the wonton skins and filling are used.

Heat the oil to 375° F. in a large skillet and deep-fry the wontons until crisp and brown, about 2 to 3 minutes. Serve with Plum Sauce (see page 34) or Sweet Hot Mustard (see page 33).

SERVES 16

Bacon-Wrapped Scallops

2 tablespoons brandy
½ teaspoon granulated sugar
1½ pounds large sea scallops, cut in half
8 fresh or canned water chestnuts, drained if canned, cut in half
4 green onions, cut into 1-inch pieces
8 slices bacon, cut in half

Combine the brandy and sugar in a bowl and marinate the scallops for 1 hour.

Preheat the broiler.

Stack 1 scallop piece, 1 piece water chestnut, and 1 green onion piece and wrap the stack with a bacon strip. Secure with a wooden pick. Repeat.

Broil for 6 to 7 minutes, turning once, or until the bacon is crisply cooked but not crumbly. Serve immediately.

US SKI TEAM The 1932 winter games in Lake Placid, New York, was the first time the Olympic winter games were held off the European continent.

MAKES 48
PIECES

Sauternes is a sweet, flower-scented, golden French wine. The American Sauterne is made from a variety of grapes and may be sweet or dry. (An alternative to Sauternes would be a German Trockenbeer-enauslese.)

Sesame Chicken Wings

3 cups soy sauce
1 teaspoon ground ginger
1 cup (packed) brown sugar
2 cups Sauternes
3 cloves garlic, crushed
4 dozen chicken wing drumettes (the meaty half)
1 cup sesame seeds

Combine the soy sauce, ginger, brown sugar, wine, and garlic in a large saucepan. Bring to a boil, then reduce the heat and simmer for 30 minutes.

Add the chicken drumettes and simmer, stirring occasionally, for 15 minutes. Remove the drumettes with a slotted spoon to a rack. Sprinkle with sesame seeds. Place the wings on baking sheets, cover with foil, and refrigerate until 30 minutes before serving time.

Preheat the oven to 400° F.

Bake the drumettes for 15 minutes, or until hot and crispy. Serve immediately.

MAKES 36
PIECES

Kanapali Crab Bites

½ pound ground lean pork
½ pound crabmeat, minced
1 egg, beaten
1 green onion, minced
1 tablespoon minced ginger root
1 clove garlic, crushed
1 tablespoon soy sauce
¾ cup minced water chestnuts
½ teaspoon salt

Preheat the oven to 350° F.

In a large bowl, combine the pork, crabmeat, egg, green onion, ginger root, garlic, soy sauce, water chestnuts, and salt. Mix well and shape into small balls.

Place on a greased jelly-roll pan and bake for 20 minutes, or until cooked through.

Serve with dipping sauces, such as Plum Sauce (see page 34) or Sweet Hot Mustard Sauce (see page 33).

MAKES 30 TO 40 PIECES

Gorgonzola-Stuffed Mushrooms

½ pound Gorgonzola cheese
½ cup butter, softened
2 tablespoons minced fresh parsley
½ cup chopped walnuts
30 to 40 medium fresh mushroom caps, wiped clean with paper toweling

Cream together the Gorgonzola and butter. Add the parsley and walnuts. Mound the mixture by small spoonsful on the mushroom caps, cover with plastic wrap and chill until serving time.

MAKES 3 CUPS

Chicken Liver Mousseline with Apples

1 medium onion, chopped
½ cup butter
½ pound chicken livers
2 packages (3 ounces each) cream cheese, softened
1 hard-cooked egg
¼ cup minced fresh parsley
salt and freshly ground black pepper to taste
mayonnaise
4 tart apples, unpeeled, but cored, sliced

GARNISH:
lettuce leaves

Sauté the onions in the butter for 2 to 3 minutes over medium heat. Add the chicken livers and sauté until the onion is transparent and the livers are cooked through, about 6 to 7 minutes.

Place the liver mixture in a food processor. Add the remaining ingredients except the apples and process until smooth and light. Pour the mixture into a mold or bowl oiled with mayonnaise. Refrigerate for 4 hours or overnight.

To serve, unmold the mousseline onto a lettuce-lined platter and surround with apple slices. Spread the mousseline on the apple slices to eat.

MAKES 64
PIECES

Cheese-Filled Tortillas

2 packages (8 ounces each) cream cheese, softened
6 ounces chopped ripe olives, drained
1 can (7 ounces) diced green chilies, drained
1 small yellow onion, diced
1 package flour tortillas (about 8 tortillas)

In a large bowl, combine the cream cheese, olives, chilies, and onion. Mix well.

Spread about ⅓ cup of the cheese mixture to within ¼ inch of the edges of each tortilla. Roll tightly. Chill until serving time, at least 2 hours. Cut into 8 pieces. The ends may be cut off for a more attractive presentation.

MAKES 50 TO
60 PIECES

A large white or Oriental-design platter is a good backdrop for crisp, colorful vegetables. Serve with a fresh flower blossom as a counterpoint.

Filled Snow Peas

50 to 60 fresh snow peas
½ pound cream cheese mixed with minced fresh vegetables
    or chopped pecans and olives or any soft spiced cheese

Drop the snow peas into 3 quarts boiling water to blanch. Remove after 15 seconds. Drain. Immediately place the peas in cold water to stop cooking and set the color. If necessary, change the water to keep it cold. Drain thoroughly.

Remove the string from the peas and cut off the stem end.

Carefully split the straight side of the peas. Pipe the cheese into the peas using a pastry bag with a small tip, or spread with a small spatula (which takes much more time).

Arrange decoratively on a china platter. Cover with plastic wrap and chill for up to 4 hours before serving.

MAKES 24
PIECES

Ham Mousse-Stuffed Eggs

1 cup ham pieces, trimmed of fat (can use leftover baked
    ham or prosciutto)
12 hard-cooked eggs, peeled and cut in half lengthwise
4 tablespoons butter, softened
2 tablespoons Dijon mustard
1 to 1¼ cups mayonnaise
dash hot pepper sauce

Process the ham in a food processor until ground. Add the egg yolks and process until crumbly.

Add the butter, mustard, and half the mayonnaise. Process until smooth, adding as much mayonnaise as needed to produce a fluffy, light consistency.

Season to taste with hot pepper sauce.

Fill the egg white halves, mounding the mousse in the center. Chill for 2 hours or overnight, covered with plastic wrap.

Avocado Mold with Caviar

SERVES 8

½ cup plus 1 tablespoon mayonnaise
2 tablespoons unflavored gelatin
¼ cup white wine vinegar
¼ cup water
½ cup diced white onion (Vidalia preferred)
2 cups sour cream
2 large ripe avocados, peeled
4 hard-cooked eggs
½ cup diced green onion with tops
2 ounces black caviar (the best you can afford)

GARNISH:
lettuce leaves

Oil a 1-quart mold with the 1 tablespoon mayonnaise. Set aside.

Soften the gelatin in the vinegar and water in a small saucepan. Heat over low heat until the gelatin is dissolved. Set aside.

In a small bowl, combine the diced onion, sour cream, and one third of the dissolved gelatin. Pour into the prepared mold and chill until set.

Mash or purée the avocado and combine with ¼ cup of mayonnaise and half the remaining gelatin mixture. Blend well and pour over the sour cream layer. Chill until set.

Dice the hard-cooked eggs and combine with ¼ cup of mayonnaise, green onions, and remaining gelatin mixture. Pour over the avocado layer and chill for 2 hours, or until set.

Unmold on a lettuce-lined platter and garnish with caviar. Serve with Melba toast rounds.

Springfield Dip

MAKES 3 CUPS

This can also be used as a dressing for crisp salad greens.

1 medium onion, cut into pieces
1 teaspoon freshly ground black pepper
1 can (2 ounces) anchovies with capers, undrained
1 clove garlic
¼ cup prepared mustard
1½ cups vegetable oil
2 eggs
salt to taste

In a food processor or blender, combine the onion, pepper, anchovies, garlic, mustard, and ½ cup of the oil. Process until well blended.

Add the eggs and process for 1 minute. Add the remaining oil and blend well. Season to taste with salt. Serve with crudités.

Summer Spread

SERVES 8

2 packages (8 ounces each) cream cheese, softened
1 cup cocktail sauce
1½ cups cooked baby shrimp
⅓ cup chopped green onions
⅓ cup chopped green bell pepper
⅓ cup sliced ripe olives
⅓ cup diced fresh tomatoes, drained
½ cup freshly grated Parmesan cheese

On a large flat, round tray (a pizza pan), spread the cream cheese evenly.

Spread the cocktail sauce on top. Sprinkle the shrimp, green onions, green pepper, olives, and tomatoes, then cheese, on top.

Chill until serving time. Serve as a spread with crackers.

The 1952 Olympics at Oslo, Norway, was the first Olympiad in which women participated in cross-country (Nordic) events as well as the alpine events.

Fresh Salsa Dip

MAKES 5 TO 6 CUPS

1 tablespoon wine vinegar
1 tablespoon vegetable oil
1 to 2 cups chopped ripe olives
4 green onions, chopped
4 fresh medium tomatoes, peeled, seeded, and chopped
1 or 2 cans (4 ounces each) chopped green chilies, drained
salt and freshly ground black pepper to taste

Whisk together the vinegar and oil in a bowl. Add the remaining ingredients and mix lightly. Season to taste with salt and pepper.

Chill for several hours. Drain and serve with tortilla chips.

Confetti Dip

MAKES 2½ TO 3 CUPS

For another dip for fresh vegetables: Blend 1 7-ounce can drained tuna with ¾ to 1 cup homemade mayonnaise. Season with minced green onion and your favorite herb. Serve with sliced cucumbers, mushrooms, or jicama.

⅔ cup plain low-fat yogurt
½ cup mayonnaise
½ pound cream cheese, softened
2 tablespoons chopped chives
2 tablespoons minced onion
2 tablespoons minced green bell pepper
2 tablespoons minced fresh parsley
2 tablespoons chopped pimiento
1 teaspoon salt
⅛ teaspoon paprika
⅛ teaspoon cayenne

In a large bowl, beat together the yogurt, mayonnaise, and cream cheese. Add the remaining ingredients and blend well. Taste and adjust the seasoning. Refrigerate for at least 3 to 4 hours to blend flavors, then let stand at room temperature 30 minutes before serving with fresh vegetables or crackers.

MAKES 24 PIECES

French Onion Tart

7 onions, sliced
½ cup olive oil
½ cup dry vermouth
3 teaspoons granulated sugar
8 tomatoes, peeled, seeded, and chopped
3 teaspoons tomato paste
1 tablespoon chopped fresh basil or 1 teaspoon dried
2 teaspoons chopped oregano or ¾ teaspoon dried
salt and freshly ground black pepper to taste
8 sheets phyllo pastry
2 to 3 tablespoons olive oil
2 cups grated Gruyère cheese
½ cup freshly grated Parmesan cheese
⅔ cup ripe olives, halved

Sauté the onions in ¼ cup of the olive oil over low heat for 15 minutes. Add the vermouth and 2 teaspoons of the sugar and sauté an additional 30 minutes, stirring often. The onions should be very soft, golden, and glazed.

Meanwhile, sauté the tomatoes in the remaining ¼ cup olive oil. Add the tomato paste, herbs, salt and pepper, and remaining 1 teaspoon sugar and cook until the mixture is thick, about 20 minutes. Combine the onion and tomato mixtures.

Preheat the oven to 350° F.

Layer an oiled 10 x 15-inch jelly-roll pan with 1 sheet of phyllo. Add the next sheet, fold the edges under, and oil again. Repeat with the remaining sheets, folding the edges under to build up the sides. Be sure to lightly oil each sheet. Top with the onion-tomato mixture. Sprinkle with the cheeses and arrange the olives on top.

Bake for 25 to 30 minutes, or until cheeses are bubbling. Let stand for 10 minutes before serving.

MAKES 5 DOZEN

Anchovy Puffs

1 package (3 ounces) cream cheese, softened
½ cup unsalted butter, softened
1 cup all-purpose flour
1 tube (2 ounces) anchovy paste

Beat the cream cheese with the butter until well blended. Add the flour and mix thoroughly. Transfer the dough to a plastic bag and flatten into a disc. Chill for at least 1 hour.

Preheat the oven to 400° F.

Roll the dough out on a lightly floured surface to a thickness of about ⅛ inch. Cut into 2-inch rounds, using a cookie or biscuit cutter. Spread each round with anchovy paste. Fold over and crimp edges with a fork. Transfer to an ungreased baking sheet. Bake until lightly golden, about 8 to 10 minutes. Serve hot.

Candied Pecans

MAKES 4 CUPS

Serve this special confection with fruit and cheese and wine, before or after dinner.

4 cups pecans
½ cup butter
2 egg whites, at room temperature
1 cup granulated sugar
½ teaspoon salt

Preheat the oven to 250° F.

Place the pecans in a jelly-roll pan and toast for 30 minutes.

Remove the nuts from the pan. Place the butter in the same pan and melt in the oven.

Beat the egg whites until stiff. Slowly add the sugar and salt. Beat until thick. Fold in the pecans.

Raise the oven temperature to 300° F.

Spread the pecans carefully in the pan with the melted butter. Bake for 45 minutes, stirring every 15 minutes. Break up large pieces.

Sweet Hot Mustard

MAKES 1½ CUPS

1 cup white tarragon vinegar
1 cup dry mustard
2 eggs, beaten
1 cup granulated sugar
1 pinch salt

Mix the vinegar and mustard together in a small bowl and let stand overnight. Combine the mustard, eggs, sugar, and salt over simmering water in the top of a double boiler. Cook, stirring constantly, over low heat until thickened, about 10 minutes.

MAKES 1¼ CUPS

Fresh vegetables are great natural containers for sauces, spreads, herb butters, and relishes. Try stuffing tiny new potatoes with egg salad seasoned with capers, or thick hollowed cucumber slices stuffed with dilled salmon salad. Try jicama or celery as a base and use your imagination for the filler— guacamole, tarragon butter.

Plum Sauce

1 jar (12 ounces) plum preserves
2 tablespoons vinegar
1 tablespoon (packed) brown sugar
1 tablespoon finely chopped green onion
1 teaspoon seeded and finely chopped dried red chili pepper
1 clove garlic, minced
½ teaspoon ground ginger

Combine all the ingredients in a small saucepan and bring the mixture to a boil, stirring constantly. Remove from the heat and cool.

Refrigerate in a covered container overnight to blend flavors.

Soups

Cuttyhunk Crab Soup

Minnesota Wild Rice Soup

SERVES 4

If canned chicken stock is used in a recipe, taste carefully for salt before adding any.

2 packages (10 ounces each) frozen white and wild rice
    combination
2 tablespoons butter
1 tablespoon minced onion
¼ cup all-purpose flour
4 cups Chicken Stock (see page 56)
¼ teaspoon salt, or to taste
1½ cups light cream

OPTIONAL:
2 tablespoons dry sherry
1 tablespoon minced chives

Prepare the rice according to package directions.

Melt the butter in a medium saucepan and sauté the onion until tender. Blend in the flour and cook for 2 minutes, stirring to blend well. Gradually add the stock, stirring constantly, until the mixture thickens. Stir in the prepared rice. Add the salt and simmer for 5 minutes. Blend in the cream and, if desired, the sherry. Heat to serving temperature, but do not boil. Each serving may be garnished with chives.

Chicken Walnut Soup

SERVES 6

¼ cup diced celery
¼ cup minced fresh parsley
4 cups Chicken Stock (see page 56)
1 egg, well beaten
1 tablespoon all-purpose flour
1 cup heavy cream
salt and freshly ground black pepper to taste

GARNISH:
½ cup heavy cream, whipped
⅓ cup ground walnuts

In a large saucepan, cook the celery and parsley in the chicken stock until the celery is tender, about 20 minutes. In a separate pan, combine the egg, flour, and cream and mix until blended. Stir about ½ cup of the hot stock into the egg-cream mixture, and then slowly return it to the pan. Cook for 3 minutes over medium heat, stirring constantly. Season to taste with salt and pepper. Serve garnished with a dollop of whipped cream, sprinkled with walnuts.

SERVES 4 TO 6

Split-Second Pea Soup

1 package (10 ounces) frozen peas
1 medium onion, sliced
1 small carrot, peeled and sliced
1 small potato, peeled and cubed
1 clove garlic, crushed
1 stalk celery with leaves, chopped
1 teaspoon salt
1 teaspoon curry powder
2 cups Chicken Stock (see page 56)
1 cup light cream

Combine the peas, onion, carrot, potato, garlic, celery, salt, curry powder, and 1 cup of the chicken stock in a small saucepan. Bring to a boil, then reduce the heat, cover, and simmer for 15 minutes. Remove from the heat and let cool for 5 minutes.

Remove the contents of the saucepan to a blender or food processor. Blend on high speed for 15 seconds. Remove the cover and, with the motor on medium speed, add the remaining cup of chicken stock and the cream. Return the soup to the saucepan and reheat. This soup is also great served cold.

SERVES 8

Bisque is a thick, rich cream soup usually made with shellfish or puréed vegetables.

Tomato Bisque

½ cup butter
1 cup chopped celery
1 cup chopped onion
¼ cup chopped carrot
⅓ cup all-purpose flour
4 cups Chicken Stock (see page 56)
6 large fresh tomatoes, peeled and chopped or
   2 cans whole tomatoes (1 pound 12 ounces each), chopped
2 teaspoons granulated sugar
1 teaspoon dried basil
1 teaspoon dried marjoram
1 bay leaf
2 cups heavy cream
¼ teaspoon paprika
¼ teaspoon curry powder
¼ teaspoon freshly ground white pepper
salt to taste

Melt the butter in a large saucepan, then sauté the celery, onion, and carrots until tender. Add the flour and cook for 2 minutes, stirring constantly. Gradually add the stock, blending well. Add the tomatoes, sugar, basil, marjoram, and bay leaf. Cover and simmer for 30 minutes, stirring occasionally.

Discard the bay leaf. In a food processor or blender, purée one third of the mixture at a time until it is liquified. Return the puréed mixture to the saucepan. Add the cream, paprika, curry powder, and pepper. Stir to blend, then season to taste with salt. If serving the soup hot, reheat after adding the cream. If serving the soup cold, refrigerate 3 to 4 hours or overnight.

SERVES 6

Curried Chicken Soup

1 frying chicken (3½ pounds), cut into pieces
salt
1½ cups peeled and chopped potato
½ cup chopped leek
½ cup chopped white onion
2 teaspoons curry powder
½ cup chopped red pimiento
2½ cups Chicken Stock (see page 56)
2 cups heavy cream
½ cup white wine

GARNISH:
chopped chives

Put the chicken pieces into a kettle with cold water to barely cover. Add 1½ teaspoons salt and bring to a rolling boil, then reduce the heat, cover, and simmer for 45 minutes, or until the chicken is tender. Let cool. Remove the skin and bones from the chicken and discard. Reserve the stock. Cut the meat into bite-sized pieces and reserve.

Bring the stock to a boil and cook over high heat until it is reduced to about 2½ cups. To this stock, add the potatoes, leek, onion, curry powder, and pimiento, then heat to a rolling boil. Cover, reduce the heat, and cook until potato and onion are tender, 15 to 20 minutes.

Remove the vegetables from the stock and place in a blender or food processor. Process until smooth. Or press the cooked vegetables through a fine sieve. Return the vegetable purée to a 1½-quart saucepan. Add the cream, wine, reserved chicken meat, and salt to taste. Serve either hot or very cold. Sprinkle chives on top of each serving.

US SKI TEAM Twenty-nine-year-old Gretchen Fraser of Vancouver, Washington, at an age when most women racers have retired from competition, became the first U.S. skier to win a major international race and a gold Olympic medal in slalom, plus a silver in the Combined in the 1948 Olympics.

SERVES 6

Mushroom and Chive Bisque

½ cup butter
2 cups sliced fresh mushrooms
¼ cup all-purpose flour
¼ teaspoon dry mustard
1 teaspoon salt
2 cups Chicken Stock (see page 56)
2 cups light cream
¼ cup sherry
¼ cup finely chopped chives

OPTIONAL:
whipped heavy cream

Melt the butter in a large kettle over medium heat. Add the mushrooms and sauté until limp. Add the flour, mustard, and salt and cook for 1 minute. Remove from the heat and gradually add the chicken stock, stirring constantly. Return to the heat and continue stirring until thickened. Add the cream, sherry, and chives and heat through. At this point, the soup can be kept warm in a double boiler on very low heat. At serving time, top each serving with a dollop of whipped cream, if desired.

**MAKES
3 QUARTS**

Mulligatawny Soup

¾ cup butter
1 cup chopped onion
1 cup chopped green bell pepper
1 cup chopped celery
3 medium carrots, peeled and chopped
1 medium potato, peeled and chopped
3 large tomatoes, peeled and chopped (about 2 cups)
1 apple, unpeeled, cored, and chopped
¾ cup all-purpose flour
1 tablespoon curry powder
1 bay leaf
6 whole cloves
6 sprigs fresh parsley
12 cups Chicken Stock (see page 56)
2 cups heavy cream
salt and freshly ground black pepper to taste

US SKI TEAM After the eight years in which no Olympic games were held because of World War II, the games resumed in 1948 at St. Moritz, Switzerland.

Melt the butter in a large saucepan or kettle. Over medium heat, sauté the onion, green pepper, celery, carrots, potato, tomatoes, and apple for 10 to 15 minutes, or until softened. Add the flour and curry powder and blend well, stirring constantly for 1 minute. Add the bay leaf, cloves, parsley, and chicken stock, stirring until thickened. Simmer, covered, for 30 minutes, or until the vegetables are tender. Remove from the heat and cool the vegetable mixture for 15 minutes.

Place the cooled vegetable mixture in a medium-fine strainer over a large bowl. Push the vegetables through the strainer with a pestle or the back of a wooden spoon. Extract as much pulp as possible, then discard the solids remaining in the strainer. Pour the strained vegetable mixture into a clean saucepan. Blend in the cream, then season to taste with salt and pepper. Serve piping hot or ice cold.

Mushroom Soup

SERVES 6

One pound of mushrooms contains about 30 medium mushrooms.

½ cup butter
½ cup minced onion
1 pound fresh mushrooms, washed, dried, and minced
2½ tablespoons all-purpose flour
4½ cups Beef Stock (see page 56)
1 cup light cream
salt

GARNISH:
paprika
minced fresh parsley

In a saucepan, over low heat, melt the butter and sauté the onion until soft but not brown, about 15 minutes. Add the mushrooms and sauté for 3 to 4 minutes. Stir in the flour and cook for 1 minute, stirring constantly. Then gradually add the stock. Cook and stir until thickened.

Add the cream and heat, but do not boil. Season with salt, then sprinkle with paprika and parsley. Serve immediately.

SERVES 8

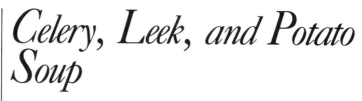

Celery, Leek, and Potato Soup

5 tablespoons butter
3 medium leeks (white part only), sliced
4 cups sliced celery
6 cups Chicken Stock (see page 56)
⅓ cup uncooked long-grain white rice
3 cups water
¾ teaspoon salt
5 to 6 medium potatoes, peeled and chopped
3 cups milk
¼ teaspoon granulated sugar
salt and freshly ground white pepper to taste
¼ cup minced fresh chervil or tarragon or
      a combination of ¼ cup minced fresh parsley and
      ¼ teaspoon crumbled dried tarragon
1 cup croutons

Melt 3 tablespoons of the butter in a large saucepan. Add the leeks and celery and cook until tender but not browned, approximately 10 minutes. Add the chicken stock and bring to a boil. Stir in the rice and reduce the heat. Simmer, uncovered, for 25 minutes.

Meanwhile, in 3 cups salted water, cook the potatoes until tender. Remove from the heat and cool for 5 minutes. Do not drain. Then pour the potato water into the leek and celery mixture.

Place the cooked potatoes and 1 cup of the milk into a blender or food processor and purée. Pour the potato purée into a large saucepan and stir in the remaining milk.

Purée the leek and celery mixture with its liquid, then pour it into the potato-milk purée. Add the sugar, salt and pepper and blend well with a wire whisk. Simmer for 5 minutes.

Mash the remaining butter and the herbs in a soup tureen. Blend the soup into the herb butter, and sprinkle the croutons on top. Serve immediately.

US SKITEAM Andrea Mead Lawrence, age 19 when the 1952 Olympics at Oslo took place, had become the world's best female skier. She won the giant slalom by 2.2 seconds over her nearest competitor, and after a bad first heat in the slalom put her 1.2 seconds behind, she came down in the second heat with the best time of the day by .8 seconds and won a second gold medal. It looked as if Andy would lead the sport for the next ten years, but instead, she went home to Vermont with her new husband, Dave Lawrence, retired from ski competition, and started raising a family.

SERVES 6

Corn Chowder

4 tablespoons butter
1 medium onion, minced
3 stalks celery, minced
2 tablespoons all-purpose flour
3 cups milk
2 cups corn kernels
1 cup (4 ounces) grated Cheddar or Gruyère cheese
freshly grated nutmeg
salt and freshly ground black pepper to taste

GARNISH:
butter

Melt the butter in a large saucepan and sauté the onion and celery until limp. Stir in the flour and blend well. Add the milk and stir until blended. Add the corn kernels and heat through. Add the cheese and stir until melted. Season to taste with the nutmeg, salt and pepper. Serve with a bit of butter on top.

SERVES 4 TO 6

Cheesy Chowder

4 tablespoons butter
½ cup chopped onion
½ cup chopped celery
½ cup chopped green bell pepper
½ cup peeled and chopped carrot
1 cup peeled and chopped potato
3 cups Chicken Stock (see page 56)
½ cup all-purpose flour
2 cups milk
3 cups shredded American or Cheddar cheese

GARNISH:
1 tablespoon chopped fresh parsley

Melt the butter in a large saucepan. Add the onion, celery, and green pepper and sauté over low heat for 10 minutes. Add the carrot, potato, and chicken stock, then bring to a boil. Reduce the heat and simmer for 30 minutes.

Whisk the flour and milk together until smooth. Stir the milk mixture into the vegetable mixture and blend well. Add the cheese and stir until thick and bubbly. Garnish with parsley to serve.

SERVES 6

Iced Papaya Soup

3 ripe papayas, peeled and seeded
¼ cup lime juice
¼ cup honey
2 cups orange juice
1 cup champagne, chilled

GARNISH:
1 kiwi fruit, peeled and cut into sixths
6 strawberries

———

Place the papayas, lime juice, honey, and orange juice in a blender and process until smooth. Pour the papaya purée into a large bowl and chill. At serving time, add the champagne and stir to blend well. Pour into chilled bowls and top each serving with a kiwi slice and a strawberry.

SERVES 4

Avocado Soup

1⅓ cups mashed avocado (about 1 large)
2 tablespoons lime juice
1⅓ cups plain yogurt
1½ cups Beef Stock (see page 56)
1 teaspoon onion juice
1 teaspoon chili powder
½ teaspoon salt, or to taste
½ cup milk

GARNISH:
1 avocado

———

Combine the mashed avocado with the lime juice. Blend in the yogurt, beef stock, onion juice, chili powder, salt, and milk. Stir until smooth. Chill 3 to 4 hours or overnight.

Peel and cube the avocado for garnish. Whisk the chilled soup to restore smoothness. Garnish with the cubed avocado and serve.

US SKI TEAM The 1980 Lake Placid games provided the third instance of a second Olympic games being held at the same site. St. Moritz, Switzerland, hosted the games in 1928 and 1948; Lake Placid, New York, in 1932 and 1980; and Innsbruck, Austria, in 1964 and 1976.

SERVES 6

Great for Mexican buffets or when serving any spicy meals. Easy to double.

Gazpacho Blanco

3 medium cucumbers, peeled, seeded, and sliced
3 cups Chicken Stock (see page 56)
3 cups sour cream
3 tablespoons white vinegar
2 teaspoons garlic salt

GARNISH:
2 tomatoes, peeled, seeded, and chopped
¾ cup slivered almonds, toasted
½ cup sliced green onions, including tops
½ cup minced fresh parsley

Combine the cucumber and 1 cup of the chicken stock in a blender or food processor. Process until blended. Add to the cucumber mixture the remaining stock, the sour cream, vinegar, and garlic salt. Stir to blend well. Chill. Serve in small bowls garnished with tomatoes, almonds, green onions, and parsley.

SERVES 4

Chilled Cucumber Soup

1 large or 2 small cucumbers, preferably unwaxed
1 cup heavy cream
½ cup plain yogurt
2 tablespoons tarragon vinegar
1 to 2 cloves garlic, crushed
1 to 2 teaspoons Dijon mustard
¼ teaspoon grated onion
¼ teaspoon minced fresh parsley
¼ teaspoon minced fresh basil
¼ teaspoon minced fresh tarragon
salt and freshly ground white pepper to taste

GARNISH:
red caviar

Wash but do not peel the cucumbers. Then grate coarsely into a bowl. Stir in the cream, yogurt, vinegar, garlic, mustard, onion, fresh herbs, and salt and pepper. Chill thoroughly. Serve garnished with red caviar.

SERVES 6

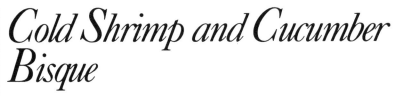

Cold Shrimp and Cucumber Bisque

3 cups water
1 teaspoon salt
¼ cup plus 2 tablespoons fresh lemon juice
1½ pounds tiny shrimp, cleaned and deveined
4 cups buttermilk
2 medium cucumbers, peeled and diced
¼ cup minced celery
½ teaspoon salt, or to taste
1½ tablespoons prepared hot mustard
¼ teaspoon garlic powder
½ teaspoon prepared horseradish
2 tablespoons minced chives

GARNISH:
chopped fresh parsley

Bring the water, salt, and the ¼ cup lemon juice to a boil in a large saucepan. Add the shrimp and cook for 2 to 3 minutes. Drain, then cool the shrimp in cold water; drain again. Dice the shrimp and set ½ cup aside.

Purée the remaining shrimp in a food processor or blender with 1 cup of the buttermilk. Combine with the remaining buttermilk, cucumber, celery, salt, mustard, garlic powder, the 2 tablespoons lemon juice, and the horseradish. Chill for 4 hours or overnight. At serving time, adjust the seasonings to taste. Stir in the chives and the reserved shrimp. Serve in chilled bowls, garnished with chopped parsley.

SERVES 4 TO 6

Strawberry Soup

2 cups strawberries
8 ounces strawberry yogurt
½ cup white wine

Wash and hull the strawberries. Put the strawberries and yogurt in a blender or food processor and purée. Add the wine and continue blending until smooth. Chill at least 3 hours.

California Chicken Stew

SERVES 8

Saffron comes from the stigma of the saffron crocus. It takes over 200,000 hand-picked stigmas to make 1 pound of saffron. It adds a delicate aroma and pale yellow color to many classic dishes.

2 frying chickens (3 pounds each), cut into serving pieces
salt and freshly ground black pepper
2 tablespoons water
1 tablespoon butter
½ cup minced fresh parsley
1 medium onion, minced
1 large clove garlic, minced
1 lemon, scored and ends cut flat
1 large tomato, peeled, seeded, and chopped
2 small green bell peppers, seeded and cut into 2½-inch squares
2 small red bell peppers, seeded and cut into 2½-inch squares, or 1 jar (4 ounces) pimientos
¾ cup white wine
¾ cup Chicken Stock (see page 56)
½ cup ripe olives, drained
2 teaspoons chopped fresh oregano or 1 teaspoon dried
½ teaspoon granulated sugar
dash of cayenne

OPTIONAL:
dash of saffron

Preheat the broiler to 450°F.

Pat dry the chicken thoroughly and sprinkle with salt and pepper. Broil the chicken approximately 4 inches from the heat until brown on both sides. Remove the chicken from the broiler pan and drain on paper toweling.

Combine the water and butter in a skillet over low heat and stir until the butter melts. Increase the heat to medium and add the parsley, onion, and garlic. Simmer until the onion is limp and water has evaporated, about 10 minutes.

Slice the lemon and reserve half of it for garnish. Combine two thirds of the tomato and peppers with half the lemon slices, the wine, chicken stock, olives, oregano, sugar, cayenne, and salt and pepper to taste. Add the tomato-lemon-wine mixture and saffron, if desired, to the parsley-onion-garlic mixture in the skillet. Mix well, and cook over medium heat. Add the dark meat of the chicken first. Baste with the sauce, then cover and simmer for 15 minutes. Add the white meat of the chicken and simmer 10 minutes more. Stir in the rest of the tomato and peppers. Cover and simmer an additional 5 minutes, or until chicken is tender. Taste and adjust the seasoning. Place on a heated platter and serve garnished with the reserved lemon slices.

SERVES 8 TO 10

To peel garlic, hold the flat side of a chef's knife on top of a clove and smack the top with your other hand. The peel is then easily removed.

Beef Stew Provençal

3 pounds beef chuck, cut into 1½-inch cubes
½ cup vegetable or olive oil
1 cup minced onion
¼ cup minced shallot or green onion
2 cloves garlic, minced
3 cups Sauterne or white wine
4 cups tomato sauce
2 cups Beef Stock (see page 56)
3 bay leaves
2 teaspoons dried rosemary, crumbled
½ teaspoon salt
freshly ground black pepper to taste
8 carrots, peeled and cut into 2-inch pieces
2 stalks celery, cut into 2-inch pieces
2 cups pimiento stuffed green olives

Pat the meat dry. Heat the oil in a Dutch oven over medium heat. Add the meat in batches and brown on all sides. Do not crowd the meat while browning. As the meat is browned, set it aside. In the same pan, sauté the onion, shallots or green onions, and garlic for 5 minutes. Add the Sauterne, tomato sauce, beef stock, bay leaves, rosemary, salt, and pepper. Cover, and bring to a boil. Reduce the heat and simmer for 1½ hours. Add the carrots and celery. Cook for 1 hour longer, or until the meat is tender. Add the olives and simmer for 1 minute. Discard the bay leaves and serve.

SERVES 6 TO 8

Kielbasa Soup

½ cup butter
½ cup chopped carrot
½ cup minced celery
3 cups ½-inch leek pieces
2 cups shredded cabbage
8 cups Chicken Stock (see page 56)
5 tablespoons all-purpose flour
2 potatoes, peeled and cut into ½-inch cubes
½ teaspoon dried marjoram
2 cups peeled and sliced kielbasa (about 1 pound)
salt and freshly ground black pepper to taste

Melt ¼ cup of the butter in a large kettle and sauté the carrot and celery until limp. Add the leeks and cabbage and sauté for 3 minutes. Stir in the stock and bring to a boil, then reduce the heat and simmer for 15 minutes.

Melt the remaining butter in a separate skillet. Add the flour and stir over low heat until well blended, about 2 minutes. Remove from the heat. Whisk in 2 cups of the hot stock and blend until smooth. Add the thickened stock to the vegetable mixture in the kettle, stirring constantly. Add the potatoes and marjoram and simmer for 10 minutes. Add the kielbasa and simmer for 15 minutes more, or until the vegetables are tender. Season to taste with salt and pepper and serve.

SERVES 6

Spicy Chili with Green Chilies

3 pounds ground beef
2 cups chopped celery
1 large onion, chopped
1 can (8 ounces) green chilies, chopped
6 tablespoons chili powder
2 tablespoons minced garlic
1 tablespoon salt
2 tablespoons sugar
2 tablespoons ground cumin
1 tablespoon coriander seeds
2 cans (1 pound 12 ounces each) whole tomatoes, puréed
1 can (1 pound) chili beans in sauce
1 cup shredded Cheddar or Monterey Jack cheese

GARNISH:
chopped green onions
shredded cheese
corn chips
chopped lettuce

Sauté the ground beef in a large saucepan until brown. Add the celery and onion and cook for 5 minutes. Drain the fat from the pan and discard. Add the chilies, chili powder, garlic, salt, sugar, cumin, coriander seeds, tomatoes, and beans. Bring the mixture to a boil, then reduce the heat, and simmer for 2½ hours. Add the shredded cheese and cook for 30 minutes. Adjust seasonings to taste. Serve with garnishes.

US SKI TEAM Back in the 1920s, U.S. ski enthusiasts numbered no more than 3,500 to 4,000. There were about 75 clubs devoted to the sport, but most were located in the northern part of the Midwest, in upper New England, and in the northern sections of New York state. The growth of the sport has been remarkable—the number of U.S. skiers is now over six million, and the number of ski clubs is over 1,000, with over 66,000 members.

SERVES 6 TO 8

This chili is better if it is made the day before it is served. It freezes well.

Cowboy Chili

2 tablespoons vegetable oil
1 pound ground beef round
1 green bell pepper, seeded and chopped
2 stalks celery
1 large onion
3 cloves garlic, minced
3½ to 4 cups peeled and chopped tomatoes (about 30 ounces)
1 cup tomato sauce
4 cups Beef Stock (see page 56)
2 tablespoons chili powder
1 tablespoon ground cumin
2 teaspoons salt
½ teaspoon freshly ground black pepper
½ teaspoon dried oregano
dash of hot pepper sauce
1 cup cooked pinto beans

Heat the oil in a large saucepan and sauté the meat, green pepper, celery, onion, and garlic. Cook this mixture until the vegetables are tender and the meat is browned, about 10 minutes.

Add the tomatoes, tomato sauce, 3½ cups of the beef stock, the chili powder, cumin, salt, pepper, oregano, and hot pepper sauce. Bring the chili mixture to a boil, then reduce the heat and simmer for 1½ to 2 hours. Add the remaining beef stock if the chili is too thick.

Add the pinto beans and continue to simmer for 30 minutes.

SERVES 8 TO 10

Hearty Hodgepodge

6 slices bacon
1 medium onion, thinly sliced
1 pound beef shank
1 ham hock (about ¾ pound)
6 cups water
2 teaspoons salt
2 cans (15 ounces each) garbanzo beans, undrained
3 cups peeled and diced potatoes
1 clove garlic, minced
¼ pound link Polish sausage, thinly sliced

Cook the bacon in a large saucepan until crisp; drain, reserving 2 tablespoons of the drippings. Crumble the bacon and set aside. Add the onion to the reserved drippings in the pan. Cook until tender but not brown, about 10 minutes. Add the beef shank, ham hock, water, and salt. Cover and simmer for 1½ hours.

Remove the beef shank and the ham hock from the pan and cut off the meat and dice; discard the bones. Carefully skim the fat from the broth. Return the diced meat to the soup; add the undrained garbanzo beans, the potatoes, and garlic. Simmer, covered, for 30 minutes more. Add the sausage and continue simmering, covered, for 15 minutes. Garnish with the reserved bacon.

Ham and Cabbage Soup

SERVES 6

4 tablespoons butter
2 to 3 tablespoons diced green bell pepper
1 cup diced celery with tops
¾ cup diced onion
2 to 3 cloves garlic, minced
2 tablespoons all-purpose flour
2 cups diced ham
1 bay leaf, crushed
1 teaspoon sugar
1 teaspoon freshly ground black pepper
1 teaspoon dried oregano
4 to 5 cups Chicken Stock (see page 56) or water
3 cups diced cabbage
1 tablespoon water

GARNISH:
sour cream
freshly grated Parmesan cheese

Melt 2 tablespoons of the butter in a 3 to 4-quart saucepan. Add the green pepper, celery, onion, and garlic and sauté until limp, about 10 minutes. Add the flour and stir to blend well. Cook for 2 to 3 minutes.

Add the ham, bay leaf, sugar, pepper, and oregano. Gradually add the chicken stock and bring to a boil. Reduce the heat, cover, and simmer for 30 minutes.

Melt the remaining butter in a large skillet and sauté the diced cabbage. Add 1 tablespoon water and cook just until the cabbage is bright green and still crisp, about 3 minutes. Add the cabbage to the soup. Put a dollop of sour cream and Parmesan cheese on top of individual servings.

US SKI TEAM There was a time when ski team travel arrangements weren't as well organized as they are now. When team members sailed to South America for summer training in 1937, Adams Carter was assigned to share a stateroom with the mother superior of a Colombian convent.

Black Bean Soup

SERVES 6 TO 8

Turtle beans are dried, black beans about the size of medium navy beans and are available in most supermarkets.

½ pound dried black turtle beans
4 cups water
¾ cup diced onion
½ cup minced green bell pepper
½ cup minced carrot
⅓ cup minced celery
1 cup diced tomato
1 smoked ham hock (about ½ pound)
4 cups Chicken Stock (see page 56)
2 teaspoons salt
1 teaspoon dried thyme
1 teaspoon dry mustard
2 cloves garlic, minced
cayenne to taste
freshly ground black pepper to taste
¼ cup sherry

GARNISH:
1 hard-cooked egg yolk, sieved
coarsely chopped onion
lemon slices

Thoroughly wash and pick over the beans. Soak the beans overnight in the water in a large, heavy stockpot.

Add the onion, green pepper, carrot, celery, tomato, and the ham hock to the beans and liquid in the stockpot. Bring to a boil, then reduce the heat. Skim off the foam that rises to the surface. Add the chicken stock, salt, thyme, mustard, garlic, cayenne, and black pepper. Simmer, covered, until beans are tender and the soup has thickened, approximately 2 to 2½ hours.

Remove the ham hock from the soup. Shred the meat and return it to the soup. Discard the bone and the fat. Stir in the sherry. Serve the soup in warmed individual bowls, garnished with chopped egg, onion, and lemon slices.

SERVES 8

Lamb Stew

2½ to 3 pounds lamb breast, cut into 2-inch pieces
2 to 3 tablespoons vegetable oil
1 tablespoon granulated sugar
2 tablespoons all-purpose flour
salt and freshly ground black pepper to taste
4 to 5 cups Beef Stock (see page 56)
3 tomatoes, peeled, seeded, and chopped
1 tablespoon tomato paste
1 clove garlic, crushed
bouquet garni (6 parsley sprigs, 1 bay leaf, 1 stalk celery, and
     6 whole peppercorns, tied in cheesecloth)
¼ teaspoon dried rosemary
1 cup 2-inch green bean pieces
16 small new potatoes, peeled
16 small white onions, peeled
3 to 4 small turnips, peeled and cut into 2-inch pieces
8 carrots, peeled and cut into 2-inch pieces
1½ cups frozen peas

GARNISH:
chopped fresh parsley

Preheat the oven to 450°F.

Pat the meat dry with paper toweling. Heat the oil in a large, heavy, ovenproof skillet over medium-high heat. Add the meat in batches and brown on all sides. Do not crowd the meat while browning. Remove the meat, as it is browned, to a large Dutch oven. When the meat is browned, return it all to the skillet and sprinkle it with the sugar. Place the skillet over high heat and stir constantly until the sugar caramelizes, about 2 minutes. Remove the skillet from the heat. Sprinkle the meat with the flour and bake, uncovered, in the preheated oven until the flour is brown, about 5 minutes. Remove from the oven and reduce the oven heat to 350°F.

Return the meat to the Dutch oven. Season with salt and pepper and add enough beef stock to cover. Add the tomatoes, tomato paste, garlic, bouquet garni, and rosemary. Bring to a simmer over medium-high heat, stirring frequently. Cook the meat in the 350° F. oven, covered, for 1 hour, stirring occasionally. Add the beans, potatoes, onions, turnips, and carrots and cook for 30 minutes, or until the vegetables are tender. Add the peas and cook for 10 minutes more. Adjust seasoning with salt and pepper. Sprinkle with parsley and serve.

 The longest downhill race is the Inferno in Switzerland, 8.7 miles from the top of the Schilthorn to Lauterbrunnen. In 1981, this famous race had a record entry of 1,401, with Switzerland's Heinz Fringen winning in a record 15 minutes, 44.57 seconds.

SERVES 8 TO 12

Lentil Soup

¼ cup vegetable oil
3 cups cooked, diced ham
¾ pound Polish sausage, cut into ½-inch slices
2 large onions, chopped
1 clove garlic, crushed
2 cups chopped celery with tops
1 large tomato, peeled and cut into wedges
1 pound lentils, washed
3 quarts Chicken Stock (see page 56)
¾ teaspoon hot pepper sauce, or to taste
1½ teaspoons salt, or to taste
½ teaspoon dried thyme
1 bay leaf
1 package (10 ounces) frozen spinach or chard,
　　thawed and chopped

Heat the oil in a large soup kettle. Add the ham, sausage, onions, and garlic and sauté for 5 minutes. Add the celery, tomato, lentils, chicken stock, hot pepper sauce, salt, thyme, and bay leaf. Partially cover the kettle with a lid, then cook for 2 hours over low heat, stirring occasionally. Discard the bay leaf. Add the spinach and cook for 10 minutes longer. Adjust the seasoning to taste with salt and hot pepper sauce, then serve.

SERVES 8 TO 10

Zuppe Italiano

1½ to 2 pounds Italian sausage (hot or mild)
olive oil, if needed
2 medium onions, chopped
3 cloves garlic, minced
3½ to 4 cups peeled and chopped tomatoes (fresh or canned),
　　including juice
5 cups Beef Stock (see page 56)
1½ cups dry red wine
¾ teaspoon dried basil
½ teaspoon dried oregano
1 medium green bell pepper, seeded and chopped
2 medium zucchini, sliced ¼-inch thick
2 cups shell or bow-tie noodles
salt and freshly ground black pepper to taste

Parmesan cheese is used extensively in the grated form. It can be grated by hand or done in a food processor. Prepackaged grated Parmesan should be used only in emergencies.

GARNISH:
¼ cup minced fresh parsley
½ cup freshly grated Parmesan cheese

Prick the sausages with a fork and place in a saucepan. Cover the sausages with water and bring to a boil. Reduce the heat and simmer for 20 minutes. Remove the sausages from the pan and allow them to cool. Discard the water.

If the casing is thick, remove it from the sausages. Cut the sausages into ¼-inch slices and sauté them in a large saucepan. Remove the sausage slices from the pan, leaving 3 tablespoons of fat in the pan (add olive oil if more fat is needed). Add the onions and garlic and sauté until limp, about 5 minutes. Add the tomatoes, beef stock, wine, herbs, and reserved sausage. Simmer for 25 minutes.

Add the green pepper, zucchini, and noodles. Cook for 20 to 25 minutes, or until the noodles are just tender. Season with salt and pepper. Sprinkle with parsley and serve with grated cheese.

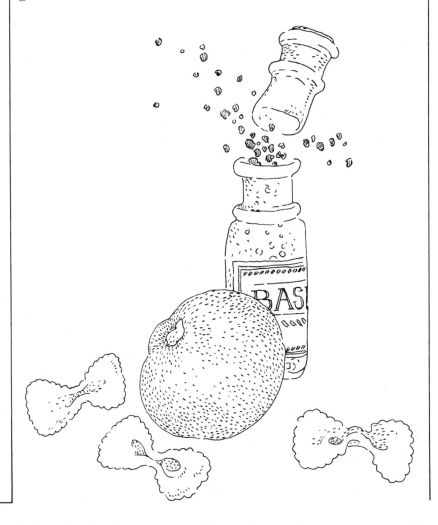

**MAKES
3 QUARTS**

Chicken Stock

3 to 4 pounds chicken pieces (backs, wings, necks, and bones
    remaining from boning chicken breasts)
2 medium carrots, cut into large pieces
2 medium onions, cut into large pieces
½ teaspoon dried thyme
1 large bay leaf
6 to 8 sprigs fresh parsley
6 to 8 peppercorns, crushed

Place the chicken with cold water to cover in a large stock pot. Add the remaining ingredients and bring to a boil. Reduce the heat. Remove scum from the top with a slotted spoon and discard.

Simmer, uncovered, for 4 to 5 hours, adding more water if necessary to keep the chicken covered with water.

Strain the stock through a large sieve into a bowl. Discard the solids. Return the strained stock to a large saucepan and cook, uncovered, over high heat until reduced by one third. Refrigerate until cold.

Remove and discard hardened fat from the surface.

The stock may be refrigerated for 2 to 3 days or frozen. Reheat to boiling before using.

**MAKES
3 QUARTS**

Beef Stock

4 to 5 pounds beef shank, rib bones, or beef soup bones
2 large carrots, cut into large pieces
2 large onions, cut into large pieces
½ to 1 teaspoon dried thyme
1 large bay leaf
6 to 8 sprigs fresh parsley
6 to 8 peppercorns, crushed

Preheat the oven to 450° F.

Place the meat and vegetables in a large, shallow roasting pan, and cook for 30 to 35 minutes, turning occasionally, until well browned.

Remove the bones and vegetables to a large soup kettle. Discard the fat in the roasting pan. Scrape the browned pieces from the pan into the kettle.

Add the seasonings to the soup kettle, along with enough cold water to cover. Bring the water to a boil, then reduce heat. Skim and discard the scum that rises to the surface.

Simmer, uncovered, for 4 to 5 hours, adding water if necessary to keep the bones and vegetables covered.

Strain the stock through a large sieve into a bowl. Discard the solids. Return the strained stock to a large saucepan and cook, uncovered, over high heat until reduced by one third. Refrigerate until cold.

Remove and discard hardened fat from the surface.

The stock may be refrigerated for 2 to 3 days or frozen. Reheat to boiling before using.

Spiced Tomato Soup

SERVES 4

1 tablespoon butter
1 medium onion, sliced
2 cups chopped, peeled, and seeded tomatoes (fresh or canned), including juice
2 cups Chicken Stock (see page 56)
pinch of ground cloves
½ teaspoon dried basil
1 teaspoon paprika
1 teaspoon sugar
1 medium bay leaf
⅛ teaspoon freshly grated nutmeg
⅛ teaspoon freshly ground black pepper
2 tablespoons chopped fresh parsley
salt to taste

OPTIONAL GARNISH:
½ cup whipped cream

In a 2-quart saucepan, over medium heat, melt the butter. Add the onion and sauté until limp, about 5 minutes. Add the tomatoes and their liquid, chicken stock, cloves, basil, paprika, sugar, bay leaf, nutmeg, and pepper. Simmer, covered, for 30 minutes. Remove from the heat and discard the bay leaf. Process half the soup in a blender or food processor until smooth. Repeat with the remaining soup. The soup may be prepared to this point and refrigerated for up to 2 days.

Just before serving, stir in the parsley, then reheat to simmering. Season to taste with salt. Serve, garnishing each serving with a dollop of whipped cream, if desired.

US SKI TEAM The champion late bloomer of alpine skiing is Zeno Colo, who won the downhill and giant slalom and was second in the slalom at the 1950 world championships when he was 30 years old. Thus encouraged, he won the Olympic downhill in 1952.

SERVES 4 TO 6

Sour and Hot Soup

Light and dark soy sauces are different in both color and flavor. Chinese, Japanese, and American brands are numerous and varied. Experiment to find your favorite taste.

¼ cup dried Chinese mushrooms (tree ears or cloud ears), measured after soaking
6 to 8 dried tiger lily buds (golden needles)
2 tablespoons cornstarch
3 tablespoons cold water or dry sherry
4 cups Chicken Stock (see page 56)
¼ cup shredded cooked pork
¼ cup bamboo shoots, cut into julienne
6 large fresh mushrooms, sliced
1 teaspoon soy sauce
½ teaspoon granulated sugar
2 tablespoons distilled white vinegar or wine vinegar
¼ teaspoon freshly ground black pepper
1 egg, beaten
½ cake tofu (fresh bean curd), cut into 1x¼x¼ = inch slices
1 teaspoon Chinese sesame seed oil

OPTIONAL:
hot pepper sauce to taste

Soak the dried mushrooms and the tiger lily buds in ¼ cup of warm water for 20 minutes. Drain the mushrooms and tiger lily buds; shred the mushrooms. Meanwhile, in a separate bowl, dissolve the cornstarch in the cold water or sherry.

Bring the chicken stock to a boil in a large saucepan. Add the pork shreds, bamboo shoots, sliced fresh mushrooms, shredded dried mushrooms, and tiger lily buds and cook for 10 minutes. Add the soy sauce, sugar, vinegar, and pepper, then add the cornstarch-water mixture and stir to thicken. Remove the pan from the heat and add the beaten egg. Stir gently two or three times. Add the sliced tofu.

Just before serving, add the sesame oil. A few drops of hot pepper sauce may be added, if desired.

SERVES 6 TO 8

Wonton Soup

1½ pounds bay or sea scallops, coarsely chopped
½ pound pork, coarsely ground
¼ pound ham, coarsely ground
8 canned bamboo shoots, drained and finely minced
6 large Chinese mushrooms, soaked in hot water for 15 to 30
    minutes, drained, dried, and finely minced
1 egg
6 tablespoons chopped shallots
2 tablespoons Chinese rice wine or dry sherry
1 teaspoon salt
freshly ground black pepper to taste
extra-thin wonton skins
8 cups Chicken Stock (see page 56)

Combine the first 10 ingredients in a bowl and mix well.

Place a wonton skin flour side down on a work surface. Put ½ teaspoon of the filling in the center of the wonton skin; don't overstuff. Gently pinch the edges to close, then twist the ends to seal. Repeat until all the filling is used.

Bring 4 quarts of water to a boil. Add the filled wontons in batches and cook for 2 to 4 minutes. Don't crowd. The wontons will float to the top and look transparent when they are done. Remove the wontons with a slotted spoon and set aside.

Pour the chicken stock into a large saucepan and bring to a simmer. Add the wontons and heat through. Serve immediately.

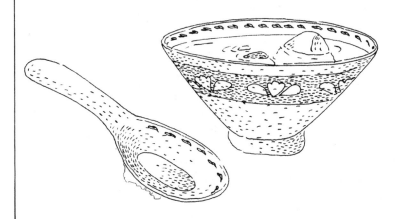

SERVES 6

Clam Chowder

½ pound bacon, diced
2 to 3 ounces diced smoked ham
3 cups chopped onion
3 tablespoons all-purpose flour
6 cups milk
3 cups peeled and diced potato
3 cups minced clams
salt and freshly ground black pepper to taste

GARNISH:
butter

Sauté the bacon and ham in a large saucepan until the bacon is crisp. Drain off the fat and discard. Add the onion and cook until limp, about 10 minutes. Stir in the flour and cook, stirring constantly, for 1 minute. Add the milk and potato and cook for 10 minutes, or until the potato is almost tender. Add the clams and cook for 5 minutes more. Season with salt and pepper to taste. Top each serving with a pat of butter and serve immediately.

SERVES 4 TO 6

Fish Chowder

Leeks are often sandy and should be sliced lengthwise and well rinsed before use.

1½ pounds halibut, haddock, or other firm-fleshed white fish
6 cups water
2 ounces salt pork, rind removed
½ cup butter
½ cup chopped onion
½ cup chopped celery
1 small leek, finely chopped (use some of the green top)
1½ teaspoons salt
½ teaspoon curry powder
3 tablespoons all-purpose flour
2 cups peeled and diced potatos
1 cup light cream
½ cup milk

GARNISH:
2 tablespoons chopped fresh parsley
freshly ground black pepper

Remove the skin and bones from the fish and cut the fish into ½-inch pieces. Put the water in a large kettle and add the fish. (If desired, the skin and bones may be securely wrapped in cheesecloth and added to the broth to improve flavor. Remove them and discard before serving.) Bring the stock to a boil, then lower the heat and simmer for 25 minutes. Drain the fish, reserving 4 cups of the stock. Remove the fine bones from the fish.

Dice the salt pork. In a clean, dry kettle, sauté the salt pork until crisp and golden brown. With a slotted spoon, remove the salt pork to paper toweling to drain. Add the butter, onion, celery, and leek to the pork drippings. Sauté the vegetables until limp, but do not let them brown. Add the salt and curry powder. Stir in the flour and cook for 1 minute, stirring constantly. Add the reserved fish stock and cook until thickened. Add the potato and cook for 25 minutes, or until tender, stirring occasionally.

Remove from the heat. Add the cream, milk, fish, and salt pork. Cover and refrigerate overnight. Reheat, but do not allow to boil. Serve sprinkled with parsley and pepper.

Cuttyhunk Crab Soup

SERVES 4 TO 6

3 tablespoons butter
2 tablespoons diced onion
2 cups crabmeat, canned or frozen, picked over
½ teaspoon salt
freshly ground black pepper to taste
3 cups milk
½ cup heavy cream
2 tablespoons Scotch

GARNISH:
chopped parsley
paprika

In a saucepan, over low heat, melt the butter. Sauté the onion until transparent, about 5 minutes. Stir in the crabmeat, salt, and pepper and cook over low heat for 10 minutes, stirring occasionally.

Place the crabmeat mixture in the top of a double boiler over simmering water. Add the milk and cook, stirring frequently, for 15 minutes. Add the cream and blend well. When the mixture is hot, stir in the Scotch. Sprinkle with parsley and paprika and serve immediately.

In 1936, at the Olympic winter games at Garmisch-Partenkirchen, Germany, the United States fielded its first women's ski team. The women skied only in the alpine events.

SERVES 4

Crab Chowder

4 slices bacon, diced
2 tablespoons all-purpose flour
1 cup milk
2 cups light cream
1 tablespoon onion juice
1 cup tomato juice
1 large clove garlic, minced
¼ teaspoon dried basil
¼ teaspoon dried marjoram
¼ teaspoon freshly ground black pepper
1 cup cooked, diced potato
2 cups flaked crabmeat, picked over
salt or celery salt to taste
paprika

OPTIONAL GARNISH:
crab legs
lemon wedges

Sauté the bacon in a large skillet until crisp. With a slotted spoon remove the bacon to paper toweling to drain. Pour off all but 1½ tablespoons of fat from the skillet. Add the flour and cook 3 minutes, stirring constantly. Gradually add the milk and the cream. Cook and stir until smooth and slightly thickened. Add the onion juice, tomato juice, garlic, and seasonings. Simmer, covered, for 10 minutes. Add the potato and the crabmeat. Adjust the seasonings to taste with salt or celery salt. Sprinkle with paprika and reserved bacon bits and serve, garnished with crab legs and lemon wedges, if desired.

Brunch Specialties

Yampa Valley Mexican Eggs

SECTION CHAIRMAN
Pat Cotsworth

TESTERS
Bill Cotsworth
Margo Crosby
Steve and Judy Fallin
Stewart and Priscilla Fry
Al and Carla Hornung
Dan and Georgia McDaniel
Vicki Michalik
Ted and Lynn Paster
Dave and Helen Robinette
Dal and Andrea Shannon
Dick and Arlene Spinelli
Al and Linda Spring
Walt and Mary Kay Stinson
Rick and Janet Weiner
Rick Yeo

SERVES 8

Sherried Strawberries

4 egg yolks
1 cup granulated sugar
2 to 4 tablespoons sherry
1 cup heavy cream
2 pints strawberries

In a small bowl, combine the egg yolks and sugar and beat until thick and lemon colored. Place in the top of a double boiler and cook, stirring constantly, for about 15 minutes, or until the mixture evenly coats a spoon. Remove from the heat and add the sherry. Chill.

Whip the cream in a chilled bowl. Fold in the chilled egg mixture and refrigerate for 2 to 4 hours.

Wash and hull the strawberries, then drain on paper toweling. Cut the strawberries in half. Just before serving, combine the cream mixture with the strawberries. Serve in parfait or champagne glasses.

SERVES 10

This is better made 24 hours before serving.

Sangria Compote

1 lemon
1 orange
12 ounces pitted prunes
12 ounces dried apricot halves
4 cups dry red wine
⅔ cup granulated sugar
3 whole cinnamon sticks
1 cup orange juice
juice of 1 lemon

GARNISH:
whipped heavy cream or sour cream or plain yogurt

Wash the lemon and the orange and cut off the ends, but do not peel. Slice the fruit into ¼-inch-thick slices, then cut each slice into quarters, or if the fruit is large, cut the slices into eighths.

Place the fruit in a heavy saucepan and add the remaining ingredients. Bring to a boil, then reduce the heat and simmer for 10 minutes, stirring occasionally. Let cool, then remove the cinnamon sticks.

Serve at room temperature in champagne glasses, or in small shallow bowls with a dollop of whipped cream, sour cream, or plain yogurt.

SERVES 8 TO 10

Curried Figs

7 to 8 cups fresh figs, or canned figs, drained
½ cup butter
½ cup (packed) brown sugar
2 teaspoons curry powder
¼ cup lemon juice
½ cup maraschino cherries

Preheat the oven to 325° F.

Place the figs in a 9 x 13-inch baking pan.

Cook the butter, brown sugar, curry powder, and lemon juice in a small saucepan over low heat for 2 to 3 minutes.

Pour the butter-sugar mixture evenly over the figs. Arrange the cherries on top. Bake for 40 minutes, or until bubbly. Serve hot.

SERVES 8

Strawberries Romanov

1 quart large ripe strawberries
granulated sugar to taste
1 cup orange juice
⅓ cup Grand Marnier or other orange flavored liqueur
1½ cups heavy cream
2 tablespoons confectioner's sugar

OPTIONAL:
candied violets

Wash and hull the strawberries. Place in a bowl and sprinkle with sugar. Add the orange juice and orange liqueur and macerate for at least 1 hour.

In a small bowl, whip the cream with the confectioner's sugar.

Place the berries and some of the juice in 8 shallow bowls or sherbet dishes. Discard the remaining juice. Top each serving with whipped cream and garnish with candied violets, if desired.

SERVES 10

Fancy Egg Scramble

1 cup (4 ounces) diced Canadian bacon
¼ cup chopped green onion
3 tablespoons butter
1 cup sliced fresh mushrooms
12 eggs, beaten
Cheese Sauce (recipe follows)
1 tablespoon butter, melted
2¼ cups soft bread crumbs (about 3 slices bread), crusts
    removed
⅛ teaspoon paprika

In a large skillet, cook the Canadian bacon and onion in the butter until the onion is tender. Add the mushrooms and cook for 2 minutes longer. Add the eggs and scramble until barely set.

Fold the cooked eggs into the Cheese Sauce. Turn the mixture into a buttered 7 x 12-inch baking dish.

Combine the melted butter, bread crumbs, and paprika and sprinkle on top of the eggs. Cover and chill until 1 hour before serving time.

Remove the egg mixture from the refrigerator and bring to room temperature. Then bake, uncovered, for 20 minutes in a preheated 350°F oven.

CHEESE SAUCE:
2 tablespoons butter
2 tablespoons all-purpose flour
½ teaspoon salt
⅛ teaspoon freshly ground white pepper
2 cups milk
1 cup shredded mild Cheddar or American cheese (4 ounces)

Melt the butter in a medium saucepan; blend in the flour, salt, and pepper. Add the milk and cook, stirring, until bubbly. Stir in the cheese and blend until the cheese is melted.

SERVES 4

Omelet fillings are limited only by your imagination. Try fresh herbs and diced tomatoes, ratatouille, caponata, prepared chili and sour cream, or raw spinach and crumbled bacon with soy sauce.

Deluxe Vegetarian Omelet

¼ cup vinaigrette (see page 107)
½ cup shredded carrot
¼ cup chopped green onion
½ cup peeled, seeded, and sliced cucumber
1 tomato, peeled, seeded, and chopped
8 eggs
¼ cup milk
1 teaspoon salt
¼ teaspoon freshly ground black pepper
¼ cup butter
1 cup alfalfa sprouts

GARNISH:
plain yogurt
snipped chives

Combine the vinaigrette, carrot, and onion in a small saucepan. Cook over medium-high heat until the vegetables are tender, stirring frequently. Stir in the cucumber and tomato. Keep warm over low heat while preparing the omelets.

Combine the eggs, milk, salt, and pepper in a medium bowl. Beat with a fork or whisk until mixed well, but not frothy.

Melt 1 tablespoon of the butter in an 8-inch omelet pan or skillet over medium-high heat. When a drop of water sizzles in the pan, pour in one fourth of the egg mixture. Cook, gently lifting the edges so the uncooked portion flows underneath, until the eggs are set. Spoon about ¼ cup of the vegetable mixture onto the omelet and top with ¼ cup alfalfa sprouts. Fold the omelet and place on a plate. Repeat with remaining butter, egg mixture, and vegetable mixture to make 3 more omelets. Garnish each with a spoonful of yogurt and a sprinkling of chives. Serve immediately.

SERVES 4

Yampa Valley Mexican Eggs

tortilla chips, crushed
2 tablespoons butter
8 eggs, beaten
1 cup shredded cooked ham
1 cup picante sauce
1 cup grated Cheddar cheese (4 ounces)

Preheat the broiler to medium.

Cover the bottom of an ovenproof serving dish with the crushed tortilla chips.

Melt the butter in a sauté pan and scramble the eggs, leaving them moist but not runny. Spread the eggs over the tortilla chips. Next, layer the ham, picante sauce, and the cheese.

Place the casserole 6 to 8 inches from the broiler heat and broil until the cheese is bubbly and lightly browned. Serve immediately.

SERVES 6

Ranch Eggs

8 slices bacon
3 green bell peppers, thinly sliced
2 large onions, peeled and thinly sliced
4 tomatoes, peeled, seeded, and quartered
1 clove garlic, minced
½ teaspoon salt
¼ teaspoon freshly ground black pepper
12 eggs
½ cup heavy cream
5 tablespoons butter
¼ teaspoon freshly ground white pepper
6 slices bread, crusts removed
1 to 2 tablespoons chopped chives

Sauté the bacon in a large skillet until crisp. Remove the bacon from the skillet and drain. Reserve 4 tablespoons of the rendered bacon fat and in it sauté the peppers and onions.

When the vegetables are soft, add the tomatoes, garlic, salt, and pepper. Cook gently, and when all the vegetables are soft, mash them slightly with a fork. Set the sauce aside and keep warm.

Beat together the eggs and the cream. Melt 4 tablespoons of the butter in a skillet and in it softly scramble the eggs. Add white pepper to taste.

Toast the bread, butter it lightly with the remaining butter, and cut each piece into 4 small triangles.

Mound the scrambled eggs in the center of a warm platter. Sprinkle with chives. Crumble the bacon and sprinkle it over the eggs. Spoon the pepper and tomato sauce in a border around the eggs. Place the toast triangles around the outside edge of the platter. Serve immediately.

US SKITEAM Alpine skiing was not included in the 1924 winter games, which program included cross-country skiing, jumping, speed and figure skating, ice hockey, and a military ski race that probably was the forerunner of the present-day biathlon. Downhill and slalom were added in 1936 in Garmisch-Partenkirchen. In 1952, giant slalom became an official event at the winter Olympics in Oslo, Norway.

SERVES 4

Italian Sausage Frittata

3 hot Italian sausage links (about 1 pound)
½ cup butter
¼ cup olive oil
3 medium potatoes, peeled and cut into ⅛-inch thick
    slices (2 cups)
1½ teaspoons salt
½ cup chopped white onion
5 eggs

Olive oils vary in type and price. The first pressing, called virgin olive oil, is the most flavorful, most expensive, and the best. Lesser olive oils are from second and further pressings and have a heavy, overpowering taste. Olive oil should not be stored in the refrigerator as it becomes cloudy and thick.

Preheat the broiler to medium.

Prick the sausages with a fork. In a large saucepan, poach the sausages in water to cover for 10 minutes. Remove from the saucepan and drain. Place on a broiler rack and broil for 10 minutes, turning once. Cut the sausages into ¼-inch-thick slices and reserve.

Melt ¼ cup of the butter with 2 tablespoons of the olive oil in a large skillet. Add the potatoes. Sprinkle with 1 teaspoon of the salt and turn them several times until they are well coated with the butter-oil mixture. Cook, uncovered, over medium heat for 10 minutes, or until the potatoes are lightly browned. Push the potatoes to one side of the pan. Add the onions and cook, uncovered, for 5 minutes.

Add the sausages to the potato-onion mixture and cook for 5 minutes more. With a slotted spoon, remove the potato-sausage mixture from the skillet.

In a large bowl, beat the eggs with the remaining ½ teaspoon salt. Add the potato and sausage mixture and mix well.

Heat the remaining ¼ cup butter and 2 tablespoons oil in a 9-inch skillet over medium heat. When the butter-oil mixture is very hot, pour in the egg mixture, spreading it so it will cook evenly. From time to time remove the skillet from the heat and shake it vigorously to prevent the eggs from sticking.

When the eggs become firm (about 4 minutes), remove the skillet from the heat. Place a plate over the skillet. Press down on the top of the plate as you flip the skillet upside down, so that the frittata is now on the plate. Slide the frittata back into the skillet and place the skillet back on the heat. Cook for 4 minutes more.

Slide the frittata onto a heated platter and cut into wedges to serve.

Country Brunch

SERVES 12 TO 14

12 eggs, well beaten
9 slices white bread, crusts removed, cut into ½-inch squares
4 tablespoons butter, cut into small cubes
3 cups milk
6 scallions, chopped, including green tops
¼ cup chopped green bell pepper
2 tablespoons chopped pimiento
2 pounds pork sausage, browned, drained, and crumbled
2 cups grated Cheddar cheese (8 ounces)
1 teaspoon salt
¼ teaspoon freshly ground black pepper

Combine all the ingredients in a large bowl and blend well. Pour the egg mixture into a buttered 9 x 13-inch casserole dish and refrigerate, covered, for 8 hours or overnight.

Bake the eggs in a preheated 300° F. oven for 1 hour, uncovered. Serve immediately.

Cheese Blintzes

SERVES 6 TO 7

12 Crepes, cooked on one side only (see page 83)
6 ounces small-curd cottage cheese, well drained
3 ounces cream cheese, at room temperature
1 egg yolk
2 tablespoons granulated sugar
¼ teaspoon salt
butter

GARNISH:
sour cream
blueberries or blueberry preserves

Blend together the cottage cheese, cream cheese, egg yolk, sugar, and salt, using an electric mixer or a food processor.

Place about 2 tablespoons of the mixture in the center of each crêpe, on the cooked side. Fold the crêpe into a square (envelope style). In a sauté pan, melt the butter and in it brown the blintzes on both sides. Serve warm, topped with sour cream and blueberries.

US SKI TEAM In the 1972 Olympic winter games at Sapporo, Japan, Barbara Cochran of the United States Women's Team won the gold medal in slalom, and teammate Susan Corrock won the bronze medal in the downhill.

Tourte Milanaise

SERVES 8

Puff pastry is best made on a cool day. Heat causes the butter to melt too quickly into the flour.

5 large eggs
2 teaspoons chopped chives
1 teaspoon minced fresh parsley
1 teaspoon chopped fresh tarragon
salt to taste
1 tablespoon vegetable oil
1 tablespoon butter
1 pound fresh spinach, trimmed, blanched, and well drained
2 cloves garlic, minced
¼ teaspoon freshly grated nutmeg, or to taste
freshly ground black pepper
1 pound Easy Puff Pastry (recipe follows) or 1 pound frozen
    puff pastry, thawed
2 large red bell peppers, cut into 1-inch pieces and blanched
8 ounces Swiss cheese, thinly sliced
8 ounces baked ham, thinly sliced
1 egg, beaten

Preheat the oven to 350° F.

Combine the eggs, chives, parsley, tarragon, and salt in a bowl and beat well. In an 8-inch skillet, prepare 2 open-faced omelets, using half the egg mixture. Reserve.

Heat the oil and butter in a large skillet. Add the spinach and garlic and sauté for 2 to 3 minutes. Season to taste with nutmeg, salt, and pepper. Remove the spinach from the skillet and reserve.

Lightly butter an 8-inch springform pan. Roll out three fourths of the pastry ¼-inch thick and line the bottom and sides of the pan. Keep the remaining pastry refrigerated.

Layer ingredients in the prepared pan in this order: 1 omelet, half the spinach, half the cheese, half the ham, and all the red pepper. Repeat layering in reverse order, ending with the omelet.

Roll the remaining pastry ¼-inch thick. Cut out an 8-inch circle. Place the circle over the omelet and seal well to the pastry lining by pinching with the fingers. Decorate the top with scraps of pastry.

Brush the pastry with the beaten egg. Place the pan on a baking sheet and bake until golden brown, about 1 hour 15 minutes. Cool for 20 minutes before serving, so that the layers will set.

EASY PUFF PASTRY:
1¼ cups all-purpose flour
⅓ cup cake flour
⅓ teaspoon salt
10 tablespoons *cold* butter
⅓ to ½ cup ice water
8 tablespoons butter, softened

Mix together the flours and salt. Cut the cold butter into small pieces and mix with the flour mixture until the mixture resembles cornmeal. Add enough water to allow the dough to be gathered into a ball. Do not overwork this mixing process. Chill the dough for at least 30 minutes.

Roll the pastry into a rectangle about 18 inches long. Spread two thirds of the pastry with 2 tablespoons of the softened butter. Fold the unbuttered third over half of the buttered area. Fold the remaining third over the top of the pastry. Turn the pastry one quarter turn. Roll out as before. Spread bottom two thirds of pastry with 2 tablespoons butter and fold as before. Wrap and chill for about 25 minutes in the freezer or an hour in the refrigerator. Repeat rolling, buttering, folding, and turning process twice more. Wrap and chill for an hour or longer. The pastry is now ready to use, or it can be tightly wrapped and stored in the refrigerator for 2 days.

There were 15 centuries between the last of Hellenic Olympics in the fourth century A. D. and the first modern Olympics, held in 1896. The games were revived by Baron Pierre de Doubertin, the father of the modern Olympic games, who stated the Olympic creed, "The most important thing in the Olympic games is not to win but to take part, just as the most important thing in life is not the triumph but the struggle."

Copper Mountain Quiche

SERVES 8

This is a rich, dense quiche.

½ cup butter
4 ounces cream cheese
1 cup plus 2 tablespoons all-purpose flour
1 pound fresh spinach, washed and trimmed or 1 package (10 ounces) frozen chopped spinach
1 cup grated Cheddar cheese (4 ounces)
1 cup grated Swiss cheese (4 ounces)
3 eggs, lightly beaten
½ cup mayonnaise
½ cup milk
10 slices bacon, crisply cooked and crumbled
8 ounces fresh mushrooms, sliced
1 bunch green onions, trimmed and sliced

Combine the butter, cream cheese, and 1 cup of the flour in a small bowl. With a pastry blender or fork, cut the butter and cheese into the flour until crumbly.

Place the flour mixture in a pie plate or quiche pan and press evenly to form a crust. Refrigerate.

Preheat the oven to 350° F.

Cook the spinach, covered, in a saucepan until just tender. Drain well and chop. Drain again on paper toweling.

In a large bowl, combine the spinach with the 2 tablespoons flour and the remaining ingredients and mix well. Pour the egg-vegetable mixture into the chilled pastry shell and bake for 1 hour, or until set. Serve hot.

Glorious Grits

SERVES 6 TO 8

4 cups water
½ teaspoon salt
1 cup quick grits
1½ cups grated sharp Cheddar cheese (6 ounces)
½ cup butter, cut in small pieces
2 cloves garlic, pressed
dash of hot pepper sauce
3 eggs

Preheat the oven to 350° F.

Heat the water with the salt, in a heavy saucepan, to a boil. Stir the grits slowly into the boiling water. Return to a boil, reduce the heat, and cook for 10 minutes, stirring occasionally. Remove the pan from the heat. Whisk in the cheese, butter, garlic, and hot pepper sauce. Stir until the cheese melts. Let cool slightly.

In a large bowl, lightly beat the eggs. Add ½ cup of the grits mixture to the eggs and beat well. Then add the remaining grits and blend. Pour the grits into a buttered 2-quart casserole dish and bake for 45 minutes to 1 hour, or until set. Serve hot.

Cheese Burek

SERVES 6 TO 8

1 pound hoop or farmer's cheese, crumbled
8 ounces feta cheese, crumbled
2 cups cottage cheese, drained
4 eggs
1 teaspoon granulated sugar
1 pound phyllo leaves
1 cup butter, melted

Preheat the oven to 350° F.

In a large bowl, mix all the cheeses together until well blended.

Combine the eggs and sugar in a separate bowl and beat well with an electric mixer. Fold the eggs into the cheese mixture. Stir until creamy.

Place 2 sheets of the phyllo, folded, in a buttered 9 x 13-inch casserole dish. Brush the phyllo with melted butter. Cover with one fourth of the cheese mixture.

Repeat layering the phyllo and the cheese mixture, ending with phyllo and melted butter.

Bake for 30 to 40 minutes, or until brown and crispy. Let stand for 10 minutes before cutting into squares.

Swiss Fondue

SERVES 4

Natural hard cheese such as Cheddar and Swiss is outstanding for cooking. Processed cheese has neither the flavor nor the body of a natural cheese and is not a good substitute.

1 clove garlic, halved
2 cups dry white wine
1 pound imported natural Swiss or Gruyère cheese, shredded
2 tablespoons cornstarch or all-purpose flour
1 tablespoon kirsch or brandy
freshly grated nutmeg
salt and freshly ground white pepper to taste

OPTIONAL:
dash of cayenne

Rub a heavy earthenware fondue pot with garlic and discard the garlic clove.

Heat the wine in the pot just until air bubbles rise. Slowly add the cheese, stirring constantly with a wooden spoon.

Combine the cornstarch, kirsch, and a spoonful of the heated wine in a small bowl. Stir to dissolve the cornstarch. Pour the cornstarch into the cheese mixture and blend well. Season with nutmeg, salt, pepper, and cayenne, if desired.

Serve with fondue forks and cubed French or Italian bread.

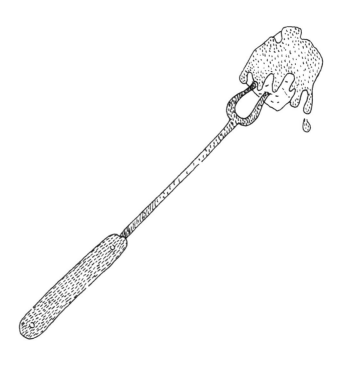

SERVES 4

These are thin, light pancakes that take only 5 minutes to make.

Cottage Cheese Pancakes

6 tablespoons butter, melted
6 eggs
6 tablespoons all-purpose flour
1 cup creamy cottage cheese

Heat a pancake griddle or heavy skillet over medium heat.

In a blender or food processor, combine all the ingredients and blend for 1 minute. Drop onto the hot griddle by tablespoonsful and cook until golden brown on both sides. Serve immediately.

SERVES 4 TO 6

Good served with link sausages for breakfast or with ice cream for dessert. The topping can be prepared ahead and reheated just before serving.

German Apple Pancake

3 large eggs
¾ cup milk
¾ cup all-purpose flour
½ teaspoon salt
5½ tablespoons butter
1 pound tart apples, peeled and thinly sliced
¼ cup granulated sugar
1 teaspoon ground cinnamon

GARNISH:
confectioner's sugar

Preheat the oven to 450° F.

Beat the eggs, milk, flour, and salt in a small bowl until smooth.

Melt 1½ tablespoons of the butter in a heavy 12-inch ovenproof skillet. As soon as it is very hot, pour in the batter and put the skillet in the oven. Bake at 450° F. for 15 minutes, then lower the oven temperature to 350° F. and continue baking for 10 minutes. The pancake should be light brown and crisp. If the pancake puffs up in large bubbles during the first 15 minutes, pierce it with a fork to deflate.

Meanwhile, in a sauté pan, melt the remaining 4 tablespoons of butter and in it cook the apples with the granulated sugar and cinnamon, just until the apples are tender.

When the pancake is done, slide it onto a serving platter and pour the apples over the top. Sprinkle with confectioner's sugar and serve immediately, cut into wedges.

SERVES 6

Potato Pancakes with Sour Cream and Lingonberries

3 large baking potatoes, peeled and grated
1 medium onion, grated
1 egg, beaten
½ cup all-purpose flour
salt and freshly ground black pepper to taste
vegetable oil

GARNISH:
sour cream
lingonberry preserves

In a bowl, mix together the potatoes, onion, egg, flour, and salt and pepper. Stir until blended.

Heat the oil in a heavy skillet over medium heat until just smoking. Spoon the potato mixture into the skillet in mounds and flatten with a spatula. Cook until the bottoms are golden brown, then turn and cook on the other sides.

Serve the pancakes immediately with a dollop of sour cream and a spoonful of preserves.

SERVES 6

Stuffed French Toast

1 package (8 ounces) cream cheese, softened
1½ teaspoons vanilla extract
¾ teaspoon granulated sugar
½ cup chopped pecans
1 loaf (16 ounces) soft French bread
4 eggs, beaten
1 cup milk
½ teaspoon freshly grated nutmeg
1 jar (12 ounces) apricot preserves
½ cup orange juice

Beat the cream cheese, 1 teaspoon of the vanilla, and the sugar in a small bowl until creamy. Stir in the pecans and set aside.

Cut the bread into 10 to 12 slices 1½ inches thick. Cut a slit in each slice, creating a pocket. Fill each pocket with 1½ tablespoons of the cheese mixture.

Beat together the eggs, milk, the remaining ½ teaspoon vanilla, and the nutmeg in a large shallow bowl. Dip the filled bread slices into the egg mixture on both sides, then cook, in batches, on a lightly greased hot griddle until both sides are golden brown. Remove to a platter and keep warm while cooking the remaining toast.

Heat the preserves and orange juice in a small saucepan. Simmer for 3 to 4 minutes, or until slightly thickened. Drizzle the hot apricot mixture over the French toast and serve immediately.

 # Skiers French Toast

SERVES 6 TO 8

The French toast may be placed in the oven overnight, with a timed setting. Awaken to a warm, wonderful breakfast.

2 tablespoons corn syrup (light or dark)
½ cup butter
1 cup (packed) brown sugar
1 loaf unsliced white bread, crusts trimmed
5 eggs
1½ cups milk
1 teaspoon vanilla extract
¼ teaspoon salt

Combine the corn syrup, butter, and brown sugar in a small saucepan and simmer until syrupy. Pour this mixture over the bottom of a 9 x 13-inch casserole dish.

Slice the bread into 12 to 16 slices and place the slices over the sugar-butter mixture in the dish.

In a bowl, beat together the eggs, milk, vanilla, and salt and pour this mixture over the bread. Cover the dish and let it stand in the refrigerator overnight.

Preheat the oven to 350° F.

Uncover the pan and bake for 45 minutes. Serve while hot or warm or the French toast will harden in the pan. This can be reheated.

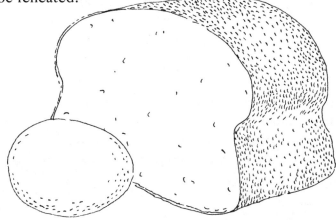

Elegant French Toast

SERVES 8

8 slices Texas toast or French bread, cut 1 inch thick
4 eggs
1 cup milk
½ teaspoon vanilla extract
1 tablespoon granulated sugar
¼ teaspoon salt
2 tablespoons Grand Marnier
2 tablespoons butter

GARNISH:
confectioner's sugar

Arrange the bread in a 9 x 13-inch casserole dish, in a single layer.

Combine the eggs, milk, vanilla, sugar, salt, and Grand Marnier in a medium bowl and beat with a rotary beater or electric mixer. Pour this mixture over the bread and turn the slices to soak evenly. Refrigerate up to 4 hours.

At serving time, melt 1 tablespoon of the butter in a large skillet over medium heat until the butter is almost smoking. Add a few slices of bread, then reduce the heat and cook on each side until golden. Repeat with the remaining butter and bread. Serve sprinkled with confectioner's sugar.

Whole-Wheat Oatmeal Waffles

SERVES 6

½ cup butter, melted
3 eggs, beaten
2 cups milk
1 cup whole-wheat flour
½ cup all-purpose flour
½ cup oatmeal
¼ cup wheat germ
1 tablespoon baking powder
½ teaspoon salt
½ teaspoon ground cinnamon

Combine the butter, eggs, and milk in a large bowl and whisk to blend. Combine the remaining ingredients in a small bowl and mix together. Pour the dry ingredients into the egg mixture and stir until blended. Do not overbeat. Bake in a preheated waffle iron. Serve immediately.

US SKI TEAM Bill Koch won the first Nordic medal ever for the United States by taking the silver in the 30-kilometer cross-country race at Innsbruck in 1976.

SERVES 10

Apple-Sausage Ring

1½ cups saltine cracker crumbs
½ cup milk
2 eggs, lightly beaten
2 pounds bulk pork sausage
⅓ cup minced onion
2 tablespoons brown sugar
1 teaspoon grated lemon zest
1¾ cups peeled, chopped tart apples

Soak the cracker crumbs in the milk in a small bowl. Add the remaining ingredients and mix well by hand. Press the mixture into a buttered ring mold. Refrigerate overnight.

Preheat the oven to 350° F.

Bake the sausage ring on a jelly-roll pan for 1 to 1¼ hours, or until browned and cooked through. If the sausage becomes too brown, cover it with foil during the last 30 minutes of cooking time.

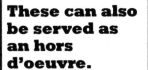

MAKES 48

These can also be served as an hors d'oeuvre.

Miniature Sausage Loaves

1 cup crushed saltine cracker crumbs
¾ cup milk
1 pound hot bulk pork sausage
1 to 2 tablespoons prepared horseradish
1 tablespoon mustard seed
1 beaten egg

Preheat the oven to 350° F.

In a small bowl, soak the cracker crumbs in the milk until soft. Add the remaining ingredients and mix well by hand. Pack the mixture into miniature muffin tins and bake for 12 to 15 minutes, or until well browned. Remove carefully from the oven and drain off the grease before serving.

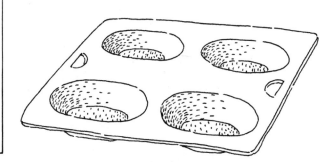

Asparagus and Ham Crêpes

SERVES 6

Make crêpes when you have a little extra time and freeze, layered with waxed paper and wrapped in foil, for up to 3 months.

48 asparagus spears
12 thin slices ham
12 Savory Crêpes (see page 83)
12 thin slices Swiss cheese
2 large tomatoes, peeled, seeded, and chopped
3 tablespoons minced shallot
4 tablespoons butter
½ cup sliced fresh mushrooms
4 tablespoons Madeira or Port
2 tablespoons all-purpose flour
½ cup Chicken Stock (see page 56)
½ cup light cream
¼ to ½ teaspoon dried tarragon or 1 tablespoon chopped
    fresh tarragon
salt and freshly ground black pepper to taste

OPTIONAL:
Dijon mustard

Preheat the oven to 350° F.

Trim the asparagus spears and cook in boiling salted water until crisp-tender, about 5 minutes. Drain.

Place a slice of ham on each crêpe. Spread a little mustard on the ham, if desired. Cover with a slice of Swiss cheese. Place 4 asparagus spears on each crêpe so that 2 tips protrude from each end when the crêpes are rolled. Top the asparagus with the chopped tomato. Roll the crêpes, then place in a single layer in a buttered 9 x 13-inch baking pan.

Sauté the shallot in 2 tablespoons of the butter until transparent but not browned. Add the mushrooms and the Madeira or Port, cover, and simmer for 1 minute. Uncover and raise the heat. Cook until almost all the liquid is evaporated.

Add the remaining 2 tablespoons butter and let melt. Mix in the flour and cook over low heat, stirring constantly, for 1 minute. Remove from the heat.

Blend the chicken stock and cream into the flour until the mixture is smooth. Return the pan to medium heat and cook, stirring, until the sauce thickens. Do not boil. Add the tarragon, salt and pepper and stir. Pour the sauce over the center of the crêpes. Bake for 20 minutes, or until the sauce is hot and bubbly.

Savory or Sweet Crêpes

**MAKES
24 CREPES**

SAVORY CRÊPES:
1 cup cold water
1 cup cold milk
4 eggs
½ teaspoon salt
2 cups sifted all-purpose flour
4 tablespoons butter, melted

SWEET CRÊPES:
1 cup light cream
1 cup club soda
4 eggs
¼ teaspoon salt
1 tablespoon granulated sugar
1 cup sifted all-purpose flour
3 tablespoons melted butter
½ teaspoon vanilla or almond or lemon extract

For either batter recipe: Place all ingredients except flavorings into a blender jar. Cover and blend at top speed for 30 seconds. Scrape down the sides of the blender jar. Mix again for a few seconds until smooth. Cover and refrigerate for at least 2 hours. Add the flavorings just before cooking and stir.

The batter should be a very light cream, just thick enough to coat a wooden spoon. If the batter seems too thick, stir in a little water, a spoonful at a time.

Cooking the crêpe: Brush the skillet lightly with oil or clarified butter. Set over moderately high heat until the pan is just beginning to smoke. Immediately remove the pan from the heat and pour a scant ¼ cup batter into the middle of the pan. Tilt pan in all directions to run the batter all over the bottom of the pan in a thin film. Return the pan to the heat for about 1 minute. Turn the crêpe over with a spatula or fingers and brown the other side for about 30 seconds. The second side will not brown evenly; use this side as the inside when preparing filled crêpes.

 It's hard to believe, but the highest speed ever claimed for any skier is 126.24 miles per hour by Franz Weber of Austria. The fastest by a woman is 111.29 miles per hour by Marty Martin-Kunz of the United States. Both were achieved at Silverton, Colorado, on April 24, 1982. The highest average race speed in Olympic downhill competition was a recorded 63.894 miles per hour in 1976 by Austria's Franz Klammer at Innsbruck, Austria.

SERVES 6

Dutch Potatoes

To make sausage: In a food processor, combine 1 pound lean pork, ¼ pound hard fatback, 1½ tablespoons coarse salt, ½ teaspoon quatre-epices, freshly ground black pepper, and 2 tablespoons parsley or thyme or sage.

4 tablespoons butter
1 tablespoon all-purpose flour
1 cup light cream
2 cups grated sharp Cheddar cheese (8 ounces)
cayenne to taste
salt to taste
4 large new potatoes, cooked, peeled, and sliced
4 hard-cooked eggs, sliced
8 ounces bulk sausage, browned and drained
½ cup fine dry bread crumbs
2 tablespoons butter, melted

Preheat the oven to 350° F.

Melt the butter in a saucepan. Stir in the flour and blend well. Add the cream and cook, stirring constantly, until thickened. Add the cheese, cayenne, and salt. Stir to blend. Remove from the heat.

Layer half the potatoes, eggs, sausage, and cheese sauce in a buttered 7 x 11-inch casserole dish. Repeat.

Top the potatoes with bread crumbs and drizzle with the melted butter. Bake, uncovered, for 30 minutes, or until bubbly.

SERVES 2 TO 4

Chocolate-Strawberry Omelet

3 large eggs
2½ tablespoons confectioner's sugar
2 tablespoons powdered cocoa
2 tablespoons coconut liqueur
1 tablespoon butter
¼ cup grated semisweet chocolate
1 cup sliced fresh strawberries
1 cup heavy cream, whipped
confectioner's sugar

GARNISH:
whipped cream
whole strawberries

In a blender or food processor, combine the eggs, confectioner's sugar, cocoa, and coconut liqueur and blend at high speed for 10 to 15 seconds.

Preheat a 10-inch shallow, nonstick omelet pan or skillet

over medium heat. Melt the butter in it, tilting pan to coat bottom and sides. Pour the egg mixture into the pan, using a wire whisk to fluff the mixture as it begins to set.

As the omelet completes cooking, the top should be moist, but not runny. Remove the omelet from the pan by loosening the edges and letting it slide out onto a heated 12 to 15-inch platter.

Sprinkle the grated chocolate over the top of the omelet. Arrange the sliced strawberries over half the omelet, then spread whipped cream on top of the strawberries. Fold the omelet in half and dust the top with confectioner's sugar. Garnish the edges with additional whipped cream and whole strawberries. Slice into 2 to 4 servings and serve immediately.

Shaker Heights Rice Pudding

SERVES 8

1 scant cup uncooked long grain rice
1 tablespoon butter
5 large eggs
1 cup granulated sugar
½ teaspoon salt
½ teaspoon vanilla extract
1 quart low-fat milk
1 cup raisins
cinnamon

Cook the rice according to package directions.

Preheat the oven to 325° F. Generously butter a shallow 2-quart baking dish.

In a large bowl, lightly beat the eggs. Add the sugar, salt, vanilla extract, and milk. Mix thoroughly.

Spread the rice evenly on the bottom of the prepared dish. Sprinkle the raisins over all. Pour the egg-milk mixture over the rice and raisins. Sprinkle with cinnamon.

Bake for 50 to 60 minutes, or until set. Serve hot or cold.

Harvey Wallbanger Soufflé

SERVES 6

1 envelope unflavored gelatin
1¼ cups orange juice
½ cup granulated sugar plus additional for sprinkling
3 eggs, separated
2 tablespoons Galliano liqueur
2 tablespoons vodka
butter
1 cup heavy cream, whipped

GARNISH:
whipped cream
3 orange slices, cut in half and twisted

In a small bowl, soften the gelatin in the orange juice.

Combine ¼ cup of the sugar and the gelatin-orange juice mixture in a medium saucepan. Stir constantly over high heat until the mixture boils and the gelatin dissolves. Remove from the heat.

In a small bowl, beat the egg yolks with an electric mixer on high speed until thick and lemon-colored, about 5 minutes. Stir ½ cup of the gelatin mixture into the egg yolks, then return the egg yolk mixture to the gelatin mixture in the saucepan. Stir constantly over medium heat until the mixture thickens and coats a spoon. Remove from the heat. Stir in the Galliano and vodka. Refrigerate until partially set, stirring occasionally.

Meanwhile, butter six 8-ounce wine glasses. Sprinkle the inside of each glass with sugar. Cut a strip of foil to fit around the outside of each glass, extending about 1 inch above the rim. Place foil collars around the glasses. If necessary, secure the collars with paper clips. Set the glasses aside.

In a medium bowl, beat the egg whites with an electric mixer on high speed until soft peaks form. Gradually add the remaining ¼ cup sugar, beating until stiff peaks form. Fold the whipped cream into the cold egg yolk mixture. Then fold the whipped cream mixture into the egg whites.

Spoon the mixture into the prepared glasses. Cover and refrigerate until firm, at least 2 hours, or overnight. Before serving, carefully remove the collars. Garnish with additional whipped cream and twisted orange slices.

Salads

Peachtree Pecan and Chicken Salad

SECTION CHAIRMEN
Jerry Cunningham
Kris Ryall

TESTERS
Vesta Brechtel
Rosemary Burris
Betty Clark
Jan DeBoer
Nancy Gerhardy
Nancy Gooding
Rusty Hayden
Charlotte Head
Barbara Knapp
Karen Kruse
Nancy Kuhl
LaNelle Lee
Ruth Logan
Fran Nabor
Barbara Nelson
Lois Nelson
Betty Shaw
Lynn Sheridan
Carmen Stansberry
Helen Winzeler
Phyllis Writz
Mimi Yen

**SERVES 10
TO 12**

Shrimp and Scallop Salad

To make
tarragon or
other herb
vinegar: Place
sprigs of the
fresh herb in a
clean glass jar
or clear wine
bottle. Fill to
the top with
white wine
vinegar. Cover
and let stand 1
week before
using.

1½ pounds uncooked medium shrimp
1½ pounds uncooked sea scallops, halved
1½ cups light olive oil
⅔ cup white wine vinegar or tarragon vinegar
2 cloves garlic, minced
3 green onions, minced
salt and freshly ground black pepper to taste
1 head cauliflower, trimmed and broken into flowerets
½ head red cabbage, cored and coarsely shredded
3 carrots, peeled and shredded
2 medium zucchini, shredded
1 package (10 ounces) frozen tiny peas, thawed
3 stalks celery, chopped
½ medium red onion, minced

OPTIONAL:
1 tablespoon Dijon mustard

GARNISH:
1 head romaine lettuce, rinsed, dried, and chilled

Bring 2 quarts of water to a boil in a large saucepan. Add the shrimp and bring to a boil again. Cook for 1 minute more, or until the shells turn bright pink. Immediately remove the shrimp with a slotted spoon and let cool. Remove the shells and discard. Reserve the shrimp in a bowl.

Place the scallops in a saucepan, cover with cold water, and simmer until they are just firm, about 3 minutes. Remove the scallops with a slotted spoon and add to the shrimp.

Combine the olive oil, vinegar, garlic, green onions, and salt and pepper to taste. Add the mustard, if desired, and whisk until well blended.

Pour half the dressing over the seafood. Marinate, covered, in the refrigerator overnight. Cover and refrigerate the remaining dressing.

Up to 3 hours before serving, prepare the cauliflower, cabbage, carrots, zucchini, peas, celery, and red onion, then combine in a large bowl. Cover and refrigerate.

At serving time, arrange the lettuce leaves on a platter. Put the vegetables in a ring around the edge and mound the seafood in the center. Serve with the remaining dressing.

Chicken Salad Pie

SERVES 6 TO 8

If desired, ⅓ cup grated Cheddar cheese may be added to a favorite pastry recipe for the pie shell.

1½ cups diced cooked chicken
1½ cups chopped fresh pineapple or 1 can (12 ounces) pineapple tidbits, drained
½ cup chopped walnuts
½ cup diced celery
⅔ cup sour cream
⅔ cup mayonnaise
1 pre-baked 8-inch pastry shell
3 tablespoons grated sharp Cheddar cheese

In a bowl, combine the chicken, pineapple, walnuts, and celery.

In another bowl, mix the sour cream and mayonnaise.

Add ⅔ cup of the sour cream mixture to the chicken mixture. Mix the salad until well blended and place in the pastry shell. Pat the mixture into the shell so that the top is as even as possible. Pour the remaining sour cream mixture onto the chicken mixture and spread it evenly. Sprinkle the grated cheese on top. Refrigerate the pie for at least 4 hours.

Macadamia Nut and Chicken Salad

SERVES 6

2 small whole chicken breasts, poached, skinned, boned, and cut into 1½-inch pieces
1 tart green apple, peeled and cut into 1-inch pieces
1 cup diced fresh pineapple
½ cup white raisins or 1 cup seedless green grapes, halved
3 tablespoons chopped chutney
1 cup mayonnaise
1½ teaspoons curry powder
salt to taste
3 chilled ripe cantaloupes, halved, peeled, and seeded
1 cup coarsely chopped macadamia nuts

GARNISH:
Bibb lettuce leaves, washed, dried, and chilled

In a bowl, combine the chicken, apple, pineapple, raisins or grapes, chutney, mayonnaise, curry powder, and salt. Taste and adjust the seasoning. Cover and refrigerate 4 hours or overnight.

At serving time, place the lettuce leaves on individual chilled plates. Cut the bottoms off each cantaloupe half to form a thick ring and place on each plate. Mound the salad in the center of the cantaloupe ring. Sprinkle the nuts on top of the salad.

SERVES 4 TO 6

Peachtree Pecan and Chicken Salad

1 cup whole pecans
1 cup strips (2x¼ inches) of cooked chicken breast
1 cup strips (2x¼ inches) of cooked ham
1 cup chopped celery
1 apple, peeled, cored, and sliced
¾ cup mayonnaise
lemon juice to taste
salt and freshly ground black pepper to taste

GARNISH:
soft-leafed lettuce for lining the platter
1 lemon, cut into wedges
1 tomato, cut into wedges
fresh parsley sprigs
minced fresh parsley

Preheat the oven to 350° F.

Spread the pecans in one layer in a jelly roll pan and toast in the oven, shaking the pan occasionally, for 8 to 10 minutes, or until they are golden brown. Transfer the nuts to paper toweling and let cool for 5 minutes.

In a large bowl, combine the toasted pecans, chicken, ham, celery, apple, and mayonnaise. Season the salad to taste with the lemon juice, salt, and pepper. Chill for 2 to 4 hours.

At serving time, line a platter with lettuce. Mound the salad in the center and garnish it with the lemon wedges, tomato wedges, parsley sprigs, and minced parsley.

From 1936 to 1940, the men on the Dartmouth College teams were the power in U.S. racing, and made the first appreciable dent in the European circuit. Dick Durrance's eighth in the combined downhill and slalom at the 1936 Olympics in Garmisch-Partenkirchen was the highest alpine racing finish by an American man until another Dartmouth man, Bill Beck, got a fifth at Oslo in 1952.

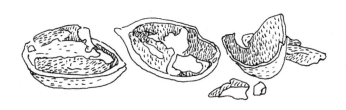

SERVES 6

Zest is the colored part of the peel of citrus fruit. Remove the zest from the fruit with a citrus zester or a grater. Be sure no pith (the white part) is included.

Creamy Crabmeat Salad

2 cups crabmeat, picked over for shells
¾ cup chopped celery
4 green onions, chopped
¼ cup minced fresh parsley
¼ cup mayonnaise
1 tablespoon prepared mustard
¼ cup heavy cream, whipped
2 tablespoons slivered almonds, toasted
seasoned salt to taste

GARNISH:
lettuce leaves
lemon zest

Combine the crabmeat, celery, onions, and parsley in a large bowl. Chill.

Combine the mayonnaise and mustard in a small bowl, then fold in the whipped cream. Add the dressing to the crabmeat mixture and mix lightly but thoroughly. Add the almonds and seasoned salt to taste. Serve on a lettuce-lined platter garnished with lemon zest.

SERVES 6

Halibut Salad

2 pounds fresh halibut fillets
2 yellow onions, peeled and quartered
bouquet garni (1 bay leaf, 4 sprigs fresh parsley, ½ teaspoon
    thyme, and 6 black peppercorns, tied in cheesecloth)
½ cup mayonnaise
½ cup chili sauce
juice of one large lemon (about 3 tablespoons)
½ cup heavy cream, whipped
4 hard-cooked eggs, chopped
4 stalks celery, chopped
salt and freshly ground black pepper to taste

In a large stainless steel sauté pan, place the fish, onions, bouquet garni, and enough water to come to the level of 1 inch in the pan. Bring the liquid to a boil, then reduce the heat. Simmer, covered, for 7 to 10 minutes, or until the fish is just cooked.

Carefully remove the fish to a rack and let it cool and drain. Discard poaching liquid or strain, reduce, and freeze for fish stock.

While the fish is cooling, combine the mayonnaise, chili sauce, and lemon juice in a small bowl. Mix thoroughly. Fold in the whipped cream and mix just until blended.

Flake the fish into large pieces and place in a large bowl. Add the eggs and celery. Pour on enough dressing to moisten the salad, then season with salt and pepper. Pour the remaining dressing into a small pitcher or bowl and refrigerate.

Refrigerate the salad for 3 to 4 hours. Serve with the remaining dressing.

SERVES 6

Oriental Shrimp Salad

8 ounces flat Japanese noodles (*udon*) or linguine (broken in half)
¼ cup sesame oil mixed with ¼ cup peanut oil
8 ounces mushrooms, sliced
1 pound small shrimp, cooked
1 bunch green onions, washed, trimmed, and thinly sliced
⅓ to ½ cup Japanese soy sauce
¼ cup sake
¼ cup toasted sesame seeds
2 tablespoons grated fresh ginger root
2 cloves garlic, mashed

Bring a large amount of salted water to a rapid boil. Add the noodles, stir, and cook until just tender but firm to the bite (al dente), about 10 minutes. Drain the noodles and rinse under cold water. Drain again and pat dry with paper toweling. Transfer the noodles to a large bowl.

Heat 2 tablespoons of the oil mixture in a large skillet over medium-high heat. Add the mushrooms and sauté for 5 minutes. Combine the sautéed mushrooms, shrimp, and onions with the noodles.

In a small bowl, combine the soy sauce, sake, sesame seeds, ginger root, garlic, and the remaining oil mixture. Pour the soy sauce mixture over the noodle-shrimp mixture and blend well. Cover and refrigerate for up to 4 hours. Remove from the refrigerator 30 minutes before serving time. Toss the salad gently to reblend.

US SKI TEAM The year 1981 was a significant one for America when Phil Mahre became the first American to win the Overall World Cup Championship, requiring top total scoring in downhill, slalom, giant slalom, and combined.

In 1982, Mahre again earned the Overall Championship title and was joined by Nordic team member Bill Koch resulting in the first U.S. men's alpine and Nordic championship sweep.

The following season Tamara McKinney became the first American woman to secure the coveted Overall World Cup Championship title in the same year Phil Mahre won his third consecutive Overall championship.

SERVES 6

Green Salad with Walnut Vinaigrette

Walnut oil has an intense, nutty flavor that competes for attention. It is best used in uncomplicated salads.

¾ cup walnut pieces
1 tablespoon granulated sugar
2 tablespoons fruit vinegar
6 to 8 tablespoons walnut oil
salt and freshly ground black pepper
2 heads Bibb lettuce, washed, dried, and chilled
2 ripe avocados, peeled and sliced

Blanch the walnut pieces in boiling water and remove with a slotted spoon to paper toweling. Quickly put the walnut pieces on foil and sprinkle with the sugar while still warm. This can be done a day in advance.

Combine the vinegar, walnut oil, and salt and pepper to taste in a small bowl.

Tear the lettuce into bite-sized pieces and put into a chilled serving bowl. Add the avocado, walnuts, and just enough of the vinaigrette to lightly coat the salad. Serve immediately.

SERVES 6 TO 8

Spinach Salad with Chutney Dressing

¼ cup wine vinegar
3 to 4 tablespoons chutney
2 cloves garlic, crushed
2 tablespoons coarsely ground French mustard or Dijon
    mustard
3 teaspoons granulated sugar
½ cup vegetable oil
salt and freshly ground black pepper to taste
8 ounces fresh spinach, washed and trimmed
8 mushrooms, sliced
1 cup sliced water chestnuts
6 slices bacon, crisply cooked and crumbled
¼ cup fresh bean sprouts
½ cup shredded Gruyère cheese
½ cup thinly sliced red onion

Combine the vinegar, chutney, garlic, mustard, and sugar in a food processor or blender. Blend until smooth. With the machine running, slowly pour in the oil through the feed tube and process until thick and smooth. Season to taste with salt and pepper. (If the dressing is prepared in advance, refrigerate it until 30 minutes before serving time. Bring to room temperature and reblend.)

Tear the spinach into bite-sized pieces.

Combine the spinach, mushrooms, water chestnuts, bacon, bean sprouts, cheese, and onion in a large salad bowl. Mix lightly. Add the dressing and toss to distribute evenly.

SERVES 6 AS A MAIN COURSE, 10 AS AN ACCOMPANIMENT

Greek Spinach Salad

6 ounces marinated artichoke hearts
1 tablespoon olive oil
2 tablespoons lemon juice
2 teaspoons chopped fresh basil or ½ teaspoon dried
½ teaspoon dry mustard
dash of freshly ground black pepper
10 ounces fresh spinach, washed and trimmed
3 to 4 green onions, thinly sliced
1 hard-cooked egg, sliced
8 to 10 cherry tomatoes, halved
4 ounces mushrooms, sliced
4 ounces feta cheese, crumbled
¾ cup Greek olives

Drain the marinade from the artichoke hearts into a small bowl and reserve the hearts. To the marinade, add the oil, lemon juice, basil, mustard, and pepper. Blend well and set aside.

Tear the spinach leaves into bite-sized pieces and place in a salad bowl. Add the onions and toss.

Arrange the egg, reserved artichokes, tomatoes, and mushrooms in rows on top of the spinach. Then sprinkle the feta cheese and olives on top.

Blend the dressing again and place in a small pitcher. After the salad presentation, pour on the dressing and toss gently.

US SKI TEAM The 1936 winter Olympics was the first winter games in which men skied alpine as well as Nordic events.

SERVES 8

Zucchini Slaw

½ cup mayonnaise
3 tablespoons white wine vinegar
1 tablespoon granulated sugar
1 teaspoon caraway seed
4 cups shredded zucchini
¼ cup thinly sliced green onion
3 large, crisp apples, cored and diced
salt and freshly ground black pepper to taste

Combine the mayonnaise, vinegar, sugar, and caraway seed in a small bowl. Whisk thoroughly.

In a large bowl, toss the zucchini, onions, and apples together. Pour the dressing over the zucchini mixture and season to taste with salt and pepper. Cover and chill for 2 to 4 hours.

SERVES 6

Santa Fe Cole Slaw

3 cups shredded cabbage
1 green bell pepper, seeded and diced
1 red bell pepper, seeded and diced, or 1 jar (4 ounces) chopped pimiento
3 tablespoons minced fresh parsley
½ to 1 small red onion, chopped
1½ tablespoons vegetable oil
¼ cup cider vinegar
1 tablespoon granulated sugar
½ teaspoon dry mustard
1 clove garlic, minced
1 teaspoon salt
1 teaspoon freshly ground black pepper

In a large bowl, combine the cabbage, green and red pepper, parsley, and onion.

In a small bowl, combine the vegetable oil, vinegar, sugar, mustard, garlic, salt, and pepper.

Pour the dressing over the cabbage mixture and mix thoroughly. Refrigerate several hours or overnight.

US SKI TEAM **The 1972 Sapporo, Japan, Olympics was the first ever held in the Far East.**

SERVES 6 TO 8

Hawaiian Salad

Salad greens should be washed, dried, and chilled for at least several hours before use. Salad spinners or plastic storage bags will keep lettuce crisp for several days in the refrigerator.

1 head red leaf lettuce, washed, dried, and chilled
1 head Bibb lettuce, washed, dried, and chilled
1 cup small fresh parsley sprigs
1½ cups bean sprouts
1 bunch green onions, sliced
1 cup fresh snow peas or 1 package (10 ounces) frozen snow peas, thawed
½ cup salted peanuts
½ cup olive oil
6 tablespoons wine vinegar
1 tablespoon soy sauce
1 teaspoon dry mustard
½ teaspoon sesame oil
¼ cup granulated sugar
2 tablespoons sesame seeds, toasted

GARNISH:
8 to 10 wonton wrappers, cut into 1-inch strips and deep-fat fried

Tear the lettuce into bite-sized pieces and place in a large salad bowl. Add the parsley, bean sprouts, green onions, snow peas, and peanuts and toss gently.

In a small bowl, combine the oil, vinegar, soy sauce, mustard, sesame oil, sugar, and sesame seeds. Blend well.

Pour the dressing over the salad and toss. Add the wonton strips and toss again. Serve immediately.

Old-Fashioned Potato Salad

SERVES 6 TO 8

For flavorful potato salad, add the dressing to warm potatoes. Cold potatoes do not absorb flavors well.

5 medium potatoes
1 slice of yellow onion
5 to 6 peppercorns
salt
freshly ground pepper to taste
2 tablespoons olive oil
2 tablespoons wine vinegar
1 tablespoon Dijon mustard or 2 tablespoons mustard sauce
3 hard-cooked eggs, sliced
2 to 3 green onions with tops, diced
2 stalks celery, sliced
1 cucumber, partially peeled, then cut into chunks
2 teaspoons capers
⅓ to ½ cup mayonnaise

Place the potatoes, onion, and peppercorns in a large saucepan. Add salted water to cover and cook until just tender. Do not overcook.

Drain the water from the pan and return the pan with the potatoes to the heat. Shake them constantly until dry, about 1 minute. Place the potatoes on a rack or platter and cool just until touchable.

Peel the potatoes while still warm. Cut them into large pieces and place in a bowl. Sprinkle with salt and pepper.

Mix the olive oil, vinegar, and mustard in a small bowl and add to the potatoes. Mix by turning the potatoes carefully so they will not be mashed. Place the potatoes in the refrigerator, uncovered, for 4 hours or overnight.

When the potatoes are cold and have absorbed the vinegar and oil, add the eggs, green onions, celery, cucumbers, and capers and mix. Add enough mayonnaise to moisten the salad and mix well. Refrigerate until serving time.

Ranch Potato Salad

SERVES 10

¾ cup Beef Stock (see page 56)
6 large, cooked potatoes, hot, peeled, and cut into large pieces
¾ cup sour cream
¾ cup mayonnaise
¾ to 1 cup chopped mild onion
⅓ cup chopped chives

Bring the stock to a boil in a small saucepan over high heat. Cook over high heat for 2 to 3 minutes, or until the stock is reduced in volume by two thirds.

Put the potatoes in a bowl and pour in the hot stock. Mix so that the stock is evenly distributed.

Combine the sour cream and mayonnaise in a small bowl. Add the sour cream mixture, onions, and chives to the potatoes. Mix gently, being careful not to mash the potatoes.

Refrigerate for 4 hours or overnight.

Dilled Apple Potato Salad

SERVES 8

6 large potatoes
½ cup mayonnaise
½ cup tiny peas, cooked briefly
2 tart green apples, peeled and cubed
2 stalks celery, chopped
2 medium dill pickles, chopped and drained
1 tablespoon chopped fresh parsley
1 tablespoon chopped fresh dill
½ cup sour cream mixed with 3 tablespoons mild vinegar
1 teaspoon salt, or to taste
white pepper to taste

OPTIONAL:
vinegar
granulated sugar
sour cream

Boil the potatoes until tender and cool slightly. Peel and chop the potatoes, then mix them carefully with the mayonnaise. Cool.

Add the peas, apple, celery, pickle, parsley, and dill. Add the sour cream mixed with vinegar, and season to taste with salt and pepper. Chill.

Taste the salad for flavor balance and adjust the seasoning with additional salt and pepper, vinegar, sugar, or sour cream. Refrigerate again until serving time.

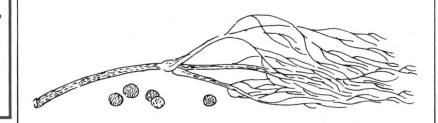

SERVES 8

Artichoke-Rice Salad

1 cup long grain rice
1 jar (6 ounces) marinated artichokes, chopped, marinade reserved
3 green onions, chopped
4 ounces pimiento-stuffed olives, drained and sliced
½ large green bell pepper, seeded and chopped
¼ cup minced fresh parsley
1 cup mayonnaise
1 teaspoon curry powder
salt and freshly ground black pepper to taste

OPTIONAL:
olive juice
mayonnaise
8 whole tomatoes, cored and drained

Prepare the rice according to package directions.

Place the cooked rice in a large mixing bowl. Add the artichokes, onions, olives, green pepper, and parsley and mix well.

Combine the mayonnaise, reserved artichoke marinade, and curry powder in a small bowl. Pour the mayonnaise mixture over the rice-artichoke mixture and mix thoroughly. Season to taste with salt and pepper. Refrigerate overnight.

Taste the salad and adjust the seasoning with olive juice if a more piquant taste is desired. If the salad seems dry, add more mayonnaise.

Serve separately as an accompaniment salad or in tomatoes as a luncheon entrée.

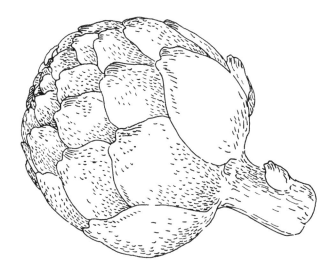

SERVES 10 TO 12

Tomatoes Diablo

½ cup sliced green onions
¼ cup olive oil
¼ cup vegetable oil
½ teaspoon freshly ground black pepper
3 tablespoons tarragon vinegar
2 teaspoons granulated sugar
2 tablespoons prepared mustard
1 teaspoon salt
7 to 8 firm, ripe tomatoes, peeled and sliced

Combine the green onions, oils, pepper, vinegar, sugar, mustard, and salt in a small bowl. Whisk until well blended.

Place the tomato slices in a large shallow bowl or glass tray. Pour the dressing over the tomatoes. Cover the dish with plastic wrap and let stand at room temperature for several hours. Serve at room temperature.

SERVES 8

Green Pea, Cashew, and Jícama Salad

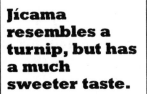

Jícama resembles a turnip, but has a much sweeter taste.

2 packages (10 ounces each) frozen tiny green peas, thawed
2 cups bean sprouts
1 large jícama, peeled and chopped into 1½-inch pieces
1 cup chopped celery
1 bunch green onions, chopped (about ¾ cup), including tops
1 cup sour cream
salt and freshly ground black pepper to taste
1 cup cashews
8 to 10 ounces bacon, crisply cooked and crumbled

Thoroughly drain the peas on paper toweling. (If the peas are not well drained, the salad dressing will be thin and watery.)

In a large bowl, combine the peas, bean sprouts, jícama, celery, green onions, sour cream, and salt and pepper; mix well. Refrigerate for 4 hours or overnight. Just before serving, add the cashews and bacon. Mix gently but thoroughly.

Green Chili Aspic with Avocado

3 tablespoons unflavored gelatin
4 cups tomato juice
3 tablespoons lemon juice
3 cans (4 ounces each) chopped green chilies, undrained
½ cup minced celery
2 medium avocados, peeled and cubed
½ teaspoon garlic salt
½ teaspoon Beau Monde seasoning
½ teaspoon onion salt
freshly ground black pepper to taste
dash of hot pepper sauce
mayonnaise for oiling mold

GARNISH:
curly endive
seedless green grapes
1 cup sour cream
2 tablespoons mayonnaise

In a small bowl, soften the gelatin in 1 cup of the cold tomato juice.

Meanwhile, heat the remaining 3 cups of tomato juice to boiling in a saucepan and remove from the heat. Add the softened gelatin mixture to the hot tomato juice and mix until the gelatin is thoroughly dissolved. Let cool.

Add the lemon juice, chilies, celery, avocados, and seasonings. Stir to mix.

Spread a film of mayonnaise on the inside of a mold. Pour in the gelatin mixture and chill for 4 hours or overnight.

Stir together the sour cream and mayonnaise in a small bowl.

Unmold the aspic onto a chilled platter. Place the endive around the edges of the mold and garnish with bunches of grapes. Serve the sour cream sauce with the aspic.

SERVES 8

Snow Cap Cheese Mold

1 teaspoon unflavored gelatin
¼ cup cold water
1½ cups cream-style cottage cheese
2 packages (3 ounces each) cream cheese, softened
¼ teaspoon salt
1 cup sliced seedless green grapes
½ cup broken pecans
2 tablespoons chopped chives
1 cup heavy cream, whipped
mayonnaise for oiling mold

GARNISH:
lettuce leaves
8 pineapple slices
Honey Dressing (recipe follows)

Soften the gelatin in the cold water.

Combine the cottage cheese and cream cheese in a large bowl. Blend until smooth and creamy.

Place the softened gelatin in a small saucepan and heat until it is thoroughly dissolved. Add the salt to the gelatin, then add the gelatin to the cheese mixture. Stir well. Add the grapes, pecans, and chives. Fold in the whipped cream.

Spread a film of mayonnaise in a 1½-quart mold or 8 individual molds. Pour the cheese mixture into the mold or molds and refrigerate 4 hours or overnight.

At serving time, place the lettuce leaves on a platter or on serving plates. Top with pineapple slices. Unmold the salad onto the pineapple. Serve with Honey Dressing.

HONEY DRESSING:
1 teaspoon dry mustard
1 teaspoon paprika
1 teaspoon celery seed
¼ teaspoon salt
⅔ cup honey
⅓ cup vinegar
1 tablespoon lemon juice
1 teaspoon grated onion
1 cup vegetable oil

Mix together the mustard, paprika, celery seed, and salt. Add the honey, vinegar, lemon juice, and onion. Pour the oil into the mixture very slowly, beating constantly with an electric mixer.

US SKI TEAM The very first ski lift was developed in the winter of 1934 when people became tired of walking uphill to ski down. Bunny Bertram, ex-captain of the Dartmouth college ski team, picked up the idea of a continuous rope lift from a fellow skier and passed the idea on to an innkeeper in Woodstock, Vermont. The innkeeper rented a slope for ten dollars for the entire season and built the first permanent ski lift in the United States. The first chairlift in the world opened on Dollar Mountain in Sun Valley, Idaho, in 1937.

SERVES 6 TO 8

Freshly grated nutmeg has a true, pungent flavor. Invest in a nutmeg grater and use a few grinds in any cheese sauce. The noticeable difference is worth the effort and expense.

Jellied Ham Bennington

3 cups Chicken Stock (see page 56)
⅔ cup dry white wine
2 pounds cooked ham, cut into julienne
freshly ground black pepper
freshly grated nutmeg
½ cup minced fresh parsley
2 tablespoons unflavored gelatin
¼ cup cold water
6 tablespoons chopped fresh parsley
2 tablespoons tarragon vinegar
1 cup sour cream
2 tablespoons Tarragon-Mustard Vinaigrette (see page 107)

GARNISH:
lettuce leaves, washed, dried, and chilled

Reduce the chicken stock to 2½ cups in a saucepan over high heat.

Reduce the heat and add the wine, ham, pepper, and nutmeg. Simmer for 5 minutes.

Remove the ham from the stock with a slotted spoon and drain well. Reserve the stock.

Rinse a 2-quart mold with cold water and drain, but do not dry. Then sprinkle the mold thickly with minced parsley. Add the ham strips to the mold.

Soften the gelatin in the cold water and stir into the hot stock. Add the chopped parsley and vinegar and stir. Cool until syrupy.

Pour the gelatin mixture over the ham. Refrigerate, covered, at least 12 hours.

At serving time combine the sour cream and vinaigrette and blend well. Unmold the aspic onto a chilled platter. Place lettuce leaves around the salad and serve with the sour cream vinaigrette.

MAKES ¾ CUP

Sesame Seed Salad Dressing

¼ cup sesame seeds
¼ cup cider vinegar
⅓ cup vegetable oil
3 tablespoons granulated sugar
2 teaspoons salt
½ teaspoon freshly ground black pepper

Place the sesame seeds in a small sauté pan over medium heat. Toast until golden, about 3 minutes, stirring frequently. Combine the toasted sesame seeds with the remaining ingredients and whisk for 1 minute. Refrigerate. Reblend before serving.

MAKES 1½ CUPS

Palm Springs Salad Dressing

1 cup sour cream
½ cup diced dates
½ teaspoon grated orange zest
2 tablespoons orange juice
dash of salt
dash of ground mace

Combine all the ingredients in a small bowl and mix well. Cover and chill for 4 hours or overnight.
Serve the dressing over a melange of seasonal fresh fruit.

MAKES 1¼ CUPS

Orange-Ginger Dressing for Fresh Fruit

8 ounces cream cheese, softened
1 tablespoon granulated sugar
1 tablespoon grated orange zest
½ to 1 teaspoon ground ginger
6 tablespoons orange juice

Beat the cream cheese in a small bowl until smooth, then stir in the remaining ingredients. Cover and chill until serving time. Pour over seasonal fresh fruit.

MAKES 2 CUPS

Golden Cream Dressing

5 tablespoons granulated sugar
5 tablespoons white wine vinegar
¼ teaspoon salt
6 egg yolks, lightly beaten
1 cup heavy cream, whipped

Heat the sugar, vinegar, and salt in the top of a double boiler over simmering water until the sugar dissolves. Add the egg yolks and cook, stirring constantly, until the mixture thickens, about 5 minutes. Cool.

When the egg mixture is at room temperature, fold it into the whipped cream. Do not overblend or the dressing will lose its volume. Serve over a mixture of fresh fruit.

MAKES 1 CUP

Good on a salad made of spinach, mushrooms, fresh bean sprouts, and crisp, crumbled bacon.

Creamy Mustard Dressing

1 cup mayonnaise, preferably homemade (see page 108)
2 tablespoons Dijon mustard
1 tablespoon plus 1 teaspoon tarragon vinegar
1 tablespoon plus 1 teaspoon granulated sugar
salt and freshly ground white pepper to taste

Combine the mayonnaise, mustard, vinegar, and sugar in a small bowl. Season to taste with salt and pepper.

MAKES 1 CUP

Garlic-Cheese Dressing

⅓ cup olive oil
2 tablespoons wine vinegar
⅓ cup freshly grated Parmesan or Asiago cheese
2 inches anchovy paste
1 clove garlic
¼ teaspoon salt
¼ teaspoon dry mustard
freshly ground black pepper
½ cup mayonnaise, preferably homemade (see page 108)
1 to 2 tablespoons water

Combine all the ingredients except the mayonnaise and water in a food processor or blender and process until well incorporated.

Combine the mayonnaise and the oil-cheese mixture in a small bowl. Thin the dressing with water. Serve on a tossed green salad or sliced tomatoes.

MAKES 1 CUP

Raspberry Vinaigrette

¼ cup light olive oil
¼ cup vegetable oil
½ cup raspberry vinegar
salt and freshly ground black pepper to taste

Combine all the ingredients in a small bowl or small covered container and mix thoroughly. Reblend at serving time if not used immediately.

MAKES 1½ CUPS

Tarragon-Mustard Vinaigrette

1¼ cups light olive oil
¼ cup tarragon vinegar
1 tablespoon Dijon mustard
½ teaspoon minced fresh tarragon
salt and freshly ground black pepper to taste

Combine all the ingredients in a small bowl or small covered container and mix thoroughly. Reblend at serving time if not used immediately.

MAKES 2 CUPS

Green Onion-Lemon Vinaigrette

1 cup light olive oil
⅔ cup fresh lemon juice
1 tablespoon Dijon mustard
½ cup minced green onion

Combine all the ingredients in a small bowl or small covered container and mix thoroughly. Reblend at serving time if not used immediately.

MAKES 1½ TO 2 CUPS

Combine minced fresh herbs, or chutney, or anchovy paste, or horseradish with homemade mayonnaise to create your own dressing.

Mayonnaise

1 large egg
1 egg yolk
1 tablespoon Dijon mustard
pinch of salt
white pepper to taste
3 to 6 tablespoons lemon juice or herb vinegar
1¼ to 1¾ cups vegetable oil or part vegetable oil and part
    olive oil

Combine the egg and egg yolk, mustard, salt, pepper, and 3 tablespoons of the lemon juice or vinegar in the work bowl of a food processor fitted with the steel blade. Process for 1 to 2 minutes.

With the motor running, add the oil, drop by drop, through the feed tube until the egg and oil are emulsified (about ½ cup oil). Then, in a steady stream with the motor running, add as much of the remaining oil as necessary to produce a thick and creamy mixture.

Taste and adjust the seasoning with the remaining lemon juice and salt and pepper.

Put the mayonnaise into a covered container and refrigerate. The mayonnaise will keep for 4 to 5 days, refrigerated.

Crème Fraîche

MAKES 1 CUP

Crème fraîche is superb on fresh fruit. It is an excellent substitute for sour cream in cooked sauces as it does not curdle when heated to the boiling point.

1 cup heavy cream (not ultrapasteurized)
1 tablespoon active-culture buttermilk

Whisk the cream and buttermilk together in a small bowl. Cover with plastic wrap and let stand at warm room temperature for 8 to 24 hours, or until thickened.

Refrigerate the cream mixture for 6 to 10 hours, or until it is as thick as sour cream. This will keep, covered and refrigerated, for over 2 weeks.

Meats

Panhandle Pork Roast

SECTION CHAIRMAN
Sharon Wilkinson

TESTERS
Susan Boettcher
Marilyn Brown
Lee Day
Sue Kintzele
Gail Nash
Linda Roberts
Elizabeth Rostermundt
Julia Secor
Judy Trumbull

MAKES ABOUT 1 QUART

Gunnison River Barbecue Sauce

For a great barbecue flavor, add branches of fresh herbs, wet fruitwood branches, or mesquite wood to your charcoal fire during the last 20 minutes of cooking.

2 tablespoons vegetable oil
1 onion, chopped
1 clove garlic, chopped
2 cups ketchup
¼ cup white wine vinegar
½ teaspoon dry mustard
2 tablespoons granulated sugar
1 teaspoon chili powder
dash of cayenne
2 tablespoons Worcestershire sauce
1 teaspoon salt

Heat the oil in a large heavy saucepan and sauté the onion for 5 minutes. Add the garlic and sauté 1 minute more. Add the remaining ingredients and bring to a boil. Reduce the heat and simmer for 30 minutes, stirring occasionally. Store, refrigerated, in a covered glass container.

MAKES 1½ QUARTS

Prairie City Barbecue Sauce

4 cups (32 ounces) ketchup
1 bottle (12 ounces) chili sauce
1 ounce celery seed
1 cup granulated sugar
1 teaspoon cayenne
1 teaspoon freshly ground black pepper
2 teaspoons salt
1 cup cider vinegar
2 teaspoons prepared mustard
2 tablespoons liquid smoke

Combine all the ingredients in a large saucepan and mix well. Simmer over low heat, stirring frequently, for 30 minutes. Remove from the heat and let cool. Store in a glass container. Does not require refrigeration.

Whiskey Sauce for Chopped Steak

MAKES 2 TO 4 SERVINGS

This sauce can be served over any steaks that have been pan-fried.

½ cup butter
2 tablespoons minced onion
1 clove garlic, minced
3 tablespoons whiskey
1 tablespoon Worcestershire sauce
½ teaspoon dry mustard
dash of hot pepper sauce or 1 tablespoon Pick-a-Pepper

Pour off any grease remaining after a steak has been sautéed.

In the same skillet used to cook the steak, melt the butter over low heat. Add the onion and garlic and cook slowly until soft. Add the remaining ingredients and simmer for 1 to 2 minutes. Pour over steaks and serve.

Creamy Mustard Sauce

SERVES 4

Good with shrimp, cold crab, hot seafood, or ham loaf.

4 tablespoons unsalted butter
1 tablespoon lemon juice
⅛ teaspoon freshly ground white pepper
½ teaspoon dry mustard
3 tablespoons sour cream

Melt the butter in a small skillet. Cool, then add the remaining ingredients and blend well.

Mustard Sauce

MAKES 1 QUART

2 cups light cream
2 egg yolks, beaten
3 tablespoons dry mustard
1 cup granulated sugar
½ teaspoon salt
2 tablespoons all-purpose flour
¾ cup vinegar

Scald 1½ cups of the cream in a double boiler.
Add the remaining ½ cup cream to the beaten egg yolks.

Combine the dry ingredients and add the egg yolk–cream mixture. Stir this mixture into the scalded cream.

Cook in a double boiler, stirring constantly until thickened, about 5 minutes. Heat the vinegar and stir into the hot mixture. Beat well. This will keep for weeks in the refrigerator.

Marinades for Meat (flank steak, pot roast, butterflied leg of lamb, rib roast)

MARINADE I:
½ cup soy sauce
½ cup peanut oil
2 to 3 cloves garlic, minced
1 tablespoon grated fresh ginger root
1 to 1½ cups dry Madeira

MARINADE II:
1¼ cups (packed) brown sugar
1 cup soy sauce
½ teaspoon ground ginger
3 cloves garlic, crushed

OPTIONAL:
⅛ teaspoon sesame oil

MARINADE III:
2 cups dry red wine
¼ cup honey
¼ cup minced fresh parsley
2 tablespoons chopped fresh thyme or oregano or 2
        teaspoons dried
freshly ground black pepper

OPTIONAL:
2 tablespoons Worcestershire sauce
4 cloves garlic, crushed

Combine all marinade ingredients and mix well.

Place meat in a shallow glass baking dish and pour the marinade over it. Cover and refrigerate for 5 to 6 hours, turning several times, or marinate at least 2 hours at room temperature.

MEATS: SAUCES AND MARINADES

SERVES 6

Horseradish Mousse

2 teaspoons unflavored gelatin
2 tablespoons cold water
½ cup heavy cream
½ cup less 1 tablespoon horseradish, drained
½ teaspoon salt
1 tablespoon minced sweet onion
1 tablespoon lemon juice
1 teaspoon granulated sugar

Soften the gelatin in the cold water for 5 minutes. Set the bowl containing the gelatin in a pan of hot water to dissolve.

Whip the cream until stiff.

Combine the horseradish, salt, onion, lemon juice, and sugar. Mix well and fold into the whipped cream. Mix in the gelatin and blend well.

Pour the mixture into a mold rinsed with cold water but not dried. Refrigerate for at least 4 hours. Serve with baked, glazed ham, or roast beef.

US SKI TEAM Andrea Mead Lawrence may still rank as the most overwhelming racer in U.S. team history. She entered 18 international races in 1951 and won 14 of them; then in 1952 she won every race she entered except one, and took two gold medals at the Olympics.

SERVES 8

This is an easy, make-ahead supper that children love.

One-Pot Dinner

1 pound ground beef round
¾ pound bacon, cut into small pieces
1 cup chopped onion
1 can (15½ ounces) pork and beans
2 cups cooked kidney beans
2 cups cooked butter lima beans
1 cup ketchup
¼ cup (packed) brown sugar
1 tablespoon liquid smoke
3 tablespoons distilled white vinegar
1 teaspoon salt
freshly ground black pepper

Brown the ground round in a large skillet. Remove with a slotted spoon and place in a heavy saucepan or crockpot.

Add the bacon and onion to the skillet and sauté for 8 to 10 minutes, or until the onion is limp and the bacon is crisp. Remove the onion and bacon with a slotted spoon and add to the saucepan.

Add the remaining ingredients to the meat mixture and mix well. Simmer (or cook in a crockpot) for 2 to 3 hours.

SERVES 10

Oklahoma Barbecued Brisket

5 pounds beef brisket
2 tablespoons liquid smoke
½ teaspoon celery salt
½ teaspoon onion salt
½ teaspoon garlic salt
¼ cup Worcestershire sauce
1 cup Barbecue Sauce (see page 111)

Place the brisket in a large glass baking dish.

Combine the liquid smoke, celery salt, onion salt, garlic salt, and Worcestershire sauce and rub on all surfaces of the meat. Cover and refrigerate the brisket overnight.

Preheat the oven to 275° F.

Place the brisket in a shallow roasting pan and bake, covered, for 5 hours. Check occasionally to see if liquid is needed. If so, add water.

Pour the barbecue sauce over the roast and bake, covered, for 1 hour longer. Let stand for 15 minutes. Slice thinly across the grain to serve.

SERVES 6

Zucchini Italiano

1 pound ground beef round
1 medium onion, chopped
3 cans (8 ounces each) tomato sauce
1 cup dry red wine
1 teaspoon Italian seasoning
dash of garlic salt
1 tablespoon granulated sugar
freshly ground black pepper to taste
2 pounds zucchini
freshly grated Parmesan cheese

Preheat the oven to 350° F.

Sauté the ground round and onion in a skillet until the meat is browned and the onion is tender. Drain off the grease and discard.

Stir in the tomato sauce, wine, Italian seasoning, garlic salt, sugar, and pepper to taste. Cover and simmer for 1 hour, stirring occasionally.

Meanwhile, wash the zucchini and trim off the ends. Cook the zucchini whole in boiling salted water for 3 to 4 minutes, or until crisp-tender, and then drain and cool.

Cut the zucchini in half lengthwise. Arrange the zucchini in a single layer, cut side up, in a buttered shallow baking dish. Pour the sauce over the zucchini and bake for 45 minutes.

Sprinkle with freshly grated Parmesan cheese and serve.

SERVES 8

Corned Beef in Foil

3 to 4 pounds corned beef
¼ cup water
2 tablespoons pickling spice
1 orange, sliced
1 onion, sliced
1 celery stalk with leaves, sliced
1 carrot, peeled and sliced

Soak the corned beef in water to cover for 30 minutes, or longer if deeply corned.

Preheat the oven to 300° F.

Remove the corned beef from the water and pat dry to remove any salt on the surface. Place a large sheet of heavy-duty foil in a shallow pan. Place the corned beef in the center of the foil and pour ¼ cup fresh water over it.

Sprinkle the meat with the pickling spice, then arrange the orange slices, onion slices, celery, and carrot over and around the meat. Bring the long ends of the foil up over the meat and seal with a tight double fold. Seal the other ends, turning them up so that liquid cannot run out. Bake for 5 to 6 hours.

Discard the cooked orange and vegetables. Let stand for 20 minutes before slicing.

Chimichangas

SERVES 4

If using fresh green chiles, wear rubber gloves while seeding and slicing them. Even jalapēnos are hot enough to burn bare hands.

2 pounds chuck roast, cut into pieces
3 cups water or Beef Stock (see page 56)
½ cup green chili strips
1 tablespoon freshly ground black pepper
1 teaspoon salt
1 cup crushed tomatoes
8 flour tortillas (each 10 inches in diameter)
2 cups vegetable oil
2 cups green chili salsa
2 cups shredded lettuce
1 large tomato, seeded and diced
2 cups grated Cheddar cheese
1 cup sour cream

Preheat the oven to 325° F.

Brown the meat on both sides in a heavy skillet. Transfer the meat to a large Dutch oven and add the water or beef stock. Cover and cook for 2½ hours, or until tender. Drain, cool, and shred the meat.

Place the shredded meat in a skillet and add the chili strips, pepper, salt, and tomatoes. Simmer over low heat for 30 minutes.

Divide the mixture evenly in the center of the tortillas. Roll up the mixture in the tortilla by folding the bottom up first, then each side over, then the top.

Heat the vegetable oil in a skillet. When it is hot, place 4 chimichangas in the oil, bottom side down first and cook for 4 minutes. Turn and cook the other side about 4 minutes. Repeat.

Place 2 chimichangas on a plate and top with equal amounts of green chili salsa, lettuce, tomatoes, cheese, and sour cream. Serve immediately.

SERVES 4 TO 6

Tomato paste is available in tubes, which are convenient when a small amount is needed. Ask for it at your market.

Hungarian Goulash

2 cloves garlic, crushed
2 teaspoons grated lemon zest
1 teaspoon caraway seed
2 teaspoons dried marjoram
¾ cup butter
3 to 4 medium yellow onions, sliced
1 tablespoon sweet paprika
2 to 2½ pounds beef chuck roast, cut into 1½-inch pieces
2 cups Beef Stock (see page 56)
1 tablespoon tomato paste
salt to taste
hot cooked noodles

OPTIONAL:
1½ to 2 cups sour cream

GARNISH:
green bell pepper, thinly sliced

Combine the garlic, lemon zest, caraway seed, and marjoram in a small bowl.

Melt the butter in a large pot, add the onions and combined seasonings, and sauté for about 15 minutes over medium heat, stirring often. Do not brown.

Add the paprika to the onions and seasonings and blend well. Add the beef, beef stock, tomato paste, and salt to taste. Cover and simmer for 1½ to 2 hours, or until the meat is tender. Stir in sour cream, if desired, and blend well. Do not boil. Top with sliced green pepper rings and serve over cooked noodles.

SERVES 6

Italian-Style Steak

1 sirloin steak (3 pounds)
4 tablespoons olive oil
1½ pounds tomatoes, peeled and diced
4 cloves garlic, minced
¼ teaspoon dried oregano
1 teaspoon salt
½ teaspoon freshly ground black pepper

GARNISH:
2 tablespoons minced fresh parsley

Cut the steak into 6 pieces and flatten slightly by pounding.

Heat 2 tablespoons of the oil in a saucepan. Add the tomatoes, garlic, oregano, ½ teaspoon of the salt, and ¼ teaspoon of the pepper. Cook over low heat for 15 minutes.

Meanwhile, heat the remaining oil in a skillet and brown the steak on both sides. Season with the remaining pepper and salt, if desired. Pour the sauce over the steak, cover, and cook over low heat for 5 minutes. Sprinkle with the parsley and serve.

Beef and Tomato Sauté

SERVES 4

For thin, even meat slices, freeze the meat for 20 to 30 minutes before slicing.

2 tablespoons sugar
3 tablespoons soy sauce
4 tablespoons vegetable oil
3 tablespoons cornstarch
2¼-inch slices fresh ginger root, minced
2 green onions, cut into 1½-inch strips, then sliced length-
    wise
1 pound lean beefsteak, such as flank steak, thinly sliced
    across the grain
1 medium onion, cut into wedges and separated
1 medium green bell pepper, seeded and cut into wedges
2 teaspoons Worcestershire sauce
1 cup tomato juice
3 large tomatoes, seeded and cut into wedges
hot cooked rice

In a small mixing bowl, combine 1 tablespoon of the sugar, 2 tablespoons of the soy sauce, 2 tablespoons of the vegetable oil, 1 tablespoon of the cornstarch, the ginger root, and green onions. Whisk until well blended. Add the beef and marinate for 1 hour or overnight in the refrigerator.

In a large skillet, over medium-high heat, heat the remaining 2 tablespoons of oil until it is smoking. Add the meat in batches and quickly stir-fry until the meat is browned. Remove the meat from the skillet and reserve.

Add the onion and green pepper to the skillet and stir-fry for 2 minutes. Return the meat to the pan. Cover and simmer for 2 to 3 minutes.

Meanwhile, prepare the sauce by combining the remaining 2 tablespoons cornstarch, 1 tablespoon soy sauce, 1 tablespoon sugar, the Worcestershire sauce, and tomato juice in a small bowl and blending well. Add the sauce and the tomatoes to the beef and vegetables in the skillet and cook until thickened and hot. Serve over hot cooked rice.

SERVES 2

Veal Sheboygan

4 veal chops, each cut about 1 to 1¼ inches thick
milk
all-purpose flour
salt and freshly ground black pepper
1 tablespoon butter
2 tablespoons vegetable oil
1 onion, chopped
1 to 2 shallots, chopped
2 cloves garlic, minced
6 to 8 mushrooms, thinly sliced
¼ cup white wine
¼ cup heavy cream
dash of Maggi seasoning

Preheat the oven to 350° F.

Dip the veal chops in the milk, then in a mixture of flour seasoned with salt and pepper.

Heat the butter and oil in a skillet. Add the veal chops and brown them on each side. Set aside.

Add the onion, shallots, garlic, and mushrooms to the skillet and sauté until the onion is limp, about 5 minutes. Add 1 tablespoon flour and stir until blended. Add the wine, cream, and Maggi seasoning and stir until thick and smooth.

Place the reserved veal chops in a gratin dish or other shallow baking dish and pour the sauce over the chops. Bake for 20 to 25 minutes. Serve hot.

SERVES 6

Veal Ragout

¼ cup olive oil
4 pounds boneless veal shoulder, cut into 1½-inch cubes
1 medium onion, chopped
3 cloves garlic, minced
½ teaspoon dried thyme
¼ teaspoon dried rosemary
4 large tomatoes, peeled, seeded, and chopped
1 bay leaf
1 cup dry white wine
½ cup Chicken Stock (see page 56) or veal stock
12 small boiling onions, blanched and peeled
salt and freshly ground black pepper to taste
¾ cup Greek olives
hot cooked rice

GARNISH:
3 tablespoons minced fresh parsley

Heat the oil in a large Dutch oven. Add the veal in batches and brown slowly on all sides. Set aside. Add the onion to the pan and cook until soft, about 5 minutes. Add the garlic, thyme, rosemary, tomatoes, and bay leaf and cook for 5 minutes. Add the wine, chicken or veal stock, boiling onions, reserved veal, and salt and pepper to taste. Cook slowly, covered, for 45 to 50 minutes.

Pour the meat and sauce into a large strainer set over a bowl. Pour the strained sauce back into the pan and reduce over high heat until syrupy. Reduce the heat and return the meat to the pan. Add the olives and heat through. Sprinkle with parsley and serve over rice.

Jackson Hole Veal Caprice

SERVES 4

Medallions of veal are also called scallops. They are thin slices usually cut from the leg.

12 scallops of veal (1½ ounces each), pounded thin
½ cup all-purpose flour
2 eggs, beaten
2 tablespoons butter
2 cups sliced mushrooms
¼ cup dry sherry
¼ cup brandy
¼ cup Beef Stock (see page 56)
salt and freshly ground white pepper to taste
paprika to taste
allspice to taste
rosemary to taste
thyme to taste
hot cooked rice

GARNISH:
1 tablespoon chopped fresh parsley

Coat the veal with flour, then dip in the beaten eggs.

Melt the butter in a skillet, add the veal, and sauté on both sides until golden, about 2 minutes per side. Remove the veal from the skillet and reserve. Add the mushrooms to the skillet and cook until tender.

Add the sherry and brandy and, over high heat, reduce the liquid by half. Add the stock and seasonings and reduce again, leaving just a glaze.

Return the veal to the pan and heat through. Serve with rice and sprinkled with parsley.

SERVES 6

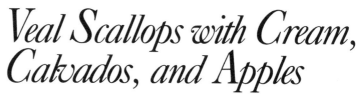

Veal Scallops with Cream, Calvados, and Apples

3 tart apples, such as Granny Smith or Pippin
juice of 1 lemon
12 veal cutlets, each cut ¼ inch thick, pounded
all-purpose flour
salt and freshly ground black pepper to taste
4 tablespoons butter
2 tablespoons vegetable oil
⅓ cup Calvados or applejack
1½ cups heavy cream

Peel and core the apples and cut into thin slices. Place the apple slices in a bowl, add the lemon juice, and mix thoroughly so that the apple slices are well coated.

Dredge the veal cutlets in flour seasoned with salt and pepper. Shake off any excess flour.

Heat the butter and oil in a large, heavy skillet. When the butter and oil are hot, add the veal, a few pieces at a time, and sauté until lightly browned on both sides, approximately 3 minutes per side. As the veal is cooked, remove it to a heated platter and keep warm.

When all the veal is cooked, add the Calvados to the skillet. Scrape the pan and cook over moderate heat, stirring frequently, for 1 minute. Add the cream and continue cooking until the mixture is an ivory color.

Reduce the heat and add the apples with lemon juice. Cook, stirring frequently, until the cream has reduced to about half and the sauce coats a spoon. Adjust the seasoning with salt if necessary. Return the veal to the skillet just until warmed through. Place the veal on a heated platter and spoon the sauce over it. Serve immediately.

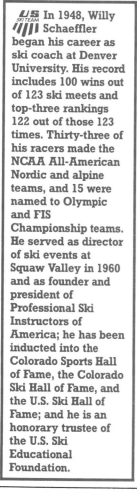

SERVES 6 TO 8

Ham Loaf

Cold ham loaf makes great sandwiches for school lunches.

2 pounds ground ham
1 pound ground pork or veal
1 teaspoon dry mustard
pinch of freshly ground black pepper
2 tablespoons minced fresh parsley
2 eggs, beaten
¾ cup milk
1 cup saltine cracker crumbs
Mustard Sauce (see page 112) or Horseradish Mousse (see
    page 114)

Preheat the oven to 325° F.

Mix the ham and pork or veal together. Add the remaining ingredients except for the sauce and mix well with hands.

Place the meat mixture in a standard loaf pan or casserole dish. Place the dish in a pan of hot water in the preheated oven and bake for 1½ to 2 hours. Serve with Mustard Sauce or Horseradish Mousse.

SERVES 4

Amana Pork Chop Casserole

4 loin pork chops (each 1 inch thick), trimmed of fat
6 slices bacon, crisply cooked, crumbled, and grease reserved
4 large potatoes, peeled and thinly sliced
1 large onion, sliced ¼ inch thick
salt and freshly ground black pepper to taste
2 cloves garlic, minced
1 cup dry white wine

GARNISH:
1 tablespoon chopped fresh parsley

Preheat the oven to 300° F.

Brown the chops in the reserved bacon grease.

Arrange half the potatoes in a deep casserole dish or Dutch oven. Top the potatoes with half the onion and bacon and season with salt and pepper. Add the pork chops in a single layer. Layer the remaining potatoes and onion over the chops and sprinkle with salt and pepper.

Mix the garlic with the wine and pour into the casserole. Sprinkle with the remaining bacon. Cover with a double thickness of foil, then with a casserole lid. Bake for 1¼ hours. Garnish with parsley before serving.

SERVES 6

Quick Pork Chops in Orange Sauce

6 pork chops
¼ cup plus 1 teaspoon all-purpose flour
salt and freshly ground black pepper to taste
1 tablespoon vegetable oil
1 cup orange juice
1 teaspoon sugar
1 tablespoon grated orange zest

Dredge the pork chops in ¼ cup of the flour seasoned with salt and pepper and brown in the oil in a heavy skillet.

Pour off all the grease from the skillet and discard. Add ½ cup of the orange juice and cook the chops, covered, for 30 minutes. Remove the chops from the skillet and keep warm on a platter in a low oven.

Combine the sugar and 1 teaspoon flour in a small bowl. Add the orange zest and remaining ½ cup orange juice and stir to blend. Stir this mixture into the skillet and cook, stirring, until the sauce is thick. Pour the sauce over the reserved chops and serve.

SERVES 6 TO 8

Basic Ribs

6 pounds country-style pork ribs or 8 pounds spare ribs
1 lemon, sliced
1 onion, sliced
salt and freshly ground black pepper to taste
2 cups Barbecue Sauce (see page 111)

Preheat the oven to 325° F.

In a large roasting pan, place the ribs on a rack in a single layer. Place the sliced lemon and onion on top and season with salt and pepper. Add ¼-inch water, cover, and bake for 1 hour.

Remove the ribs from the pan and discard the water, lemon, and onion. At this point the ribs may be finished in the oven or on a charcoal grill. Place the ribs on a baking sheet or charcoal grill. Brush 1 cup of the barbecue sauce on top and bake at 350° F. or grill for 15 minutes. Turn the ribs over and brush with the remaining sauce. Bake or grill for 10 minutes more.

Pork Schnitzel

The juice of fresh lemons is a versatile seasoning for some meats and most fish. It is especially good on pork and veal. Try omitting salt and using lemon instead.

6 pork loin cutlets (1½ pounds), cut ½ inch thick
¼ cup plus 1 tablespoon all-purpose flour
1 teaspoon seasoned salt
¼ teaspoon freshly ground black pepper
1 egg, beaten
2 tablespoons milk
¾ cup fine dry bread crumbs
1 teaspoon paprika
3 tablespoons vegetable oil
¾ cup Chicken Stock (see page 56)
½ teaspoon dried dill weed
½ teaspoon onion salt
½ cup sour cream

GARNISH:
lemon wedges

Pound the pork cutlets to ¼ to ⅛-inch thickness. Cut small slits around the edges of the cutlets to prevent curling. Combine ¼ cup flour, seasoned salt, and pepper. Dredge the cutlets in the seasoned flour.

Combine the egg and milk in a shallow bowl. Dip the cutlets in the egg mixture, then into a mixture of the bread crumbs and paprika. Refrigerate overnight so that the coating will stick well.

Heat the oil in a large skillet. Sauté the cutlets for 6 to 8 minutes on each side, or until golden brown. Remove the cutlets from the skillet and place on a heated platter to keep warm.

Pour the chicken stock into the skillet and stir, scraping to loosen brown bits.

Blend the 1 tablespoon flour, dill weed, and onion salt into the sour cream. Stir the sour cream mixture into the chicken stock. Cook and stir until the mixture thickens. Do not boil.

Garnish the cutlets with lemon wedges and serve with the sauce.

Panhandle Pork Roast

SERVES 8 TO 10

1 boneless rolled pork loin roast (4 to 5 pounds)
½ teaspoon salt
½ teaspoon garlic salt
1 teaspoon chili powder
½ cup apple jelly
½ cup ketchup
1 tablespoon vinegar
1 cup crushed corn chips

Preheat the oven to 325° F.

Place the pork roast, fat side up, on a rack in a shallow roasting pan. Combine the salt, garlic salt, and ½ teaspoon of the chili powder and rub into the roast.

Roast the meat for 2 hours, or until a meat thermometer registers 165° F. Carefully drain off the grease and discard.

Combine the apple jelly, ketchup, vinegar, and remaining ½ teaspoon chili powder in a small saucepan. Bring to a boil, then reduce the heat and simmer, uncovered, for 2 minutes.

Brush the roast with the glaze and sprinkle with the corn chips. Continue roasting for 10 to 15 minutes longer, or until the meat thermometer registers 170° F.

Remove the roast from the oven and let it stand for 10 minutes before carving.

Add water to the pan drippings, including any corn chips, to make 1 cup of liquid. Heat this liquid to boiling and serve as a sauce with the roast.

l'Oeuf may be an essential ingredient of an omelet, but it was also the first visible evidence of the French Revolution of the 1960s when France put its team on the year-round work basis that lead to the 1966 world championships, where they took 16 of 24 medals, and to Killy's triple gold performance at the 1968 Olympics. George Joubert was the guiding light of the French technical development program, and *profile d'un oeuf* (egg position) was his name for the downhill racing tuck developed by using wind tunnel tests to find the most streamlined racing position for a downhill racer. French teammate Jean Vuarnet used the technique and took a gold medal in the 1960 Olympic downhill in Squaw Valley, California.

Mushroom-Stuffed Pork Rolls

Asiago is a very hard cheese with a sharp, tangy flavor somewhat reminiscent of Parmesan.

5 tablespoons unsalted butter
¼ pound mushrooms, finely chopped
2 tablespoons finely chopped shallot
2 teaspoons lemon juice
freshly ground pepper to taste
4 thick, boneless pork chops, butterflied
4 tablespoons freshly grated Asiago cheese
all-purpose flour
1 cup dry white wine

Heat 2 tablespoons of the butter in a large stainless-steel skillet over medium heat. When the foam subsides, add the mushrooms, shallot, lemon juice, and pepper to taste. Raise the heat to medium-high and cook, stirring constantly, until liquid has evaporated, about 4 to 5 minutes. Transfer the mixture to a small bowl and let cool for 3 to 4 minutes.

Pound the pork chops to ¼-inch thickness.

Spread 1½ tablespoons of the mushroom-shallot mixture over each pork chop, leaving a ½-inch border on all sides. Sprinkle 1 tablespoon of the cheese over each chop. Roll each chop up and secure with a toothpick. Dredge the chops in flour.

In the skillet, heat the remaining 3 tablespoons of butter over medium-high heat. Add the pork rolls and brown on all sides. Add the wine and heat to boiling, scraping up brown bits from the bottom of the skillet with a wooden spoon.

Reduce heat and cook the rolls, covered, until meat is done and sauce is slightly thickened, about 15 to 20 minutes.

Remove the rolls to a heated platter. Degrease the sauce and pour over the rolls. Serve hot.

SERVES 6 TO 8

Fruit-Stuffed Pork Loin Roast

20 large pitted prunes
1 cup dry white wine
12 large dried apricot halves
1 boned loin of pork (3½ to 4 pounds), tied at 1 to 2-inch
    intervals
3 tablespoons salted butter
2 tablespoons vegetable oil
6 tablespoons Cognac
1½ cups Beef Stock (see page 56)
¾ cup heavy cream
2 tablespoons currant jelly
2 tablespoons orange juice
salt and freshly ground black pepper to taste
4 tablespoons unsalted butter
¼ cup all-purpose flour

Soak the prunes in the wine in a medium bowl for 1 hour. Drain, reserving the wine.

Preheat the oven to 350° F.

Using a wooden spoon handle, push a prune, then 2 apricot halves, into the cavity of the roast and repeat until the cavity is filled. Reserve the remaining prunes.

Melt the salted butter with the oil in a skillet large enough to hold the roast comfortably. Brown the roast on all sides, turning with wooden spoons, about 20 minutes.

Warm the Cognac, then pour it over the roast and ignite. Allow the flames to subside, then remove the roast to a roasting pan. Bake, uncovered, until a meat thermometer reads 165° F., about 1½ hours. Remove the meat to a heated platter and let stand for 15 minutes while making the sauce.

Combine the beef stock, reserved wine, cream, and jelly in a saucepan. Cook over high heat until the mixture is reduced by one-third. Skim the grease from the pan juices, if necessary, then deglaze the roasting pan with a little of the prepared sauce. Return the deglazed juices to the saucepan. Add the orange juice and season with salt and pepper.

Combine the unsalted butter and flour and whisk into the sauce, 1 teaspoon at a time, until thickened (all of the butter and flour mixture may not be needed). Simmer the sauce for a few minutes. Add the reserved prunes.

Spoon some of the sauce over the roast, then carve into 1-inch slices. Serve the remaining sauce with the roast.

US **SKI TEAM** Alf Engen, in the opinion of many, was the greatest all-around skier the United States has ever known. In his prime during the years preceding World War II, he also beat the veterans while in his youth and beat the youngsters while an old-timer. He won more than a dozen national titles of one kind or another. A favorite of colleagues and competitors alike, Engen became the men's coach for the 1948 winter games.

SERVES 8

Butterflied Leg of Lamb

1 leg of lamb (4 to 5 pounds), boned and
  slit lengthwise to spread flat
2 cloves garlic, minced
¼ cup grated onion
1 teaspoon salt
1 teaspoon *fines herbes*
½ teaspoon freshly ground black pepper
½ teaspoon dried thyme
½ cup vegetable oil
½ cup lemon juice

Trim any excess fat from the leg of lamb and place the meat in a large shallow dish. Combine the remaining ingredients, mix well, and pour over the lamb. Marinate the lamb for at least 1 hour, preferably overnight, refrigerated.

Remove the meat and reserve the marinade. Insert skewers at right angles in the meat to keep it flat while broiling. On the broiler rack, broil 3 inches from the heat for 8 minutes on each side, brushing once or twice with the marinade. Carve across the grain in thin slices.

SERVES 6 TO 8

Lamb Espresso

Strong perked coffee is a flavor enhancer when used as part of the braising liquid for any stewed beef or lamb.

1 leg of lamb (4 pounds)
3 cloves garlic
2 tablespoons dry mustard
2 tablespoons ground ginger
salt and freshly ground black pepper to taste
1 jar (10 ounces) currant jelly
⅓ cup tawny port wine
½ cup brewed espresso coffee

Preheat the oven to 350° F.

Cut 3 slits in the lamb and insert the garlic cloves.

In a small bowl, combine the mustard, ginger, salt and pepper and rub this mixture over the lamb. Place the roast in a roasting pan and bake for 20 minutes.

Meanwhile, in a saucepan, combine the jelly, wine, and coffee and mix well. Bring to a boil over high heat and stir until the jelly is dissolved. Reserve.

Baste the roast every 10 minutes with the sauce, until the roast is the desired internal temperature (about 30 minutes more for medium rare). Total roasting time is 50 minutes.

**SERVES
10 TO 12**

Leg of Lamb with Tomato Conserve

5 carrots, coarsely chopped
2 medium white onions, coarsely chopped
2 tablespoons olive oil
5 to 7 pounds prepared leg of lamb
3 garlic cloves, slivered
salt and freshly ground black pepper to taste
1 cup chopped parsley
1½ to 2 cups water
¼ cup red wine vinegar
1½ tablespoons all-purpose flour
1 cup ketchup
1 tablespoon freshly ground black pepper
Tomato Conserve (recipe follows)

Preheat the oven to 325° F.

In a skillet over high heat, sauté the carrots and onions in olive oil just until well coated. Reserve.

Cut slashes in the lamb and insert the garlic slivers. Season with salt and pepper.

Put the lamb in a roasting pan and place the onion, carrots and parsley on top. Add 1½ cups water and the vinegar to the pan and bake for 2 hours.

In a small saucepan, whisk together the flour and ¼ cup water to make a paste. Add the ketchup and pepper and simmer, stirring, until thickened, about 5 minutes. Pour the sauce around the lamb in the roasting pan and return it to the oven. Continue roasting until desired temperature is reached (about 25 minutes per pound for medium) for a total roasting time of about 3 hours. Serve the lamb with the vegetable topping undisturbed, surrounded by the sauce. Pass the Tomato Conserve separately.

TOMATO CONSERVE:
1 can (28 ounces) whole tomatoes
1 large unpeeled lemon, thinly sliced
1 cup granulated sugar
12 whole cloves

Combine all the ingredients in a saucepan. Bring to a boil and stir well. Then reduce heat and simmer, covered, for 1 hour. Chill until serving time. The conserve will be thin.

 The longest regularly scheduled race the U.S. team has entered is the Parsenn Derby, 7.5 miles long, with a vertical drop of 6,500 feet. The course runs through fences, hay barns, bridges, even a small town. To keep up its strength, our team stationed injured mate Vern Goodwin halfway down with a pitcher of beer.

Lamb Shanks with Fruit

SERVES 4

A 3-ounce serving of lean lamb provides 158 calories, 85 milligrams of cholesterol, and zinc, iron, and B complex vitamins.

4 lamb shanks
salt and freshly ground black pepper to taste
all-purpose flour
1½ cups rośe or red wine
1 package (12 ounces) dried mixed fruit, cut into 1-inch pieces
½ cup seedless raisins
2 tablespoons vinegar
2 tablespoons lemon juice
½ cup honey
½ teaspoon ground cinnamon
½ teaspoon allspice

Preheat the oven to 350° F.

Season the lamb shanks with salt and pepper and dust with flour. Place the meat in a 9 x 13-inch baking pan. Cover and bake for 1½ hours, or until the meat is tender. Drain off the grease from the pan and discard.

In a small saucepan, combine the remaining ingredients. Bring to a boil over high heat, then reduce the heat and simmer for 5 minutes.

Increase the oven temperature to 400° F.

Pour the sauce over the lamb shanks and return them to the oven. Cover and bake for 20 to 30 minutes. Serve the meat with the sauce.

SERVES 8

Venison Paprika

3 pounds boneless venison, cut into 1-inch pieces
½ cup all-purpose flour
salt and freshly ground black pepper
½ cup butter
1 cup sliced celery
2 medium onions, quartered
1½ teaspoons paprika
2 cups Chicken Stock (see page 56)
2 cups sour cream
cooked rice or noodles

Dredge the venison in flour seasoned with salt and pepper.

Melt the butter in a Dutch oven, add the venison, and brown on all sides. Add the celery, onions, and 1 teaspoon of the paprika and stir for 1 minute. Stir in the chicken stock. Cover and simmer gently for 1 hour.

Stir in the sour cream and heat through, but do not boil. Sprinkle with the remaining paprika. Serve over cooked rice or noodles.

SERVES 6

This method of roasting takes the "gamey" flavor out of the meat and makes it very moist.

Roasted Elk with Lingonberry Sauce

1 large elk or venison roast, about 4 pounds
2 medium onions, quartered
6 carrots, peeled and cut into pieces
6 stalks celery, cut into pieces
2 bay leaves
salt and freshly ground black pepper to taste
Lingonberry Sauce (recipe follows)

Preheat the oven to 300° F.

Place the roast in a deep, heavy baking pan. Add all the vegetables and seasonings to the roasting pan and pour in enough water to completely cover the roast. Cover and bake in the oven for 5 to 6 hours.

When the meat is done, discard the broth and vegetables and place the meat on a heated platter.

Serve Lingonberry Sauce over the roast.

LINGONBERRY SAUCE:
1 jar (7 ounces) lingonberries in syrup
3 ounces currant jelly
1 tablespoon Worcestershire sauce
2 tablespoons lemon juice
3 dashes hot pepper sauce, or to taste
salt and freshly ground black pepper to taste

Combine all the ingredients in a small saucepan and mix well. Bring to a boil and reduce the heat. Simmer for 3 to 5 minutes to blend flavors. Good served over antelope, venison, or duck.

SERVES 6

Silver Bow Elk

2 to 2½ pounds elk, trimmed
all-purpose flour
vegetable oil
6 ounces mushrooms, sliced
1 shallot, finely chopped
¼ cup brandy
½ cup red wine
2 cups Beef Stock (see page 56)
1 teaspoon freshly ground black pepper

GARNISH:
2 ounces hazelnuts, ground
2 strips bacon, crisply cooked and crumbled

Cut the elk into 18 medallions and pound with a mallet to tenderize. Dredge the medallions in flour. Heat oil in a skillet and brown both sides of the medallions, a few at a time, and set aside.

To the skillet, add the mushrooms, shallot, and brandy and sauté for 1 minute. Add the red wine. Cook over high heat and reduce until the alcohol has evaporated. Add the beef stock and pepper. Reduce the liquid over high heat for 3 to 4 minutes.

Add the elk to the skillet and cook to desired doneness. Remove to a heated platter. Reduce the sauce by cooking over high heat until syrupy. Pour the sauce over the elk, garnish with ground hazelnuts and bacon, and serve.

Poultry

Fargo Pheasant Stew

SECTION CHAIRMAN
Sally Clayton

TESTERS
Lucy Achenbach
Alice Bosworth
Lorraine Coleman
Brigit Davis
Mary Eiseman
Sharon Ferlie
Nancy Gart
Sally Gart
Joy Hilliard
Dottie Hopeman
Sally Hovanic
Joy Jackson
Joanne Keener
Puddy Leidholt
Helene Malek
Cynthia Nagel
Helene Weisbart

Monterey Chicken

SERVES 8

This recipe can be made in advance for dozens of guests and is easy to transport.

8 large, whole chicken breasts, skinned and boned
    (7 to 8 ounces each)
1 can (7 ounces) chopped mild green chilies
½ pound Monterey Jack cheese, cut into 8 strips
½ cup fine dry bread crumbs
¼ cup freshly grated Parmesan cheese
1 to 3 teaspoons chili powder
½ teaspoon salt
¼ teaspoon ground cumin
¼ teaspoon freshly ground black pepper
6 tablespoons butter, melted
Tomato Sauce (recipe follows)

GARNISH:
sour cream
fresh limes

Pound the chicken breasts between 2 sheets of waxed paper until thin. Spread each breast with 1 tablespoon of the green chilies. Place one cheese strip on top of each portion of chilies. Roll up each chicken breast and tuck ends under.

Combine the bread crumbs, Parmesan cheese, chili powder, salt, cumin, and pepper in a shallow dish.

Dip each stuffed breast into the melted butter and roll in the bread crumb mixture. Place the breasts in a baking dish, seam side down. Drizzle with remaining butter. Cover and chill at least 4 hours or overnight.

Preheat the oven to 400° F.

Bake for 25 to 40 minutes, or until done. Serve with the tomato sauce and garnish with sour cream and fresh limes.

TOMATO SAUCE:
1 can (15 ounces) plain tomato sauce
½ teaspoon ground cumin
⅓ cup sliced green onion
salt and freshly ground black pepper to taste

OPTIONAL:
hot pepper sauce to taste

In a small saucepan, combine the tomato sauce, cumin, green onion, salt, pepper, and hot pepper sauce, if desired. Bring to a boil and cook, stirring constantly, until slightly thickened.

SERVES 6 TO 8

Chicken Piccata

4 whole chicken breasts, halved, skinned, and boned
½ cup all-purpose flour
salt and freshly ground black pepper to taste
4 eggs, beaten
2 tablespoons freshly grated Parmesan cheese
½ cup butter
1 tablespoon capers

GARNISH:
1 lemon, cut into wedges

Dredge the chicken in the flour seasoned with the salt and pepper. Combine the eggs and Parmesan cheese, then dip the chicken into the mixture.

Heat the butter in a large skillet until golden brown and sauté the chicken breasts on both sides until crisp and brown, about 3 to 4 minutes on each side. Remove the chicken to a warm platter.

Add the capers to the butter and heat through. Spoon the capers and butter over the chicken. Garnish with the lemon wedges and serve.

SERVES 4

Suprèmes de Volaille aux Tomates

This can be prepared up to the broiling stage and held for an hour. Bring to room temperature before broiling.

2 whole chicken breasts, halved, skinned, and boned
lemon juice
salt and freshly ground black pepper to taste
3 tablespoons unsalted butter
¼ cup Chicken Stock (see page 56)
¼ cup dry white wine
1 cup heavy cream
freshly grated nutmeg
8 slices ripe but firm avocado, peeled
12 slices tomato, peeled and seeded
¼ cup Gruyère cheese, grated

Lightly rub the chicken breasts with lemon juice and sprinkle with salt and pepper.

Heat the butter in a medium skillet until foamy and sauté the chicken breasts, turning to keep coated with butter.

Cook for 7 to 8 minutes, or until done. When cooked through, remove the breasts to a gratin dish. Do not overcook.

Add the stock and wine to the butter in the pan and reduce over high heat until syrupy. Add the cream and continue cooking over high heat until the mixture is thickened and coats a spoon. Remove from the heat and season with salt, pepper, and nutmeg.

Arrange the chicken breasts, avocado, and tomato slices alternately, in an attractive pattern, in a shallow baking dish. Cover with the sauce and top with cheese. Heat under the broiler until glazed and bubbly.

Quick Saucy Chicken

SERVES 4

To make a rice mold, place hot cooked and buttered rice in a small, well-buttered mixing bowl or ring mold. Pack down well with a spoon and let stand for 5 minutes. Turn upside down to unmold.

4 small chicken breasts, halved, skinned, and boned (about 1 pound)
2 tablespoons butter
1 clove garlic, pressed
3 green onions, finely chopped
1 tablespoon all-purpose flour
½ cup heavy cream
2 tablespoons chopped fresh parsley
¾ cup grated Swiss cheese
⅓ cup freshly grated Parmesan cheese
½ teaspoon salt
freshly ground black pepper to taste
hot cooked pasta or rice

Cut the chicken into very thin strips.

Heat the butter in a heavy skillet. Add the chicken and stir constantly over moderate heat for about 3 minutes, or until the chicken is firm and white. Add the garlic and onions and cook for 2 more minutes. Stir in the flour and cook for 1 minute, stirring constantly.

Add the cream, parsley, and cheeses and stir just until blended. Remove the pan from the heat as soon as the cream is hot and the cheese has melted. Do not let the mixture boil after adding the cream. The total cooking time is about 6 minutes. Season with salt and pepper and serve over hot pasta or rice.

SERVES 4

Crab-Stuffed Chicken Breasts

4 whole chicken breasts, skinned and boned
½ cup finely chopped green onion
½ cup chopped mushrooms
4 tablespoons butter
3 tablespoons all-purpose flour
pinch of oregano
½ cup Chicken Stock (see page 56)
½ cup milk
½ cup dry white wine
salt and freshly ground black pepper to taste
8 ounces crabmeat, picked over for shells
⅓ cup chopped fresh parsley
⅓ cup fine dry bread crumbs
1 cup shredded Swiss cheese

Preheat the oven to 400° F.

Pound the chicken breasts between 2 sheets of waxed paper until thin.

In a skillet, sauté the green onion and mushrooms in the butter until the onion is transparent, about 5 minutes. Stir in the flour and oregano and blend well.

Combine the stock, milk, and wine and add to the onions and mushrooms. Cook, stirring constantly, until the sauce is thick. Season with salt and pepper and set aside.

Mix together ¼ cup of the sauce, the crabmeat, parsley, and bread crumbs. Spoon onto the chicken breasts. Roll up the breasts and place them seam side down in a buttered casserole dish.

Pour the remaining sauce over the chicken and sprinkle with the cheese. Cover and bake for 25 minutes. Uncover and bake for 15 minutes longer. Serve hot.

Willy Schaeffler originated two notorious training activities. While at the University of Denver, ski team members were required to climb the stadium steps carrying a team member on their shoulders piggyback fashion. Those same loyal skiers complied with Willy's requirement that every team member eat a raw egg for "extra protein and energy" immediately prior to competition. One Norwegian former student recently remarked that the clocked times would have been even faster if the egg were reserved for those who did *not* improve their times during a meet!

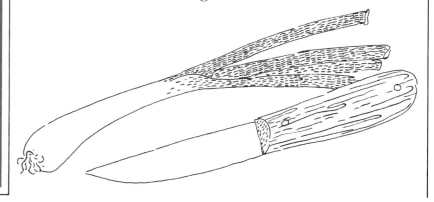

SERVES 4

Basic Chicken Sauté

1 frying chicken (3 pounds), cut into serving pieces
2 tablespoons butter
1 tablespoon vegetable oil
salt and freshly ground black pepper to taste
1 tablespoon minced shallot
½ cup dry white wine
½ cup Chicken Stock (see page 56)
1 tablespoon softened butter

To sauté properly requires a high heat. Butter burns at a lower temperature than oil, so a combination of both provides the butter flavor at the preferred higher heat. Sautéing at too low a temperature will allow the chicken or meat to absorb the oil.

Rinse the chicken pieces under cold running water and pat dry with paper toweling.

In a large skillet, heat the butter and oil until foamy. Add the chicken pieces to the pan without crowding, and brown on each side, about 3 minutes per side. Remove pieces as they are browned and repeat with the remaining chicken.

Return only the dark meat to the pan, season and cover. Cook over moderate heat for 10 minutes.

Add the white meat to the pan, season and cover. Cook for about 20 minutes, basting at intervals. When the chicken is cooked through, remove to a serving platter.

Remove all but 2 tablespoons of the fat from the pan. Add the shallot and cook slowly for 1 minute, then add the wine and chicken stock. Increase the heat and reduce the liquid, scraping the bottom of the pan. Taste for seasoning and correct with salt and pepper, then remove from the heat (the sauce should be syrupy). Swirl in the softened butter and pour over chicken. Serve immediately.

BASIC SAUTÉ WITH HERBS:

Add 2 teaspoons fresh green herbs when first seasoning the chicken. Thyme or tarragon or a mixture of favorite herbs can be used.

BASIC SAUTÉ WITH CREAM:

Substitute 1 cup heavy cream for the chicken stock in the basic recipe. Cook down the wine to a syrupy stage, then add the cream and reduce until thickened.

SERVES 4

Lemon Chicken is tangy served hot and equally flavorful served cold.

Lemon Chicken

1 frying chicken (2½ to 3 pounds), cut into serving pieces
1 cup lemon juice
¼ cup all-purpose flour
salt and freshly ground black pepper to taste
½ cup vegetable oil
2 tablespoons (packed) brown sugar
1 tablespoon grated lemon zest

GARNISH:
thinly sliced lemon

Combine the chicken pieces with the lemon juice in a bowl. Marinate, covered, in the refrigerator overnight.
Preheat the oven to 350° F.
Drain the chicken well and pat dry with paper toweling. Dredge the chicken in a mixture of the flour, salt, and pepper. Heat the oil in a large skillet and brown the chicken pieces on all sides.
Arrange the chicken in one layer in a large shallow casserole dish. Sprinkle with the brown sugar and lemon zest. Bake for 35 to 45 minutes, or until the chicken is tender. Serve hot.

SERVES 4 TO 6

Sherried Chicken

2 frying chickens (2½ pounds each), halved
½ cup butter
1 teaspoon salt
½ teaspoon freshly ground black pepper
1 onion, minced
½ cup dry sherry
¼ cup honey

Preheat the oven to 350° F.
Spread the butter on the chicken and sprinkle with the salt and pepper. Arrange the chicken in one layer in a roasting pan. Add the onion, cover, and bake for 45 minutes to 1 hour.
Combine the sherry and honey in a small saucepan and bring to a boil over medium-high heat. Pour the sauce over the chicken and bake for 15 minutes more, uncovered, or until the chicken is tender. Serve hot.

Herbed Chicken with Cognac

SERVES 8 TO 10 ◼

Fresh herbs always taste better than dried. If you are using dried herbs, crush them with your fingers, or steep them in a tablespoon of dry white wine for 20 minutes.

2 tablespoons butter
2 tablespoons vegetable oil
2 frying chickens (2½ to 3 pounds each), cut into
    serving pieces
3 tablespoons Cognac
3 medium onions, quartered
2 cloves garlic, minced
2 tablespoons all-purpose flour
1 teaspoon fresh rosemary leaves
1 teaspoon chopped fresh oregano
1 teaspoon chopped fresh thyme
½ teaspoon fresh sage leaves
1 cup Chicken Stock (see page 56)
1 cup dry white wine
1 cup sliced mushrooms
1 cup heavy cream
2 tablespoons Dijon mustard
1 teaspoon Beau Monde seasoning
salt and freshly ground black pepper to taste

Preheat the oven to 350° F.

Heat the butter and oil in a heavy Dutch oven or large heatproof casserole over medium heat. Add the chicken, a few pieces at a time, and brown on all sides. When all the chicken is browned, return all pieces to the pan. Pour the Cognac into the pan and ignite carefully, spooning the Cognac over the chicken until the flames subside. Remove the chicken from the pan and reserve.

Add the onions and garlic to the pan and sauté until limp. Stir in the flour and cook for approximately 2 minutes. Add the rosemary, oregano, thyme, and sage, then add the chicken stock and wine and blend well.

Return the chicken to the Dutch oven and bring to a boil. Place the chicken in the oven and bake, covered, for 20 minutes. Add the mushrooms and cook for another 30 minutes. Remove from the oven and transfer the chicken to a warm serving dish.

On the range top, bring the sauce to a boil and cook, uncovered, until reduced by two thirds, stirring constantly. Then add the cream, mustard, Beau Monde, and salt and pepper to taste. Simmer until the sauce has been reduced by one half cup. Pour the sauce over the chicken and serve.

SERVES 3 TO 4 ●

Curried Baked Chicken

Curry powder is a mixture of many spices and varies by brand. Like some other spices and most herbs, it loses its potency with age and has a pantry shelf-life of about 6 months.

1 frying chicken (2½ to 3 pounds), cut into serving pieces
1½ to 2 tablespoons curry powder
2 tablespoons soy sauce
½ cup prepared mustard
½ cup honey

Preheat the oven to 350° F.

Place the chicken in a shallow casserole dish. Mix together the curry powder, soy sauce, mustard, and honey and spread over the chicken parts. Let the chicken stand for 30 minutes.

Pour off the extra sauce from the casserole and reserve for basting. Bake for 1 hour, turning after 30 minutes and basting occasionally. Serve hot.

SERVES 8 ●

Southern Fried Chicken and Gravy

2 frying chickens (2½ pounds each), cut into serving pieces
milk
¾ cup all-purpose flour
salt and freshly ground black pepper to taste
1 cup vegetable oil (not a light oil)
3 cups milk, scalded

OPTIONAL:
1 egg, beaten

Cover the chicken pieces with milk in a bowl and let stand for 1 hour.

Drain the chicken and discard the milk.

Pour ¾ cup of fresh milk into a shallow bowl (or mix 1 beaten egg with the milk, if desired). Combine ½ cup of the flour with salt and pepper in a shallow bowl. Dip the chicken first in the milk (or egg-milk mixture), then dredge it in the seasoned flour.

Heat ½ cup oil in each of 2 large heavy skillets. When oil is almost smoking, add the chicken, a few pieces at a time, and cook until golden brown on both sides, turning once. Cover the skillets, reduce the heat, and cook for 15 minutes.

Remove the lids, turn the chicken pieces over, and cook for 15 to 20 minutes more, or until the chicken is tender. Remove the chicken to a warm platter.

Drain off all but ¼ cup of the oil. Add the remaining ¼ cup of flour and stir, scraping the browned pieces off the bottom. Slowly add the scalded milk and stir until thickened. Season with salt and pepper.

Serve the chicken with the gravy and mashed potatoes or biscuits or both.

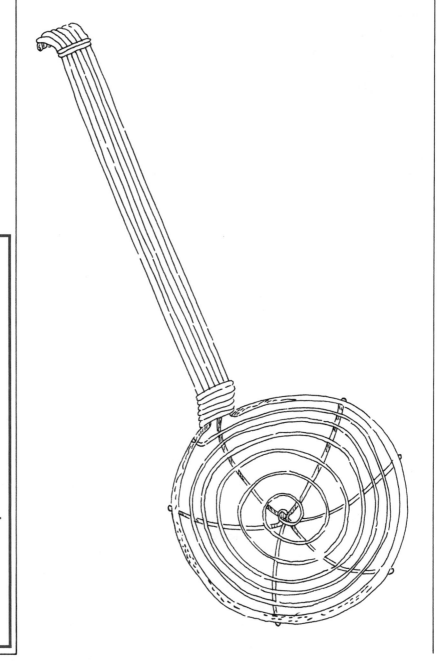

Willy Schaefflers's 1972 Olympic team secured gold and bronze medals and also brought home 23 separate medals in four years' competition in the World University Games. Willy and Aspen orthopedic surgeon Robert Oden developed the medical support program which operates today, providing full time medical coverage of the U.S. Ski team by an American surgeon. Fifty orthopedic and general surgeons from around the country currently comprise that volunteer support team, under the coordination of Dr. Richard Steadman.

SERVES 4

Stir-Fry Chicken with Cashews in Chili Sauce

Fresh water chestnuts resemble a small flower bulb and are available in Oriental markets. They are tedious to peel, but have a fresh, crisp, nutty flavor that is well worth the effort.

6 tablespoons soy sauce
4 tablespoons rice wine or dry sherry
2 tablespoons water
3 tablespoons cornstarch
4 teaspoons sesame oil
1½ pounds skinned, boned chicken breasts, cut into bite-sized pieces
3 tablespoons minced green onion
3 tablespoons minced garlic
2 tablespoons minced fresh ginger root
2 tablespoons chili paste
½ cup Chicken Stock (see page 56)
2 tablespoons granulated sugar
2 teaspoons black vinegar
1 pound fresh spinach
1 teaspoon salt
7 tablespoons peanut oil
1 cup halved water chestnuts
1½ cups cashews (about 6 ounces)

In a bowl combine 3 tablespoons of the soy sauce, 2 tablespoons of the rice wine, the water, 1 tablespoon of the cornstarch, 1 teaspoon of the sesame oil, and the chicken. Set aside.

Combine the green onion, 2 tablespoons of the garlic, the ginger root, and chili paste in a separate bowl and set aside.

In a third bowl, combine the chicken stock, remaining 3 tablespoons soy sauce, remaining 2 tablespoons rice wine, the sugar, remaining 2 tablespoons cornstarch, the black vinegar, and 2 teaspoons of the sesame oil. Set aside.

Wash and trim the spinach. Cook the spinach in the water that clings to the leaves over high heat for 1 minute, or until the spinach begins to wilt. Rinse under cold water and squeeze out the moisture. In a bowl combine the spinach with the remaining 1 tablespoon garlic, the salt, and remaining 1 teaspoon sesame oil. Set aside.

Heat a wok over high heat until it is hot. Add 4 tablespoons of the peanut oil and heat until it is very hot. Add the chicken mixture and stir-fry until the pieces separate and change color, then transfer to a plate.

Add the remaining 3 tablespoons oil to the wok and heat until it is very hot. Add the green onion mixture and stir-fry until it is fragrant. Add the water chestnuts, chicken, and the broth mixture and stir-fry until the sauce begins to thicken. Add the cashews and stir-fry for 30 seconds.

Mound the mixture in the center of a heated platter and surround with the spinach. Serve immediately.

Stir-Fry Orange Chicken

SERVES 2

½ pound chicken breast, skinned, boned, and cut into
     bite-sized pieces
¼ cup all-purpose flour
salt and freshly ground black pepper to taste
4 tablespoons butter
1 medium carrot, peeled and cut into julienne
1 tablespoon lemon juice
2 tablespoons orange juice
½ teaspoon dried rosemary, crumbled
1 tablespoon chopped fresh parsley
hot cooked rice

Dredge the chicken pieces in the flour seasoned with salt and pepper.

Melt the butter in a skillet over medium heat. Add the chicken and carrot to the skillet. Increase the heat to medium-high and cook, stirring constantly, until the chicken juices run clear when pierced with a fork, about 3 to 5 minutes. Add the lemon juice, orange juice, and rosemary and stir for 2 minutes. Sprinkle with the parsley and serve over rice.

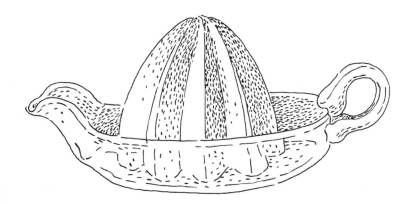

Roast Chicken with Mushrooms and Cream

SERVES 6

For simple roast chicken, place 2 to 3 cloves garlic, sprigs of fresh tarragon or thyme, and salt to taste in the cavity of a 3-pound chicken and roast at 350° F. until the juices run clear, about 1½ hours.

1 roasting chicken (about 5 pounds)
salt and freshly ground black pepper to taste
garlic salt to taste
1 orange, unpeeled, quartered
1 cup heavy cream
½ pound small mushrooms

GARNISH:
fresh parsley

Preheat the oven to 425° F.

Rub the inside and outside of the chicken with salt, pepper, and garlic salt. Place the orange in the chicken cavity. Place the chicken, breast side up, in a buttered casserole dish and roast for 20 minutes.

Reduce the heat to 350° F. and pour half the cream over the chicken. Roast for 20 minutes longer. Pour the remaining cream over the chicken and continue roasting for 1 hour.

Place the mushrooms alongside the chicken in the pan juices and continue roasting for 15 minutes longer. Garnish with fresh parsley and carve at the table.

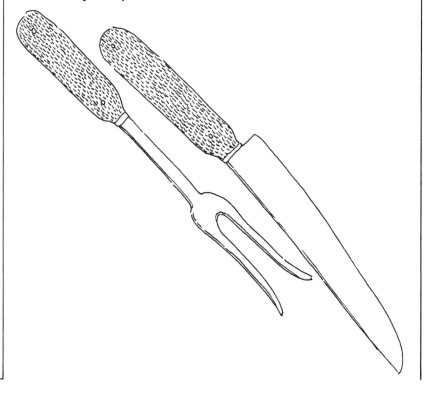

SERVES 4

Chicken alla Roma

½ pound hot Italian link sausage, sliced into ½-inch pieces
½ pound sweet Italian link sausage, sliced into ½-inch pieces
all-purpose flour for dredging
¼ teaspoon garlic pepper
¼ teaspoon dried oregano
¼ teaspoon salt
2 whole chicken breasts, skinned, boned, and split
2 tablespoons olive oil
1 medium onion, diced
1 green bell pepper, diced
1 red bell pepper, diced or 1 jar (2 ounces) diced pimientos
¼ pound mushrooms, sliced
3 cloves garlic, minced
1 can (16 ounces) Italian plum tomatoes, drained and halved,
    liquid reserved
½ cup red wine
1 teaspoon chopped fresh basil or ¼ teaspoon dried
freshly ground black pepper to taste

Brown the sausages in a large, heavy skillet over medium-high heat. Remove the sausages from the skillet with a slotted spoon and drain on paper toweling.

Combine the flour, garlic pepper, oregano, and salt. Dredge the chicken in the seasoned flour. Sauté the chicken in the grease left in the skillet until browned on both sides. Remove the chicken from the skillet and set aside.

Drain the grease from the pan and discard. Add the olive oil to the pan. Stir in the onion, green pepper, red pepper, mushrooms, and garlic and sauté until golden, about 5 minutes.

Return the sausages and chicken to the pan. Add the tomatoes, wine, basil, and pepper to taste. Cover and simmer over low heat for 30 minutes. Add the reserved tomato liquid if the sauce is too thick. Serve hot.

US Bob Beattie was the first year-round director of the U.S. ski team, operating out of a room at the Denver, Colorado, airport. His first team won the 1962 world championship. Bob went on to co-found the World Cup circuit. Later, he organized and administered World Pro skiing with its parallel race format; developed and promoted the NASTAR citizens racing program; was a prime mover in establishing the seeding system used in all international racing; and created the penalty point system used throughout the world to score FIS races. (FIS stands for the French Federation Internationale du Ski, the organization responsible for scoring international ski competitions.)

Chicken Sausage Jambalaya

SERVES 10 TO 12 ■

Rice is an economical source of carbohydrates and B vitamins. Because of its bland taste, rice can be used as a base or combined with sweet and savory flavors. Try it with olives and pine nuts; pineapple, curry, and butter; chutney, green onions, and raisins; or shredded cheese and minced parsley.

3 tablespoons vegetable oil
1 pound smoked sausage links, sliced into ¼-inch lengths
2 frying chickens (2½ to 3 pounds each), cut into serving pieces and breasts halved
2 pounds cooked ham, cubed
¼ cup all-purpose flour
2 to 2½ cups finely chopped white onions
1 medium green bell pepper, cored and chopped
4 stalks celery, finely chopped
1 can (6 ounces) tomato paste
1 cup Beef Stock (see page 56)
6 cups Chicken Stock (see page 56)
2 bay leaves
1 teaspoon dried basil
½ teaspoon chili powder
¼ teaspoon cayenne
freshly ground black pepper to taste
1 teaspoon salt
3 to 4 cloves garlic, chopped
2 cups rice
6 green onions with tops, chopped
fresh parsley
dash of hot pepper sauce

Heat the oil in a heavy kettle and brown the sausage over medium heat. Remove the sausage with a slotted spoon and set aside.

Brown the chicken, a few pieces at a time, in the same kettle. Remove as browned and set aside.

Add the ham to the same kettle and brown, adding more oil if necessary. Remove from the kettle and set aside.

Add the flour to the kettle and cook, scraping brown bits from the bottom, for 4 to 5 minutes, or until the mixture is medium brown. Add the white onions, green pepper, and celery and cook until tender, stirring occasionally. Add the tomato paste and stir well. Add the beef stock and gradually add the chicken stock, stirring constantly.

Bring to a slow boil and add the bay leaves, basil, chili powder, cayenne and black pepper, salt, and chopped garlic and stir well. Add the chicken, sausage, and ham. Bring to a boil over high heat. Reduce the heat to low, then cover and simmer for 20 minutes, stirring occasionally. Add the rice and stir well. Raise the heat, return the mixture to a slow boil, then reduce the heat, cover, and simmer for 25 to 30 minutes. Turn off the heat and allow to stand for at least 1 hour.

Thirty minutes before serving, reheat slowly over medium-low heat. Stir in the green onions and parsley. Add a dash of hot pepper sauce to taste and serve.

SERVES 6

Chicken and Spinach Enchiladas

2 eggs, beaten
1 cup minced, cooked chicken
1 cup chopped, cooked, well-drained spinach
¼ cup heavy cream
1 clove garlic, minced
2 tablespoons hot salsa
1 cup grated Monterey Jack cheese
⅓ cup freshly grated Parmesan cheese
1 can (4 ounces) green chilies
1 can (7 ounces) mild green chile salsa
6 Flour Tortillas (see page 248)
1 tomato, diced
1 cup grated Cheddar cheese

GARNISH:
chopped green onion
picante sauce
sour cream

Preheat the broiler. Combine the first 9 ingredients in a bowl and mix well. Add 2 tablespoons of the green chile salsa and transfer the mixture to a saucepan. Warm over medium heat until the cheeses are melted and well blended.

Fill each tortilla with one sixth of the chicken-salsa mixture. Divide the tomato evenly between the tortillas and fold the tortillas, one side over the other, to close. Place the tortillas side by side in a buttered casserole dish. Sprinkle the top with Cheddar cheese and pour the remaining salsa on top.

Place the enchiladas on the lowest level of the broiler and broil for 5 to 10 minutes, or until the cheese on top is melted and bubbly. Don't allow the tortillas to become crisp. Serve immediately, garnished with green onion, picante sauce, and sour cream.

US 1948 Olympic downhiller Steve Knowlton continues to promote American skiing with the same enthusiasm he had during his competitive years. Founder of Colorado Ski Country, U.S.A., an organization that promotes Colorado ski areas and protects land designated for ski areas within the state, Steve currently owns Café Kandahar and Ski Museum in Littleton, Colorado, a first-class establishment.

SERVES 8

Chicken and Artichoke Casserole

1 chicken (2½ to 3 pounds), poached, skinned, boned, and cut into pieces
2 packages (9 ounces each) frozen artichoke hearts, cooked and drained
6 tablespoons butter
½ pound mushrooms, sliced
¼ cup all-purpose flour
2 cups Chicken Stock (see page 56)
3 cups grated Cheddar cheese
½ teaspoon freshly grated nutmeg
½ cup fine dry bread crumbs
1 teaspoon dried savory
1 teaspoon dried thyme

To poach chicken: Place the chicken pieces in water to cover with 2 stalks celery, 1 carrot, and 1 onion (all unpeeled and cut into pieces), 1 bay leaf, and a few peppercorns. Heat to a simmer and cook, covered, until tender. Cool in broth.

Preheat the oven to 350° F.

Place the chicken and artichoke hearts in a 3-quart casserole dish. Melt 4 tablespoons of the butter in a saucepan and sauté the mushrooms for 4 to 5 minutes. Blend in the flour, then add the chicken stock gradually and cook until thickened. Add the cheese and nutmeg and stir until the cheese is melted. Pour the mushroom-cheese sauce over the chicken.

Combine the bread crumbs with the savory and thyme, then sprinkle over the chicken. Dot with the remaining 2 tablespoons butter.

Bake, uncovered, for 30 minutes. Place under the broiler briefly just to brown the bread crumbs. Serve immediately.

SERVES 10 TO 12

Chicken, Ham, and Shrimp Casserole

This casserole can be made a day in advance and reheated. It is easy to double.

6 tablespoons butter
1 small onion, chopped
½ pound mushrooms, sliced
6 tablespoons all-purpose flour
½ teaspoon salt
1½ cups milk
1½ cup Chicken Stock (see page 56)
1 cup shredded sharp Cheddar cheese
½ cup chopped green bell pepper
3 cups cubed, cooked chicken
1 pound cooked ham, diced
1½ pounds shrimp, cooked, shelled, and deveined
2 tablespoons pimiento strips

Melt the butter in a large skillet and sauté the onion until tender. Add the mushrooms and cook for 3 minutes. Stir in the flour and salt and cook and stir for 2 minutes. Add the milk and stock gradually, stirring until smooth. Cook the sauce until thickened. Add the cheese and stir until the cheese is melted and the sauce is smooth.

Stir in the green pepper, chicken, ham, shrimp, and pimiento and cook until heated through. Serve.

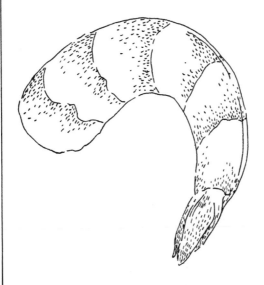

SERVES 3 TO 4

Pheasant in Green Peppercorn Sauce

4 tablespoons butter
1 pheasant, quartered
2 tablespoons minced onion
½ cup dry white wine
4 teaspoons green peppercorns, rinsed and drained
1 cup heavy cream
½ teaspoon dried tarragon
salt and freshly ground black pepper to taste

Melt the butter in a skillet over medium heat. Add the pheasant and sauté until golden. Cover and cook over low heat for 30 minutes, or until tender. Remove to a plate and keep warm.

Add the onion to the skillet and sauté over low heat until limp. Add the wine. Increase the heat and boil until the wine is reduced by half, scraping up any brown bits of pheasant. Mash 2 teaspoons of the peppercorns, leaving the remainder whole. Stir the cream, mashed and whole peppercorns, and tarragon into the skillet. Continue boiling until the sauce is syrupy. Remove from the heat and season with salt and pepper to taste. Pour the sauce over the pheasant and serve.

SERVES 3 TO 4

Fargo Pheasant Stew

1 pheasant, cut into serving pieces
all-purpose flour for dredging
salt and freshly ground black pepper to taste
butter
⅓ cup chopped onion
⅓ cup chopped celery
⅓ cup chopped carrot
2 bay leaves
½ cup dry white wine
1 cup Chicken Stock (see page 56)

Preheat the oven to 250° F.

Dredge the pheasant in the flour seasoned with salt and pepper. Brown the pheasant in butter in a skillet, then remove to a roasting pan.

POULTRY: GAME BIRDS

Add the onion, celery, carrot, bay leaves, wine, and chicken stock to the pan. Cover and bake for 5½ to 6 hours. Serve hot.

Duck with Raspberry Sauce

SERVES 6

Raspberry vinegar can be made with fresh or frozen berries. Heat 2 cups white wine or rice vinegar and add 1½ cups fresh or frozen raspberries. Let cool and stand for 24 hours at room temperature. Strain and pour into a clear glass bottle.

6 duck breasts
3 tablespoons butter
3 tablespoons framboise (raspberry brandy)
¼ cup raspberry vinegar
¾ cup white wine
1 tablespoon chopped shallots
1 tablespoon beef base
1 teaspoon tomato paste
½ cup Beef or Chicken Stock (see page 56)
1 package (10 ounces) frozen raspberries, thawed
4 kiwi fruit, peeled and sliced

Sauté the duck breasts in the butter in a skillet. Pour in the brandy and ignite carefully. Sauté until the flame subsides.

Combine the vinegar, wine, and shallots in a small saucepan. Cook over high heat to reduce by half. Add the beef base, tomato paste, and the beef or chicken stock. Add the sauce to the breasts and cook over low heat for 15 to 20 minutes.

Purée the raspberries and sieve, discarding the seeds.

To serve, add a few tablespoons of the sauce to the raspberry purée. Place the purée on a serving platter and place the breasts on the purée. Place the kiwi slices on and around the duck. Spoon the sauce over the breasts and serve immediately.

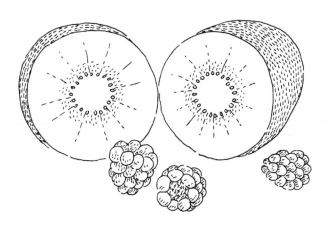

SERVES 6

Turkey Risotto

1 cup chopped onion
1 cup chopped celery
2 tablespoons vegetable oil
3 cups cubed, cooked turkey
1 can (16 ounces) tomatoes
1½ teaspoons salt
1 teaspoon granulated sugar
½ teaspoon dried rosemary, crushed
¼ teaspoon freshly ground black pepper
1 cup water
¾ cup tomato juice
¾ cup cooked rice
2 cups shredded sharp Cheddar cheese

Preheat the oven to 350° F.

Sauté the onion and celery in the oil in a large sauté pan until limp, about 5 minutes; push the onion-celery mixture to one side of the pan. Add the turkey to the pan and brown lightly. Stir in the tomatoes, salt, sugar, rosemary, pepper, water, and tomato juice. Heat to boiling.

Spoon half of the mixture into a buttered 2-quart baking dish. Spread the rice and half of the cheese on top. Next layer the remaining turkey mixture and cheese. Cover and bake for 1 hour, or until the rice is tender and the liquid is absorbed. Serve immediately.

Seafood

Kodiak-Style Salmon

SECTION CHAIRMAN
Sally Clayton

TESTERS
Lucy Achenbach
Alice Bosworth
Lorraine Coleman
Brigit Davis
Mary Eiseman
Sharon Ferlic
Nancy Gart
Sally Gart
Joy Hilliard
Dottie Hopeman
Sally Hovanic
Joy Jackson
Joanne Keener
Puddy Leidholt
Helene Malek
Cynthia Nagel
Helene Weisbart

SERVES 3 TO 4

Fillet of Fish Florentine

Fish should be cooked about 10 minutes per inch. Watch the time carefully and do not overcook.

1¼ to 1½ pounds fish fillets (red snapper, turbot, sole, or flounder)
salt and freshly ground black pepper to taste
¾ cup sour cream
⅓ cup mayonnaise
2 tablespoons all-purpose flour
2 tablespoons lemon juice
¼ teaspoon ground coriander
1½ pounds spinach, stemmed and well rinsed
paprika

Preheat the oven to 400° F.

Season the fish fillets with salt and pepper, then place in a buttered 9 x 13-inch baking pan.

In a small bowl, blend together the sour cream, mayonnaise, flour, lemon juice, and coriander. Spread this mixture over the fish. Bake the fish for 10 minutes, or just until the fish is opaque when flaked in the center.

Meanwhile, cook the spinach in a large skillet, covered, until wilted, about 4 minutes.

Place the spinach on a platter. Put the fish fillets on top of the spinach and drizzle any extra sauce from the baking pan over the fish. Sprinkle with paprika and serve.

SERVES 3 TO 4

Broiled Fish with Dijon Sauce

½ cup mayonnaise
2 tablespoons Dijon mustard
3 tablespoons freshly grated Parmesan cheese
freshly ground black pepper to taste
1 pound firm fish fillets

In a small bowl, mix the mayonnaise, mustard, cheese, and pepper. Spread this mixture over the fish fillets.

Broil the fillets for 4 to 7 minutes, depending on the size and thickness of the fish, or just until the fish flakes with a fork. Do not overcook. Serve immediately.

SERVES 8

 # *Snapper Stuffed with Crab*

¼ cup chopped onion
7 tablespoons butter
3 ounces mushrooms, chopped
½ pound crabmeat, picked over for shells
½ cup crushed saltine crackers
2 tablespoons fresh snipped parsley
freshly ground black pepper to taste
8 red snapper fillets (about 2 pounds)
3 tablespoons all-purpose flour
1½ cups milk
⅓ cup white wine
salt and freshly ground white pepper
freshly grated nutmeg
1 cup shredded Swiss cheese
paprika

Preheat the over to 400° F.

Sauté the onion in 4 tablespoons of the butter in a medium skillet over medium heat until the onion is soft. Stir in the mushrooms, crabmeat, cracker crumbs, parsley, and pepper. Spread this mixture over the fish fillets and roll up. Place seam side down in a buttered casserole dish.

Melt the remaining 3 tablespoons butter in a saucepan. Add the flour and stir until well blended. Cook and stir until blended. Slowly add the milk and wine and stir until thickened. Season the sauce with salt, pepper, and nutmeg.

Pour the sauce over the fish and bake for 25 minutes. Sprinkle with the cheese and paprika and return to the oven for 10 minutes. Serve hot.

SERVES 6

 # *Lemon Sole with Beurre Blanc and Raspberries*

1 cup dry white wine
1 tablespoon chopped shallot
1 teaspoon whole peppercorns
½ cup raspberry vinegar
1 cup heavy cream
1 pound sweet butter, cut into small pieces
18 small lemon sole or other fish fillets

GARNISH:
1 bunch watercress
1½ cups fresh raspberries

Cook the wine, shallot, peppercorns, and raspberry vinegar together in a small saucepan and reduce until syrupy. Add the heavy cream and reduce again by half.

Blending with a wire whisk over low heat, add the butter, one piece at a time, until all the butter is used. Strain the sauce through cheesecloth into the top of a double boiler and keep warm.

Put water in a steamer and bring to a boil. Fold the fish fillets, shiny side in, and place in the steamer. Cook until done, about 2 to 3 minutes. Do not overcook.

Place the fish fillets on a hot platter. Pour some of the butter sauce over each fillet and garnish with watercress. Sprinkle some fresh raspberries over each fillet and mix the remaining berries into the remaining sauce. Serve with the sauce.

Whole Grilled Fish

SERVES 8

Whole fish can also be cooked directly on a grill. Place herbs and lemon slices inside the fish. Lightly oil the grill and the fish and cook over medium heat.

1 whole fish (6 to 8 pounds) (salmon, striped bass, etc.), slit, cleaned, head and tail removed after weighing
12 slices bacon
10 sprigs fresh parsley
salt and freshly ground white pepper to taste
1½ to 2 cups dry white wine

Heat outdoor grill.

Lay 8 slices of bacon and the parsley inside the fish. Season the inside of the fish with salt and pepper. Lay 4 slices of bacon on top of the fish.

Place the fish on a double thickness of heavy-duty aluminum foil with enough additional foil to make a tight package. Shape the foil so that it will hold the wine.

Pour the wine over the fish. Secure the package tightly and place 4 to 5 inches from medium-hot coals. Cook for 45 minutes to 1 hour, or until the fish flakes easily when tested. Remove the foil, bacon, and parsley. Remove the bones and serve.

SERVES 6

Lemon Swordfish

3 to 4 lemons
6 slices swordfish (about ½ pound each)
salt and freshly ground white pepper to taste
milk
all-purpose flour
12 tablespoons peanut oil
1 teaspoon salted butter
5 tablespoons unsalted butter
¼ cup drained capers

GARNISH:
2 tablespoons chopped fresh parsley

Carefully peel the lemons, discarding all of the white pith. Cut the white membrane from the lemon sections. Remove the segments, then dice. Set aside.

Generously season the swordfish with salt and white pepper. Dip each slice in milk. Coat with flour, shaking off excess.

Heat 6 tablespoons of the peanut oil in a large skillet over medium-high heat. Stir in ½ teaspoon of the salted butter. Add 3 slices of fish and sauté until lightly browned on both sides. Reduce the heat and continue cooking until the fish is opaque and feels firm to the touch. Transfer the fish to a heated serving platter and keep warm. Repeat with the remaining oil, ½ teaspoon salted butter, and fish.

Wipe out the skillet with paper toweling. Add the 5 tablespoons of unsalted butter and cook over medium heat until lighty browned. Stir in the diced lemons and capers. Pour over the fish, garnish with chopped parsley and serve immediately.

SERVES 4

Grilled Salmon with Pistachio Butter

3 to 4 tablespoons shelled natural pistachio nuts
4 tablespoons unsalted butter, softened
1 tablespoon finely minced fresh parsley
1 teaspoon lime or lemon juice
2 tablespoons vegetable oil
4 salmon steaks (½ pound each), each about 1 inch thick

Chop the pistachio nuts in a food processor or blender. Do not overprocess.

Beat the butter until fluffy in a small bowl. Stir in the nuts, parsley, and lime or lemon juice. Shape the butter into a log about 3 inches long. Wrap tightly in waxed paper or foil and refrigerate until firm, about 1 hour in the refrigerator or 20 minutes in the freezer.

Heat the broiler or grill. Brush 1 tablespoon of the oil on the broiler or grill. Brush the remaining 1 tablespoon oil on both sides of the salmon steaks. Broil about 5 inches from the heat for 3 to 4 minutes on each side. Serve with several slices of pistachio butter on top.

Kodiak-Style Salmon

SERVES 4

4 salmon steaks (½ pound each)
¼ cup (packed) brown sugar
4 tablespoons butter
lemon juice to taste

Broil or poach the salmon for 8 to 10 minutes, or until done. Remove to a hot platter.

Combine the sugar, butter, and lemon juice in a small saucepan and heat until the sugar dissolves. Pour over the salmon to serve.

Lake Huron Perch

SERVES 4

An easy sauce for broiled or fried fish is 2 parts homemade mayonnaise to 1 part Dijon mustard. Sharpen the flavor with fresh lemon juice or hot pepper sauce, if desired.

vegetable oil
2 eggs, beaten
saltine cracker crumbs
flour
salt and freshly ground black pepper to taste
12 freshly caught perch, filleted

In a large, heavy skillet (preferably over a campfire on the shore), heat the vegetable oil until hot.

Dip the fish in egg and then in a mixture of cracker crumbs and flour seasoned with salt and pepper.

Fry the fish on both sides until crisp. Serve immediately.

SERVES 4

Gulf Coast Shrimp

2½ tablespoons butter
1½ tablespoons all-purpose flour
2 cups Beef Stock (see page 56)
½ teaspoon minced garlic
1½ tablespoons minced onion
1½ pounds large shrimp, cooked, peeled, and deveined
2 cups chopped fresh mushrooms
1½ tablespoons lemon juice
⅓ cup Madeira
1½ tablespoons minced fresh parsley

GARNISH:
lemon wedges

Melt 1½ tablespoons of the butter in a saucepan. Blend in the flour and cook over low heat until browned, about 10 minutes, stirring occasionally. Stir in the beef stock, bring to a boil, and cook for 3 to 5 minutes. Reduce heat to a simmer and cook, uncovered, for 30 minutes, stirring occasionally.

When the brown sauce is ready, melt the remaining 1 tablespoon butter in a skillet. Add the garlic and onion and sauté until tender. Add the shrimp, mushrooms, and lemon juice. Sauté for 2 minutes, then add the Madeira, brown sauce, and parsley. Heat thoroughly.

Remove the shrimp with a slotted spoon and place on heated serving dishes.

Bring the sauce to a boil over high heat and reduce until syrupy. Pour the sauce over the shrimp, garnish with lemon wedges and serve.

SERVES 4

Scallops Provençal

5 tablespoons butter
2 cloves garlic, minced
½ cup dry white wine
2 large tomatoes, peeled, cored, and chopped, or 1 can (15 ounces) tomatoes, diced
3 tablespoons chopped fresh parsley
½ teaspoon salt
freshly ground black pepper to taste
2 cups soft fresh bread crumbs, toasted (about 4 slices)
3 tablespoons freshly grated Parmesan cheese
1 pound fresh sea scallops

Place 3 tablespoons of the butter in a large skillet and sauté the garlic over medium heat for about 3 minutes. Add the wine and simmer for 3 minutes. Add the tomatoes, parsley, salt, and pepper and simmer for 10 to 12 minutes until very thick.

In a small skillet, toss the bread crumbs with 2 tablespoons melted butter. Add the Parmesan cheese and stir.

Add the scallops to the tomato sauce and cook for 3 to 5 minutes, or until the scallops are opaque.

Sprinkle the scallops with the bread crumb-cheese mixture and serve.

SERVES 3 TO 4

Stir-Fry Apricot Shrimp

½ cup diced dried apricots
⅓ cup apricot brandy
1 tablespoon lemon juice
1 tablespoon soy sauce
2 teaspoons cornstarch
⅛ teaspoon freshly ground black pepper
2 tablespoons butter
1 tablespoon vegetable oil
1 green bell pepper, seeded and cut lengthwise into ¼-inch
    strips
½ cup thinly sliced green onion with tops
1 clove garlic, minced
¾ pound shrimp, shelled and deveined

GARNISH:
¼ cup toasted slivered almonds
hot cooked rice

OPTIONAL:
1 package (10 ounces) frozen snow peas

Combine the apricots and brandy in a small bowl and let stand, covered, for 15 minutes.

Mix the lemon juice, soy sauce, cornstarch, and pepper in a small bowl.

Heat the butter and oil in a skillet over high heat. Add the green pepper, green onion, garlic, and snow peas, if desired. Cook, stirring constantly, for 3 minutes. Add the shrimp and cook 2 minutes. Add the apricot mixture and cook 2 minutes.

Stir the cornstarch mixture into the shrimp mixture and cook 2 minutes more.

Serve over rice and sprinkle with toasted almonds.

Shrimp and Mushrooms Au Gratin

SERVES 8

1 pound mushrooms, sliced
3 tablespoons butter
1 tablespoon all-purpose flour
3 ounces dry sherry or Marsala
2 cups light cream
¼ teaspoon grated lemon zest
1 teaspoon onion juice
1 tablespoon chopped fresh parsley
salt and freshly ground black pepper to taste
2 pounds shrimp, cooked, shelled, and deveined
½ cup fine dry bread crumbs
freshly grated Parmesan cheese

Preheat the oven to 400° F.

Sauté the mushrooms in the butter in a medium sauce-pan until tender. Sprinkle in the flour and stir until well blended. Add the sherry or Marsala, the cream, lemon zest, onion juice, parsley, and salt and pepper. Stir over low heat until smooth and thickened. Add the shrimp and heat through.

Transfer the mixture to 8 individual buttered ramekins or a buttered casserole dish. Top with crumbs and cheese. Bake for 5 to 15 minutes, or until hot and lightly browned.

Mussels Sailor Style

SERVES 4

This is a favorite late night supper served with lots of French bread, a crisp green salad, and a cold Muscadet.

4 dozen mussels
cornmeal
2 cloves garlic, minced
2 tablespoons minced fresh parsley
4 whole black peppercorns, finely crushed
3 green onions with tops, minced
1 cup dry white wine
1½ cups heavy cream
salt to taste

Soak the mussels in cold water with about ¼ cup corn-meal for 1 hour.

Wash the mussel shells with a stiff brush and remove the beards (the seaweedlike attachments).

In a heavy saucepan with a lid, combine the mussels, garlic, 1 tablespoon of the parsley, the peppercorns, green onions, and wine. Bring to a boil. Cover the pan and cook over high heat until the mussels open up, 1 to 2 minutes. Remove the mussels from the pan with a slotted spoon and set aside. Discard any mussels that do not open.

To the liquid in the saucepan, add the cream and cook until reduced and thick. Watch carefully so that the cream does not burn. Return the mussels to the pan, add the remaining 1 tablespoon parsley and stir. Remove the mussels with a slotted spoon and place in soup plates. Carefully pour the sauce over the mussels, discarding the last ¼ cup of sauce in the bottom of the pan (it could be gritty).

Chinatown Shrimp

SERVES 4

½ cup minced green onions with tops
½ cup minced bamboo shoots
½ to 1 teaspoon minced fresh ginger root
3 large cloves garlic, minced
¼ teaspoon crushed red pepper
2 tablespoons sugar
½ cup ketchup
3 tablespoons dry sherry
1 tablespoon soy sauce
1 tablespoon sesame seeds
1 tablespoon cornstarch
3 tablespoons water
1 cup vegetable oil
1 pound medium raw shrimp, shelled and deveined
hot cooked rice

Combine the green onions, bamboo shoots, ginger root, garlic, and hot pepper flakes in a small bowl and set aside.

In another small bowl, combine the sugar, ketchup, sherry, soy sauce, and sesame seeds.

Mix the cornstarch and water together in a third bowl.

Heat the oil in a wok or large skillet to 400° F. Have ready a strainer with a bowl underneath. Add the shrimp to the oil and stir-fry for 2 minutes. Pour the oil and shrimp into the strainer to drain off the oil.

Return 1 tablespoon of the strained oil to the wok. Add the green onion mixture and stir-fry for 1 minute. Add the shrimp and stir-fry for 30 seconds more. Add the ketchup mixture and stir-fry for 1 minute. Add the cornstarch and stir until the sauce is thickened. Serve over hot cooked rice.

US SKI TEAM **Racers need to concentrate. When a reporter tried to get some quotes from Betsy Snite while she was bearing down before the second run of the 1960 Olympic slalom, she threw him over the fence of the start enclosure. Betsy took the silver medal, totally forgetting about the reporter until someone later reminded her of the incident.**

Scallop Mousse

SERVES 8

Throughout most of the year, canned plum tomatoes are more flavorful than those available fresh. Fresh red tomatoes can be ripened in a brown paper bag at room temperature. Fresh tomatoes are diminished in flavor if stored in the refrigerator.

MAKES 2 CUPS

1 pound scallops
salt and freshly ground white pepper to taste
2 large egg yolks
20 medium shrimp, peeled and deveined
1 cup heavy cream
Tomato Sauce (recipe follows)

Preheat the oven to 375° F.

Set aside ½ cup of scallops. Place the remaining scallops in the container of a food processor or blender. Add salt and pepper to taste and blend for about 20 seconds. While blending, add the egg yolks and half of the shrimp. Add the cream and blend until thoroughly smooth.

Butter a 5- or 6-cup ring mold and spoon half the mousse mixture into it. Cut the reserved shrimp into ½-inch pieces and sprinkle these over the mixture in the mold. Scatter the reserved scallops over this. Cover with the remaining mousse mixture and smooth it over. Cover tightly with a ring of waxed paper, pressing down to get out the air bubbles. Place the mold in a basin of boiling water and bake for 20 minutes, or until set. Unmold and serve with Tomato Sauce.

TOMATO SAUCE:
1½ tablespoons butter
1 tablespoon chopped onion
1 teaspoon finely chopped shallot
1 cup fresh tomatoes, peeled, seeded, and cubed, or 1 can
    (15 ounces) tomatoes, drained and diced
salt and freshly ground black pepper to taste
½ cup fish stock or bottled clam juice
2 tablespoons finely chopped fresh parsley

Heat the butter in a medium saucepan over medium heat and add the onion, shallots, and salt and pepper to taste. Cook until the onion is wilted, then add the tomatoes. Stir and simmer for 5 minutes. Add the fish stock or clam juice. Cook over high heat until the mixture is reduced almost by half. Reduce heat and simmer, stirring often, for about 10 minutes. Add the parsley and adjust seasonings, if desired.

SERVES 6 TO 8

Seafood Au Gratin

1 large bay leaf
2 stalks celery, cut in half
3 to 4 crushed black peppercorns
1 pound medium shrimp
1 pound bay scallops
5 tablespoons butter
1 clove garlic, minced
3 large shallots, minced
½ pound mushrooms, sliced
¼ cup all-purpose flour
1 tablespoon minced fresh dill weed or 1 teaspoon dried
¾ cup light cream
¾ cup dry white wine
2 cups grated Monterey Jack cheese (8 ounces)
salt and freshly ground black pepper to taste
1 package (9 ounces) frozen artichoke hearts, cooked
    and drained
¼ cup soft fresh bread crumbs

Preheat the oven to 375° F.

In a large kettle, bring 2 quarts of water, the bay leaf, celery, and peppercorns to a boil. Add the shrimp and cook for 3 minutes, or until the shrimp shells are pink. Remove the shrimp with a slotted spoon. Peel and devein. Set aside.

Add the scallops to the cooking water and bring to a boil. Immediately reduce the heat. Poach the scallops until just opaque, about 1 minute. Remove and set aside.

Melt the butter in a large skillet and sauté the garlic and shallots for 2 to 3 minutes over medium heat. Add the mushrooms and sauté until lightly browned, about 5 minutes.

Add the flour and dill and cook until well blended. Add the cream and wine and cook and stir until thick. Add half the cheese and season to taste with salt and pepper. Stir until smooth. Add the seafood and artichokes to the sauce and mix well.

Pour the gratin mixture into a buttered shallow casserole dish. Top with bread crumbs and the remaining cheese. Bake for 25 to 30 minutes, or until bubbly and light brown.

US SKI TEAM The 1964 alpine team won the most Olympic medals for the United States in Innsbruck, Austria. Billy Kidd and Jim Heuga placed second and third in the slalom, and Jean Saubert tied for second in the grand slalom and was third in the slalom. In 1960, Penny Pitou was second in both the downhill and the grand slalom, and Betsy Snite was second in the slalom. Betsy was leading in the downhill by 2.5 seconds when she fell near the bottom of the course.

**MAKES ABOUT
2 CUPS**

Marinade for Barbequed Fish

½ pound unsalted butter
⅔ cup beer, at room temperature
6 tablespoons ketchup
6 tablespoons lemon juice
¼ cup Worcestershire sauce
6 cloves garlic, minced
grated zest of 1 lemon
½ teaspoon salt
½ teaspoon freshly ground black pepper

Melt the butter over low heat in a small saucepan. Stir in the remaining ingredients. Let the marinade cool before using.

Marinate the fish for at least 1 hour before broiling.

SERVES 6

Seafood Sausage Boudin with Shrimp Beurre Blanc Sauce

1 pound fresh sole fillets, cut into pieces
3 egg whites
1½ cup heavy cream
1 tablespoon lemon juice
1 tablespoon chopped fresh tarragon or 1 teaspoon dried
1½ teaspoons salt
6 ounces salmon fillets, cut into pieces
6 ounces shrimp, shelled (reserve shells for Beurre Blanc Sauce), cut in half
6 ounces scallops
2½ quarts water or fish stock
Shrimp Beurre Blanc Sauce (recipe follows)

GARNISH:
caviar

In a food processor, place the sole and egg whites and process 2 minutes, or until smooth. Add the cream slowly until well incorporated. Add the lemon juice, tarragon, and salt. Place the fish mousse in a large mixing bowl.

Place the salmon, shrimp, and scallops in the food processor and process a few seconds to coarsely chop. The fish should stay in pieces and not be puréed. Add the chopped fish to the mousse mixture and blend well.

Form ½ cup of the fish mixture into a sausage shape about 5 inches long, then wrap in plastic wrap and tie at the ends. Repeat with the remaining fish mixture.

Poach the sausages in water or fish stock for 15 minutes. Cool 5 minutes before unwrapping. Serve each piece of sausage with Shrimp Beurre Blanc Sauce and caviar.

SHRIMP BEURRE BLANC SAUCE:
1 cup unsalted butter
shells reserved from the 6 ounces shrimp
½ cup dry white wine
¼ cup lemon juice
1 large shallot, minced
¼ cup heavy cream
1 tablespoon chopped fresh tarragon or 1 teaspoon dried

Melt the butter in a small skillet. Add the shells and sauté until pink. Cool. Place the shells and butter in the food processor and process until the shells are finely chopped. Strain the shrimp butter and discard the shells. Chill.

In a heavy small saucepan, boil the wine, lemon juice, shallot, cream, and tarragon until the liquid is reduced to 2 tablespoons. Remove from the heat and whisk in 2 tablespoons of the shrimp butter. Return to low heat and stir in the remaining shrimp butter, 2 pieces at a time, combining well after each addition. Do not allow the sauce to boil or it will separate.

When making a beurre blanc sauce, maintain the proper heat level by moving the saucepan onto and off the burner. Too much heat will break down the sauce.

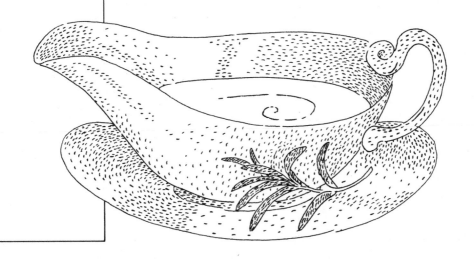

SERVES 4 TO 5

Crab-Zucchini Casserole

4 tablespoons butter, plus additional for dotting
1 small onion, chopped
3 small zucchini, unpeeled and sliced
½ medium clove garlic, crushed or minced
3 large fresh tomatoes, cut into small pieces
½ pound shelled crab, cut into small pieces
1⅓ cups shredded Swiss cheese (about 6 ounces)
1 cup fresh bread crumbs
1 teaspoon salt
1 teaspoon freshly ground black pepper, or to taste
1 teaspoon dried basil, crushed

Preheat the oven to 375°F.

Melt 4 tablespoons butter in a large saucepan and add the onion, zucchini, and garlic. Sauté until the onion is transparent, stirring frequently.

Combine the onion-zucchini mixture with the tomatoes, crab, 1 cup of the cheese, ¾ cup of the bread crumbs, salt, pepper, and basil. Mix lightly but thoroughly. Turn the mixture into a 2-quart casserole dish. Sprinkle the top with the remaining ⅓ cup cheese and ¼ cup of bread crumbs. Dot with additional butter.

Bake, uncovered, for 30 to 40 minutes, or until browned and bubbly. Serve hot.

US Good equipment was hard to find in the 1930s, even if you could afford to buy it. Don Fraser was a member of both the alpine and Nordic teams, and before he left for Europe for the 1936 Olympics he made all his own equipment—skis, poles, and boots for all the events. Unfortunately, an injury kept him out of the competition.

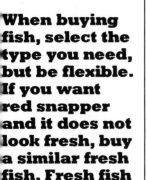

Cioppino (West Coast Bouillabaisse)

6 SERVINGS

When buying fish, select the type you need, but be flexible. If you want red snapper and it does not look fresh, buy a similar fresh fish. Fresh fish should be firm to the touch and should *not* smell fishy.

¼ cup olive oil
2 tablespoons butter
2 medium onions, minced
3 large garlic cloves, minced
½ pound whole mushrooms
1 can (28 ounces) Italian plum tomatoes
1 can (6 ounces) tomato paste
1 medium green bell pepper, chopped
1 tablespoon chopped fresh basil or 1 teaspoon dried
1 teaspoon chopped fresh oregano or ¼ teaspoon dried
½ cup lemon juice, or to taste
2 cups dry red wine
2 pounds firm-fleshed white fish such as red snapper or halibut
½ pound scallops
2 dozen medium shrimp, shelled and deveined, with tails left on
1 Dungeness crab, cracked
1 dozen clams
1 unpeeled lemon, sliced and seeded

OPTIONAL:
1 dozen mussels, debearded, scrubbed, and soaked

In a large kettle heat together the oil and the butter. Add the onions and garlic and cook slowly for about 5 minutes. Do not brown. Add the mushrooms and sauté for about 5 minutes.

Add the tomatoes, tomato paste, green pepper, basil, oregano, lemon juice, and wine and stir well. Bring to a boil, then reduce the heat, and simmer for 1 hour or more. Taste and adjust the seasoning with more lemon juice, if necessary. This recipe can be made ahead to this point up to 2 days in advance.

Twenty minutes before serving, add the fish. Cook the stew for 10 minutes and add the scallops, shrimp, crab, clams, sliced lemon, and mussels, if desired. Cover and simmer until the clams open, about 5 to 10 minutes. Discard any clams or mussels that do not open.

Serve with plenty of French or sourdough bread, a light red wine, and large napkins.

Plantation Point Shrimp Gumbo

SERVES 4

Chili powder is available in two forms. One is a combination of spices usually including chili pepper, allspice, coriander, cumin, and cloves. The other is pure chili pepper. There is a vast difference between them, so be sure to know which you want.

½ cup butter
1 package (10 ounces) frozen cut okra
1 can (15 ounces) tomatoes
½ green bell pepper, diced
2 onions, sliced
2 tablespoons all-purpose flour
1 cup Beef Stock (see page 56)
2 cloves garlic, minced
1 can (8 ounces) tomato sauce
4 teaspoons Worcestershire sauce
⅛ teaspoon ground cloves
½ teaspoon chili powder
⅛ teaspoon dried basil
1 bay leaf
⅛ teaspoon freshly ground black pepper
1 pound medium shrimp, peeled and deveined
hot cooked rice

Melt the butter in a large pan and add the okra, tomatoes, green pepper, and onions. Sauté until the onion is transparent, about 5 minutes. Blend in the flour and stir until smooth. Gradually add the beef stock until thickened.

Add the remaining ingredients, except for the shrimp and rice, and simmer, covered, for 35 minutes.

Add the shrimp and cook for 7 to 10 minutes longer. Serve with hot cooked rice.

Pasta

Capellini with Chesapeake Oysters

MAKES 1 POUND

To serve pasta as a main course, allow 1 pound for 4 to 5 persons. For first-course servings, 1 pound will serve 8 to 10, depending on the sauce.

Egg Pasta

2 cups all-purpose flour, approximately
2 large eggs
½ teaspoon salt
1 tablespoon vegetable or olive oil

Place the flour in a large mixing bowl or on a pastry board and make a well in the center. Add the eggs, salt, and oil and blend with a fork or fingers until the dough can be gathered into a rough ball.

Knead the dough on a floured board for about 10 minutes, or until the dough is smooth and shiny; or combine all the ingredients in a food processor and process until the mixture leaves the sides of the bowl.

Cover and let the dough rest for 25 minutes before rolling.

Roll to desired thickness and cut into the desired shape by hand or with a pasta machine.

TO COOK PASTA:
In a large kettle, bring 3 quarts of salted water to a boil. Add the pasta and bring back to a boil.

Cook uncovered, stirring occasionally to prevent sticking, just until tender (al dente): 3 to 4 minutes for fresh pasta, 7 to 10 minutes for dried pasta. Do not overcook. Drain well, but do not rinse.

MAKES 1 POUND

The measurements in making pasta are not exact because egg sizes vary and determine the amount of flour or added moisture needed.

Spinach Pasta

To the basic Egg Pasta recipe (see above) add 6 to 8 ounces spinach, cooked, drained, squeezed dry, and minced. Additional flour or water may be needed.

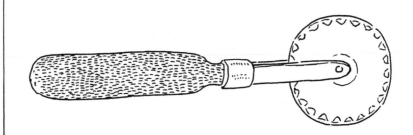

MAKES ABOUT
1½ CUPS

Pesto Sauce

Pesto is good on hot pasta, cooked vegetables, blended into homemade mayonnaise, or spread on French bread as an appetizer.

2 cups (packed) fresh basil leaves
3 cloves garlic
2 to 4 tablespoons pine nuts
1 teaspoon salt
¾ cup light olive oil
½ cup freshly grated Parmesan cheese
¼ cup freshly grated Romano cheese

In a food processor or a blender, combine the basil, garlic, pine nuts, and salt. Process until smooth. With the motor running, add the oil through the feed tube and process until well blended. Pour the basil mixture into a bowl and mix in the cheeses.

SERVES 4

Shrimp and Clam Sauce

2 cups dry white wine
1 pound medium shrimp
2 cans (6½ ounces each) chopped clams, drained and juice reserved
1 cup additional clam juice
4 tablespoons butter
4 tablespoons all-purpose flour
6 ounces soft herb and garlic cheese

Bring the wine to a boil in a large pot. Add the shrimp and cook until the shells are pink all over, about 4 minutes. Remove shrimp and reserve liquid. Shell and devein the shrimp and set aside.

Add the reserved clam juice, plus 1 cup additional clam juice to the reserved wine. Boil over high heat for 5 minutes to reduce by one half. Set aside.

Melt the butter in a sauté pan and add the flour. Cook over medium heat for 3 minutes, stirring constantly. Add the clam-wine stock and cook, stirring constantly, over medium heat until thickened. Whisk in the cheese. If the sauce is too thick, add more clam juice. Fold in the shrimp and clams and heat through. Serve over hot fettuccine or linguine with freshly grated Parmesan cheese.

**MAKES ABOUT
2 QUARTS**

Italian Tomato Sauce

2 tablespoons olive oil
¼ cup minced onion
1 small clove garlic, minced
¼ cup minced celery
3½ cups peeled fresh tomatoes or 1 can (28 ounces) Italian
    plum tomatoes
2 cans (6 ounces each) tomato paste
1½ teaspoons salt
1 teaspoon granulated sugar
⅛ teaspoon freshly grated nutmeg
1 teaspoon dried oregano
⅛ teaspoon freshly ground black pepper
¼ cup chopped fresh parsley
¼ cup freshly grated Italian cheese (Parmesan or Romano)

Heat the oil in a large sauté pan and sauté the onion, garlic, and celery over medium heat for 5 minutes.

Put the tomatoes through a food mill and discard the seeds, or crush the tomatoes with a potato masher.

Place the tomatoes and the onion-garlic mixture in a large, heavy stainless-steel saucepan. Add the remaining ingredients, except for the cheese, and bring to a boil. Reduce the heat, add the cheese and stir well to blend.

Simmer, covered, for about 1 hour, stirring frequently so that the sauce does not scorch. Water may be added if the sauce is too thick.

MAKES 3 CUPS

Tomato-Basil Sauce

¼ cup olive oil
4 cloves garlic, minced
4 cups canned plum or whole-pack tomatoes, coarsely chopped
    but not drained
¼ cup minced fresh basil or 2 tablespoons dried
1 teaspoon granulated sugar
salt and freshly ground black pepper to taste

Heat the oil in a stainless-steel saucepan over low heat. Add the garlic and cook 2 minutes. Add the tomatoes, basil, and sugar and cook over high heat, stirring frequently, to reduce the liquid by half. Add salt and pepper to taste.

**MAKES ABOUT
7 CUPS**

Marinara Sauce

¼ cup olive oil
2 medium onions, diced
6 cloves garlic, minced
2 cans (28 ounces each) Italian plum tomatoes
salt and freshly ground black pepper to taste
½ cup chopped fresh parsley
1 tablespoon chopped fresh basil or 1 teaspoon dried
1 tablespoon chopped fresh oregano or 1 teaspoon dried
1 tablespoon fresh rosemary leaves or 1 teaspoon dried

In a large, heavy stainless-steel saucepan, heat the olive oil and sauté the onions for 5 minutes. Add the garlic and sauté for 2 minutes.

Drain the tomato juice into the saucepan. Coarsely chop the tomatoes and add to the saucepan. Add the remaining ingredients and simmer, uncovered, for about 2 to 3 hours, stirring occasionally.

SERVES 8 TO 10

Marinara Sauce with Meatballs and Sausage

1 can (28 ounces) Italian plum tomatoes
1 can (28 ounces) tomato purée
1 can (12 ounces) tomato paste
1 cup water
1 bay leaf, crumbled
2 cloves garlic, chopped
½ teaspoon sugar
2 pounds link Italian sausage, cut into 3-inch pieces
1 pound ground beef round
¾ cup fine dry bread crumbs
2 eggs, beaten
1 teaspoon dried thyme
1 small onion, chopped
salt and freshly ground black pepper to taste
vegetable oil

In a large, heavy stainless-steel saucepan, combine the tomatoes, tomato purée, tomato paste, water, bay leaf, 1 clove garlic, and sugar and mix well. Add the sausage and cook over high heat until the sauce comes to a boil. Reduce the heat and simmer. Skim the grease from the top of the sauce and discard.

In a small bowl, combine the ground round, bread crumbs, eggs, thyme, onion, remaining garlic, and salt and pepper. Shape the meat into 1½-inch balls.

Brown the meat balls in oil in a heavy skillet, turning to brown evenly. When all the meatballs (16 to 18) are browned, add them to the sauce and simmer gently for 2 hours. Stir the sauce often, but gently, so the meatballs do not break.

Creole Shrimp or Clam Sauce

SERVES 6

For a simple clam sauce, sauté minced garlic in olive oil. Add the liquid from fresh clams, some white wine, and a handful of minced parsley. Add chopped fresh clams and freshly ground black pepper and heat through.

3 tablespoons butter
3 tablespoons vegetable oil
6 tablespoons all-purpose flour
2 cups chopped onion
1 cup chopped green bell pepper
1 cup chopped celery
4 to 5 cloves garlic, minced
1 can (6 ounces) tomato paste
2 cups Beef Stock (see page 56)
2 cups water
3 bay leaves
1 tablespoon chopped fresh basil or 1 teaspoon dried
2 teaspoons chopped fresh thyme or ½ teaspoon dried
1 teaspoon chili powder
¼ teaspoon cayenne
¼ teaspoon freshly ground black pepper
1 teaspoon salt
2 cans (7 ounces each) clams, or 2 pounds medium shrimp, shelled and deveined
1 cup chopped shallot or green onion
2 tablespoons chopped fresh parsley

Melt the butter and heat with the oil in a 2-quart saucepan. Add the flour and stir over low heat until browned, about 8 to 10 minutes. Add the chopped onion, green pepper, celery, and garlic and sauté until soft.

Add the tomato paste and mix well. Add the beef stock, water, and seasonings and simmer uncovered for 45 minutes. Add the clams or shrimp, shallot, and parsley. Simmer for 20 minutes. Remove from heat and let stand for at least 1 hour for the seasonings to blend.

Reheat gently at serving time.

Cold Fettuccine with Shrimp

**SERVES 6 TO 8
AS A FIRST
COURSE, 4 AS A
MAIN COURSE**

¾ pound fettuccine, cooked al dente and drained
1 pound medium shrimp, cooked, shelled, and deveined
½ cup walnut pieces
⅓ to ½ cup lemon juice
¼ cup vegetable oil
1 tablespoon red wine vinegar
2 tablespoons chopped fresh basil or 2 teaspoons dried
salt and freshly ground black pepper to taste

Combine the fettuccine, shrimp, and walnuts in a large bowl.

In a small bowl, combine the lemon juice, oil, vinegar, and basil and whisk to blend.

Pour the lemon dressing over the shrimp and pasta and toss. Season to taste with salt and pepper.

Serve at cool room temperature.

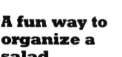

Pot-Luck Salad

SERVES 6 AND UP

**A fun way to
organize a
salad
luncheon is to
have everyone
bring an
ingredient for
the salad.**

2 tablespoons red wine or fruit vinegar
1 cup sour cream
1 teaspoon granulated sugar
1 teaspoon salt
½ teaspoon celery seed
1 tablespoon chopped fresh basil or 1 teaspoon dried
¼ cup chopped fresh parsley
1 cup peeled, seeded, and diced cucumber
1 cup chopped celery
4 green onions, with tops, sliced
¼ cup chopped green bell pepper
¼ cup chopped red bell pepper or pimiento
10 ounces thin spaghetti, cooked al dente and drained

OPTIONAL:
sliced ripe olives
chopped marinated artichoke hearts
cubed Cheddar cheese
julienne strips of prosciutto ham
stemmed cherry tomatoes
crisply cooked and crumbled bacon
chopped hard-cooked eggs

In a large bowl, whisk together the vinegar, sour cream, sugar, salt, celery seed, and basil.

Add the remaining ingredients and mix well. At this point, add as many of the optional ingredients as you wish to create your own salad. If you wish to serve 12 or 18 or more, increase the basic salad proportionately.

Refrigerate several hours before serving. Toss again. Serve at cool room temperature.

Cold Pasta and Chicken Primavera

SERVES 4

½ pound vermicelli or spaghetti, cooked al dente and drained
½ cup light olive oil
½ cup wine vinegar
1 teaspoon Dijon mustard
1 clove garlic, crushed
10 mushrooms, sliced
1 cup broccoli florets, blanched
1½ cups fresh snow peas, blanched, or 1 package (10 ounces) frozen snow peas, thawed
12 cherry tomatoes or 1 red bell pepper, chopped
2 cups cubed, poached chicken
⅓ cup chopped fresh basil or 1 tablespoon dried
⅓ cup pine nuts
salt and freshly ground black pepper to taste

Pasta salads are best when served lightly chilled, but not ice cold. If pasta salads are refrigerated for several hours, let them stand at room temperature for 30 minutes before serving.

Put the drained pasta in a large bowl.

Combine the olive oil, vinegar, mustard, and garlic in a small bowl and whisk well to make a vinaigrette dressing. Pour one third of the vinaigrette over the pasta. Toss and let the pasta cool; chill at least 3 hours.

Place the remaining dressing in another bowl and add the mushrooms, broccoli, snow peas, and tomatoes or red pepper. Stir gently to coat the vegetables thoroughly. Refrigerate up to 3 hours.

When ready to serve, bring the pasta to room temperature. Add the chicken, vegetables, basil, and pine nuts. Toss gently and season with salt and freshly ground black pepper to taste, then serve.

Ham and Pasta Salad

SERVES 4

10 ounces vermicelli or thin spaghetti
3 hard-cooked eggs, chopped
5 stalks celery, chopped
5 small sweet pickles, diced
⅓ cup sliced green onion with tops
1½ cups mayonnaise
¼ cup pickle juice
½ teaspoon dry mustard
salt and freshly ground black pepper to taste
2 cups diced cooked ham

GARNISH:
¼ cup chopped fresh parsley

Break up the pasta into thirds. Cook in boiling, salted water according to package directions. Drain and place in a large bowl. Add the eggs, celery, pickles, and green onions to the vermicelli.

Combine the mayonnaise, pickle juice, dry mustard, and salt and pepper in a small bowl and mix well. Add to the pasta, then cover and chill overnight.

Add the ham and mix well. Bring to cool room temperature before serving. Garnish with chopped parsley.

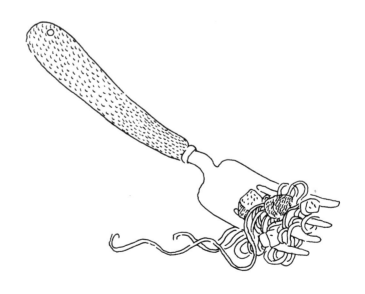

SERVES 6

This special salad should be made only when fresh dill is available.

Salmon Salad

1½ pounds salmon steak, or 1½ pounds canned salmon
Court Bouillon (recipe follows)
½ pound small shell pasta, cooked al dente and drained
½ cup sliced celery
¼ cup sliced green onion
1½ cups cooked tiny green peas
¾ cup mayonnaise, preferably homemade
salt and freshly ground black pepper to taste
1 tablespoon minced fresh dill, or to taste

GARNISH:
fresh dill
lemon wedges

Add the fresh salmon to the court bouillon and bring to a boil. Reduce the heat and simmer covered, for 8 to 10 minutes. Drain the salmon. Allow to cool. Remove the bones and skin from the salmon and discard. Flake the salmon into a small bowl and chill for 1 hour.

In a large bowl, combine the pasta with the celery, green onion, peas, and mayonnaise. Add the salmon and mix gently. Season to taste with salt, pepper, and dill. Chill until serving time.

COURT BOUILLON:
1 bay leaf
1 carrot, sliced into 2-inch pieces
2 stalks celery, cut into 2-inch pieces
1 medium onion, sliced
¼ cup (packed) parsley sprigs
8 to 10 black peppercorns
1 cup white wine
2 cups fish stock or bottled clam juice

Combine all the ingredients in a saucepan and bring to a boil. Reduce heat and simmer for 30 minutes.

SERVES 6

Try canned roasted red peppers as a substitute for seasonal red bell peppers.

Pasta with Tuna Sauce

2 onions, chopped
2 cloves garlic, crushed
¼ cup butter
¼ cup olive oil
¼ cup diced red bell pepper
½ cup diced green bell pepper
5 cups canned Italian plum tomatoes, drained
1 bay leaf
1 can (12½ ounces) tuna packed in oil, drained
1 can (2 ounces) flat anchovy fillets, drained and chopped
12 stuffed green olives, chopped
salt and freshly ground black pepper to taste
1 pound pasta, cooked al dente and drained

Sauté the onions and garlic in the butter and olive oil in a large skillet until golden. Add the red and green peppers and cook over moderate heat, stirring, for 5 minutes. Add the tomatoes and bay leaf. Reduce the heat and simmer the mixture for 20 minutes, stirring several times.

Add the tuna, anchovies, and olives. Simmer for 3 to 4 minutes, or until the tuna is hot. Season with salt and pepper to taste. Serve the sauce over cooked pasta.

SERVES 4

Capellini with Chesapeake Oysters

½ pound capellini
2 tablespoons butter
1 tablespoon Worcestershire sauce
2 dozen oysters, shucked and chopped, liquid reserved
¼ cup all-purpose flour
2 cups warm milk
⅓ cup Marsala
salt and freshly ground black pepper to taste
paprika to taste
4 tablespoons butter, melted
½ cup soft fresh bread crumbs
½ cup freshly grated Parmesan cheese

Preheat oven to 375° F.

Cook the capellini in boiling salted water until just tender. Drain well and place in a large bowl.

In a small saucepan, heat the butter, the Worcestershire sauce, and ⅓ cup reserved oyster liquid. Add the flour and cook, stirring constantly, until smooth. Add the warm milk all at once and cook over low heat until thickened. Add the Marsala and blend well.

Add the oysters, salt, pepper, and paprika to the capellini. Pour the sauce over the pasta and mix well. Place the pasta in a buttered shallow casserole dish.

In a bowl, mix together the butter, bread crumbs, and Parmesan cheese. Sprinkle the cheese mixture over the top of the pasta. Bake for 30 minutes. Serve hot.

Green Fettuccine with Scallop and Parsley Sauce

SERVES 10 AS A FIRST COURSE, 6 AS A MAIN COURSE

¼ cup minced fresh parsley
1 shallot, minced
4 tablespoons butter
½ cup dry white wine
1 pound sea scallops, cut horizontally into ¼-inch slices
1 cup light cream
½ cup heavy cream
1 cup freshly grated Parmesan cheese, plus additional for serving
⅓ cup plus 2 tablespoons minced fresh parsley
freshly grated nutmeg
salt and freshly ground black pepper to taste
1½ pounds green fettuccine
2 tablespoons unsalted butter, softened

In a stainless-steel or enameled skillet, cook the ¼ cup parsley and the shallot in the butter over moderate heat, stirring, for 5 minutes. Add the wine and reduce over high heat to about 6 tablespoons liquid.

Add the scallops and cook, stirring, for 1 minute. Then add the light and heavy cream and simmer for 2 minutes. Remove from the heat and add the 1 cup Parmesan cheese, ⅓ cup minced parsley, nutmeg, and salt and pepper to taste. Keep warm.

Cook the pasta in boiling salted water until al dente. Drain well and toss with the unsalted butter.

Transfer the pasta to a heated serving dish and spoon the sauce over. Toss gently to distribute the sauce. Sprinkle with 2 tablespoons of minced parsley and the additional Parmesan cheese. Serve hot.

Spaghetti alla Puttanesca

SERVES 4 TO 6

Al dente ("to the tooth") is an Italian phrase meaning pasta that is cooked until it is just tender—not mushy.

¾ cup olive oil
6 to 8 cloves garlic, minced
½ cup drained capers
1 can (12 ounces) flat anchovy fillets, drained
1 can (6 ounces) pitted ripe olives, coarsely chopped
1 tablespoon dried basil
2 cups Marinara Sauce (see page 180)
1 tablespoon crushed hot red chilies
1 pound spaghetti, cooked al dente and drained

Heat the oil in a large sauté pan and sauté the garlic over low heat for 1 to 2 minutes. Add the capers, anchovies, olives, basil, and marinara sauce. Mix well and simmer for 10 minutes. Serve over the hot spaghetti.

Summer Pasta with Pesto

SERVES 4

2 tablespoons butter
1 small onion, minced
½ pound cooked ham, cut into julienne
½ pound tiny peas, cooked
4 to 6 small new potatoes, peeled, cooked, and halved
1 cup Pesto Sauce (see page 178)
1 pound fettuccine, cooked al dente and drained
freshly grated Parmesan cheese

Melt the butter in a large skillet and sauté the onion over medium heat for 5 minutes. Add the ham, peas, potatoes, and pesto sauce to the skillet and heat through.

Place the hot pasta in a large, heated serving bowl. Add the potato-pesto mixture and toss gently to mix. Sprinkle with Parmesan cheese and serve.

Mostaccioli e Broccoli

SERVES 4

¾ to 1 cup light olive oil
6 to 8 cloves garlic, crushed
2 packages (10 ounces each) chopped broccoli, thawed and well-drained, or 4 cups chopped fresh broccoli
1 pound mostaccioli, cooked al dente and drained
freshly grated Parmesan cheese

Heat the oil in a skillet and sauté the garlic over low heat for 2 to 3 minutes without browning. With a slotted spoon, remove the garlic and discard. Add the broccoli to the oil and cook for 2 to 3 minutes, or until crisp tender.

Place the cooked pasta in a large, heated serving bowl. Pour the oil-broccoli sauce onto the pasta and mix well. Sprinkle with Parmesan cheese and serve.

Cheesy Noodles and Chives

SERVES 8

12 ounces vermicelli or other thin noodles
2 cups sour cream
2 cups small-curd cottage cheese
4 tablespoons butter
½ cup chopped chives
salt and freshly ground black pepper to taste

GARNISH:
chopped chives

Preheat the oven to 375° F.

Cook the noodles according to package directions and drain well. Add the remaining ingredients and stir gently. Pour into a buttered 9 x 9-inch casserole dish and bake for 45 minutes. Sprinkle with more chopped chives and serve.

Fettuccine Florentine

SERVES 8

1 pound fettuccine
½ cup butter
1 package (10 ounces) chopped spinach, thawed and drained, or fresh spinach, chopped
1 pound bacon, crisply cooked and crumbled
1½ cups heavy cream
1 egg, lightly beaten
2 cups freshly grated Parmesan cheese (8 ounces)
salt and freshly ground black pepper to taste

Cook the pasta in boiling salted water until al dente.

Melt the butter in a large saucepan. Add the spinach and bacon and sauté until heated through. Add the fettuccine and toss.

Combine the cream and egg in a small bowl, then pour over the pasta. Add the cheese and mix well. Season with salt and pepper to taste. Heat thoroughly but do not cook. Serve immediately.

Linguine with Spring Vegetables

SERVES 6 TO 8

2 tablespoons light olive oil
½ cup unsalted butter
1 medium onion, minced
2 large cloves garlic, minced
½ pound mushrooms, thinly sliced
1 medium zucchini, thinly sliced
1 medium carrot, peeled and cut into strips
1 pound fresh, thin asparagus, sliced diagonally
½ cup Chicken Stock (see page 56)
1 cup heavy cream
3 green onions with tops, thinly sliced
1 cup frozen peas, thawed, or 1 cup broccoli florets
¼ cup fresh basil, chopped, or 2 to 3 teaspoons dried
salt and freshly ground black pepper to taste
1 pound linguine, cooked al dente and drained
½ cup freshly grated Parmesan cheese
¼ cup minced fresh parsley

Heat the oil and butter in a large skillet over medium heat and sauté the onion and garlic until limp. Add the mushrooms, zucchini, carrot, and asparagus. Sauté for 2 to 3 minutes.

Add the chicken stock and the cream and cook for several minutes to reduce the liquid. Stir in the green onions, peas, and basil and season to taste with salt and pepper. Cook for 1 minute more.

Add the hot pasta and the cheese to the skillet and mix well. Sprinkle with the parsley and serve.

Eggs alla Spaghetti

SERVES 2

This children's favorite is a good way to use leftover spaghetti.

2 cups leftover cooked spaghetti
butter
2 to 3 eggs, beaten
salt and freshly ground black pepper to taste

Sauté the leftover cooked spaghetti in a small amount of butter. Stir until heated through. Add the eggs and stir until the eggs are cooked. Season with salt and pepper to taste and serve.

SERVES 4

Linguine Carbonara

2 tablespoons butter
¼ pound bacon, chopped
½ cup chopped onion
1 tablespoon chopped shallot
¼ cup dry white wine
3 eggs, beaten
½ cup freshly grated Parmesan cheese
½ teaspoon freshly ground black pepper
2 tablespoons chopped fresh parsley
1 pound linguine

Melt the butter in a skillet and sauté the bacon, onion, and shallot until lightly browned, about 5 minutes. Add the wine and cook, uncovered, over low heat until the wine evaporates. Reserve and keep warm.

In a large bowl, beat together the eggs, cheese, pepper, and parsley. Set aside.

When ready to serve, cook the linguine in boiling salted water until just tender. Drain well. Place the linguine in a large heated bowl and toss quickly with the egg mixture. Pour the bacon mixture over and toss. Serve immediately.

SERVES 6

Fettuccine with Gorgonzola

½ pound fresh spinach
1 cup heavy cream
3 ounces Gorgonzola cheese
4 tablespoons butter
1 ounce vodka
salt and freshly ground black pepper to taste
¼ pound ricotta cheese
1 pound fettucine, cooked al dente and drained
3 ounces freshly grated Parmesan cheese

Wash the spinach and shake off excess water. Cook the spinach in the water clinging to the leaves; drain, chop, and set aside.

In a saucepan, bring the cream to a simmer, then add the Gorgonzola, butter, and vodka. Blend well and season with salt and pepper. Add the spinach and ricotta and simmer and stir until well blended.

Pour the sauce over the hot fettuccine and toss. Sprinkle with Parmesan cheese and toss again. Serve immediately.

**SERVES 8 AS A
FIRST COURSE,
4 AS A MAIN
COURSE**

Fettuccine à la Crème

1 pound fettuccine
½ cup butter
1 clove garlic
¼ cup dry white wine or dry sherry
salt and freshly ground black pepper to taste
2 tablespoons freshly chopped parsley
1 teaspoon chopped fresh basil or ½ teaspoon dried
1 cup heavy cream
½ cup freshly grated Parmesan cheese

GARNISH:
1 tablespoon chopped chives (optional)

Cook the fettuccine in boiling salted water until al dente. Drain well.

Melt the butter in a large skillet and sauté the garlic for 3 to 4 minutes over low heat. Remove the garlic from the skillet and discard. Add the wine, salt and pepper, parsley, and basil and simmer for 5 minutes. Add the cream and heat through.

Place the fettuccine in a heated serving bowl. Pour the cream sauce and Parmesan cheese over the pasta and mix well. Garnish with chives, if desired, and serve.

SERVES 8

Terrific Lasagne

1 pound bulk Italian sausage
½ pound ground beef round
½ cup chopped onion
2 cloves garlic, minced
1 tablespoon granulated sugar
1 teaspoon salt
1½ teaspoons dried basil
½ teaspoon fennel seeds
¼ teaspoon freshly ground black pepper
¼ cup minced fresh parsley
1 can (28 ounces) Italian plum tomatoes
3 cans (6 ounces each) tomato paste
½ cup water
2 cups ricotta cheese or 3 cups creamed cottage cheese
3 eggs, beaten
½ teaspoon salt
12 lasagne noodles
¾ cup freshly grated Parmesan cheese
¾ pound mozzarella cheese, thinly sliced

Sauté the sausage in a Dutch oven over medium heat for 3 to 4 minutes. Add the ground round, onion, and garlic and sauté, stirring, until browned. Drain off the grease and discard.

Add the sugar, salt, basil, fennel seeds, pepper, and half the parsley to the meat and stir well.

Mash the tomatoes with a spoon or potato masher. Combine the tomatoes with the tomato paste and water. Add this mixture to the meat mixture in the Dutch oven and simmer, covered, for 1½ hours.

In a bowl, combine the ricotta cheese, eggs, salt, and the remaining parsley.

Preheat the oven to 350° F.

Cook the lasagne noodles according to package directions. Drain.

Place a layer of noodles in a buttered 9 x 13-inch casserole dish. Cover with 1½ cups of the sauce, half the cottage cheese mixture, ¼ cup of the Parmesan cheese, and half of the mozzarella cheese. Repeat layering, ending with sauce sprinkled with the remaining ¼ cup Parmesan cheese. Cover and bake for 25 minutes. Remove the cover and bake for 20 minutes longer, or until hot and bubbly. Let stand for 5 to 10 minutes before serving.

The U.S. men's team planned to unveil its newly-invented racing tights at the world championships in Are, Sweden. But the first race was the women's giant slalom. Jannette Burr was close enough to Buddy's size and, always ready, she borrowed his revolutionary pants for the giant slalom. She placed third in the event, but her female teammates were so embarrassed by her scandalous attire that they refused to pose for pictures until Jeanette changed her clothes.

SERVES 8

Ham and Mushroom Lasagne

Dried Boletus mushrooms would work well here, but choose your favorite.

1½ ounces imported dried mushrooms
½ cup minced onion
¼ cup vegetable oil
2 medium tomatoes, peeled, seeded, and chopped
3 tablespoons chopped fresh parsley
1 pound fresh mushrooms, sliced
salt and freshly ground black pepper to taste
9 or 10 lasagne noodles
2 cups Béchamel Sauce (recipe follows)
¾ pound ham, cut into thin strips
⅔ cup freshly grated Parmesan cheese
4 tablespoons butter

Prepare the dried mushrooms by soaking them in warm water for 45 minutes; remove them from the water and trim and chop. Strain the water and reserve.

In a large skillet, sauté the onion in the oil. Add the soaked mushrooms and the reserved water, the tomatoes, and the parsley. Cook over moderate heat until the liquid has evaporated. Add the fresh mushrooms and salt and pepper and mix well. Set aside.

Preheat the oven to 350° F.

Cook the lasagne noodles according to package directions. Drain the noodles on paper toweling.

Butter a 9 x 13-inch casserole dish. Place a layer of lasagne noodles in the bottom of the dish, followed by a layer of half of the mushroom mixture. Next, spread a thin layer of bechamel sauce and then a layer of ham; sprinkle with Parmesan cheese. Repeat the layers and top with a layer of noodles. Pour the remaining béchamel sauce on top and dot with butter.

Bake uncovered for 25 to 30 minutes, or until hot and bubbly. Let stand 5 to 10 minutes before serving.

BÉCHAMEL SAUCE:
4 tablespoons butter
3 tablespoons all-purpose flour
2 cups milk, heated
salt and freshly ground black pepper to taste

Melt the butter in a saucepan. Add the flour and stir until smooth. Cook over low heat, stirring constantly, for 3 to 4 minutes. Slowly add the milk, stirring constantly, and season with salt and pepper. Cook over low heat until thickened.

SERVES 5

Canelloni with Chicken, Cheese and Mushroom Filling

1 pound Egg Pasta (see page 177)
6 tablespoons butter
2 tablespoons all-purpose flour
2 cups milk
1 tablespoon chopped onion
¼ pound mushrooms, chopped
2 cups chopped, cooked chicken
3 egg yolks, beaten
4 tablespoons Parmesan cheese
salt and freshly ground black pepper to taste
freshly grated nutmeg to taste

Roll out the pasta and cut into ten 6-inch squares. Cook in boiling salted water for 20 seconds and remove with a slotted spoon. Drain on paper toweling.

Melt 2 tablespoons of the butter in a sauté pan. Add the flour and stir until well blended, about 2 minutes. Add the milk and stir until a smooth white sauce is produced, about 4 minutes. Set aside.

In a large sauté pan, melt 2 tablespoons of the butter and sauté the onion until transparent. Add the mushrooms and sauté 3 minutes more. Add the chicken, half the white sauce, the egg yolks, and 2 tablespoons of the cheese and mix well. Season with salt, pepper, and nutmeg. This should be a fairly smooth paste.

Preheat the oven to 400° F.

Mound the filling on the pasta squares, roll up and place side by side in a buttered shallow casserole dish.

Pour on the remaining white sauce and sprinkle with the remaining 2 tablespoons cheese.

Dot with the remaining 2 tablespoons butter and bake for 20 minutes, or until bubbly and lightly browned. Serve hot.

US SKI TEAM Slalom racing was formalized by Sir Arnold Lunn, a protean figure in the early days of skiing. It was urged on American organizers in 1925: "The Association suggests that whenever possible a new event called the slalom race be added to your competitions. This is a downhill race, the competitors having to follow a course marked by flags. This necessitates proficiency in making Telemarks and Christiana swings and brings out the all-round ability of the ski-runner. It helps to develop the sport. It is very interesting to spectators."

SERVES 4 TO 6

Cheese-Filled Tortellini

1¼ cups ricotta cheese
1 cup freshly grated Parmesan cheese (4 ounces)
¼ cup chopped flat-leaf parsley
1 egg yolk
½ teaspoon salt
¼ teaspoon freshly grated nutmeg
¼ teaspoon grated lemon zest
1 pound Egg Pasta (see page 177)

Combine the cheeses, parsley, egg yolk, salt, nutmeg, and lemon zest in a bowl and mix well.

Roll and stretch the pasta dough as thin as possible. Cut the dough into 2-inch circles with a biscuit cutter or drinking glass.

Wet the edges of a circle, then place ¼ to ½ teaspoon filling slightly off center, and fold over. Gently press edges together with fingertips to seal. Wrap the folded edges around the tip of the little finger, overlapping the 2 ends slightly; press overlap to seal. Slip the tortellini off your finger and onto a clean towel. Repeat filling, folding, and wrapping with remaining circles.

Heat 4 quarts of salted water in a large kettle to boiling. Drop the tortellini into the water and stir gently with a wooden spoon. Cook until al dente, about 2 minutes.

Serve with Italian Tomato Sauce (see page 179) or Tomato Basil Sauce (see page 179).

SERVES 4

Ham-Stuffed Manicotti with Cheese Sauce

¼ pound manicotti shells (8 shells)
¼ cup chopped onion
2 tablespoons vegetable oil
¼ pound mushrooms, sliced
3 cups ground cooked ham (½ pound)
3 tablespoons freshly grated Parmesan cheese
¼ cup chopped green bell pepper
3 tablespoons butter
3 tablespoons all-purpose flour
2 cups milk
1 cup grated Swiss cheese (4 ounces)

Cook the manicotti in boiling salted water for 15 to 20 minutes, or just until tender; drain. Rinse with cold water and drain again. Set aside.

Sauté the onion in the oil in a small skillet until tender, about 5 minutes. Add the mushrooms and sauté for 3 to 4 minutes more. Remove from the heat and stir in the ham. Let the mixture stand until cool. Stir in the Parmesan cheese and set aside.

In a small saucepan, sauté the green pepper in the butter until tender, about 3 to 4 minutes. Blend in the flour and cook over moderate heat for 1 to 2 minutes. Add the milk and stir constantly to make a smooth sauce. Add the Swiss cheese and stir to blend.

Preheat the oven to 350° F.

Stuff the manicotti with the ham mixture. Place the stuffed shells in a buttered 9 x 13-inch casserole dish. Pour the sauce over all. Bake for 30 to 40 minutes, or until bubbly and lightly browned. Serve immediately.

Stuffed Pasta Shells

SERVES 6

This dish can be frozen if cooked before freezing.

1 pound jumbo pasta shells
1 pound mozzarella cheese
1 pound ground beef round
½ pound bulk Italian sausage
⅔ cup soft bread crumbs
½ cup milk
2 tablespoons chopped fresh parsley
1 egg, beaten
salt and freshly ground black pepper to taste
4 cups Italian Tomato Sauce (see page 179)
¾ cup freshly grated Parmesan cheese

Cook the shells in salted boiling water for 10 minutes. Drain and rinse in cold water.

Preheat the oven to 350° F.

Dice half the mozzarella cheese, slice the rest.

In a large skillet, brown the ground round and sausage and drain off the grease. Add the bread crumbs, milk, parsley, egg, and diced mozzarella cheese to the meat and mix well. Season to taste with salt and pepper.

Fill the cooked shells with the meat mixture.

Place half the tomato sauce in a shallow 3-quart baking dish. Place the stuffed shells in the dish; top with the remaining sauce and the sliced mozzarella. Cover and bake for 30 minutes. Serve with Parmesan cheese.

SERVES 8 AS A
FIRST COURSE,
6 AS A MAIN
COURSE

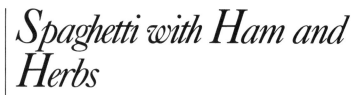

Spaghetti with Ham and Herbs

¾ cup olive oil
4 ounces cooked ham, Canadian bacon, or prosciutto, coarsely
      chopped
2 cloves garlic, minced
½ cup chopped fresh parsley
2 teaspoons minced fresh marjoram or ½ teaspoon dried
6 to 8 leaves fresh basil, chopped, or 1 teaspoon minced fresh
      thyme or ¼ teaspoon dried
1½ pounds spaghetti or other pasta
salt and freshly ground black pepper to taste

Heat the oil in a skillet and add the ham, bacon, or prosciutto and the garlic and sauté gently, without browning, for 4 to 5 minutes.

Add all the herbs and stir them into the oil. Sauté for 2 to 3 minutes more. Turn off the heat and let the herbs steep in the oil while the spaghetti is cooking.

Cook the spaghetti in boiling salted water until it is just done. Drain and place in a hot serving dish. Pour the sauce over the spaghetti and season with salt and pepper. Serve immediately.

SERVES 8

Brie and Bacon Pasta

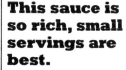

**This sauce is
so rich, small
servings are
best.**

2 cups heavy cream
1 pound linguine
1 pound Brie cheese, rind removed and cubed
¼ pound bacon, crisply cooked and crumbled

Cook the cream, uncovered, in a heavy saucepan over medium heat until reduced by one fourth.

Cook the linguine in boiling salted water until just tender. Drain well and place in a heated serving bowl.

Add the Brie to the hot cream and stir until the cheese is melted. Pour the cheese sauce over the hot pasta and toss to coat. Sprinkle with the bacon and toss again. Serve immediately.

Vegetables

Coal Creek Canyon Corn

SECTION CHAIRMAN
Helen Powell

TESTERS
Margaret Bekins
Jean Berney
Alline Buttrill
Lorraine Coryell
Barbara Foncannon
Marilyn Heslip
Hanna Holt
Carolyn Longmire
Lynn Moyle
Laura Snyder

SERVES 6 TO 8

Artichoke and Spinach à la Crème

This dish can be prepared one day ahead of baking and refrigerated. Bring to room temperature before baking.

2 packages (10 ounces each) frozen chopped spinach
4 tablespoons butter
1 medium onion, chopped
2 tablespoons all-purpose flour
1 cup light cream
1 can (16 ounces) artichoke hearts, drained
butter
½ cup fine dry bread crumbs

Preheat the oven to 350° F.

Cook the spinach and drain well. Place in a clean linen towel and squeeze dry. Reserve spinach.

Melt the butter and sauté the onion until translucent, about 5 minutes. Add the flour and blend well. Add the cream and whisk until a smooth sauce is produced. Add the spinach and mix well.

Put the artichoke hearts in a buttered 12-inch casserole dish. Pour the spinach mixture over the artichoke hearts and top with the bread crumbs. Bake for 30 minutes, or until bubbly. Serve hot.

SERVES 6

Asparagus with Hazelnut–Butter Sauce

2 pounds asparagus, washed, ends trimmed, and peeled
salt
½ cup butter
4 ounces hazel nuts (filberts) finely chopped
2 teaspoons tarragon wine vinegar

Steam the asparagus over salted water until crisp-tender and drain well. Reserve and keep warm.

Melt the butter in a small saucepan and when it is hot but not yet brown, add the chopped nuts. Cook and stir just until the nuts are light brown, about 1 minute. Add the vinegar; there will be a loud hissing. Stir once more and serve immediately over the warm asparagus.

Green Beans Polonaise

6 tablespoons butter
¼ cup fine dry bread crumbs
3 tablespoons minced fresh parsley
3 hard-cooked eggs
3 pounds fresh green beans, trimmed, stringed, and sliced

In a small saucepan melt the butter. Remove and reserve 4 tablespoons of the butter. Add the crumbs to the butter in the saucepan and cook, stirring often, until golden brown. Remove the pan from the heat. When crumb mixture is cool, stir in the parsley.

Separate the egg whites from the yolks. Finely chop the whites and force the yolks through a sieve. Reserve separately.

Steam the green beans until just tender. Drain well and place in a serving dish. Top with the crumb-parsley mixture, the egg whites, then the egg yolks. Drizzle with the reserved melted butter and serve immediately.

Lima Beans Fermière

1 pound dried baby lima beans
2 cups Beef Stock (see page 56)
2 cups water
8 ounces salt pork, cut into fine julienne
2 cups chopped onion
6 carrots, peeled and sliced
1 bay leaf
1 teaspoon dried chervil
1 teaspoon fennel seed
½ teaspoon freshly grated nutmeg
½ cup dry vermouth
¼ cup brandy
salt and freshly ground black pepper to taste
½ cup chopped fresh parsley

Soak the beans overnight in water to cover. Drain the beans and place them in a large, heavy pan with the beef stock and water. Simmer, covered, until tender, about 1 to 1½ hours.

Preheat the oven to 350° F.

Sauté the salt pork until crisp and golden brown. Add the onions and carrots and sauté just until the onions are translucent, about 5 minutes.

Combine the onion-carrot mixture, beans, seasonings, vermouth, and brandy in a large buttered casserole dish. Bake for 1 hour. To serve, season to taste with salt and pepper and stir in the parsley.

SERVES 10

Molded Broccoli

1 package (1 ounce) unflavored gelatin
¼ cup cold water
1 cup Chicken Stock (see page 56)
3 tablespoons lemon juice
salt and freshly ground black pepper to taste
½ teaspoon Worchestershire sauce
3 cups chopped broccoli, slightly cooked and drained
4 hard-cooked eggs, chopped
3 green onions, sliced
¾ cup mayonnaise

Soften the gelatin in the cold water.

Bring the chicken stock to a boil in a saucepan. Remove from the heat. Stir in the softened gelatin and let cool slightly, then stir until dissolved.

Add the lemon juice, salt, pepper, and Worchestershire sauce and whisk until well blended. Add the broccoli, eggs, green onions, and mayonnaise and blend well. Pour the mixture into an oiled mold. Chill until set, 4 hours or overnight. Unmold to serve.

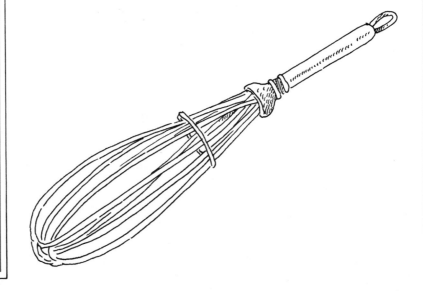

US SKI TEAM Gretchen Fraser, Andrea Mead Lawrence, Joan Saubert, and Susie Corrock, representing seven Olympic medals, gathered at Stratton Mountain, Vermont, in January 1980 for a Women's Way Seminar and Pro Race, and they all entered a team race there. The weather was awful: heavy rain all night, solid freeze and high winds for the race. Wanting to be ready for anything, Andrea drew on her long experience and wore a diver's wet suit in the race.

SERVES 8 TO 10

Scalloped Cabbage

1 small head cabbage (1½ pounds)
5 tablespoons butter, softened
3 tablespoons all-purpose flour
2 cups milk
¼ cup diced ham
4 slices bacon, crisply cooked and crumbled
¼ cup chopped green bell pepper
1 cup saltine cracker crumbs

Preheat the oven to 375° F.

Wash and core the cabbage. Cut into ½-inch slices. Steam for 5 to 7 minutes, or until tender. Drain well, then place in a casserole dish.

Melt 3 tablespoons of the butter in a saucepan. Add the flour and stir for 2 minutes. Add the milk all at once and blend quickly with a whisk. Cook over medium heat for 3 or 4 minutes until the sauce is smooth. Remove from the heat.

In a small bowl, mix together the ham, bacon, remaining 2 tablespoons butter, and green pepper. Spread evenly over the cabbage in the casserole dish. Sprinkle in the cracker crumbs and top with the white sauce. Bake, uncovered, for 25 minutes, or until light brown and bubbly. Serve hot.

SERVES 4 TO 6

Apricot Carrots

4 tablespoons butter
3 to 4 green onions, cut into julienne
10 to 12 carrots, peeled and cut into julienne
4 ounces dried apricots, cut into julienne
1 tablespoon honey
1 tablespoon sherry wine vinegar or other wine vinegar
½ cup water
salt and freshly ground black pepper to taste

Melt the butter in a large sauté pan over medium heat. Add the onions and carrots and sauté for 3 to 4 minutes, until the onions are translucent.

Add the apricots, honey, vinegar, and water and cook, covered, for 4 to 5 minutes. Remove from the heat and season with salt and pepper to taste. Serve hot.

SERVES 6 TO 8

Dilled Carrots

3 tablespoons butter
2 pounds carrots, peeled and cut into julienne
2 teaspoons chopped fresh dill or 1 teaspoon dried
½ cup Chicken Stock (see page 56)
1 teaspoon honey
3 tablespoons sour cream

Melt the butter in a large skillet over medium heat. Add the carrots and stir well to coat. Sauté the carrots, stirring frequently, for 3 minutes.

Add the dill, chicken stock, and honey. Cover and cook just until the carrots are barely tender. Remove the carrots with a slotted spoon and place in a serving dish.

Over high heat, reduce the liquid in the skillet until syrupy. Stir in the sour cream and pour the sauce over the carrots. Serve immediately.

SERVES 6

Carrot Soufflé

2 cups sliced carrots, cooked
4 tablespoons butter, melted
1 teaspoon salt
¼ cup honey
2 tablespoons cornstarch
1¼ cups light cream
3 eggs, separated

Preheat the oven to 400° F.

In a food processor or blender, purée the carrots and mix in the butter, salt, and honey.

Dissolve the cornstarch in the cream and add to the carrot mixture. Add the egg yolks and mix well.

In a small bowl, beat the egg whites until stiff but not dry and fold them into the carrot purée.

Pour the mixture into a buttered 1½-quart soufflé dish. Place the soufflé dish in a larger pan containing 1 inch of hot water and bake for 45 minutes, or until done. Serve immediately.

US SKI TEAM Barbara Ann Cochran won the 1972 Olympic slalom by 0.1 second, despite having lost a whole second in the start house when she accidentally tripped the timing mechanism before her second run.

SERVES 4

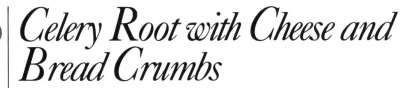

Celery Root with Cheese and Bread Crumbs

3 cups celery root (celeriac), cut into julienne
½ clove garlic
3 tablespoons butter
¼ cup fine dry bread crumbs
1 cup grated Gruyère cheese (4 ounces)
salt and freshly ground black pepper to taste
pinch of freshly grated nutmeg

Preheat the oven to 425° F.

In a large pot of boiling salted water, cook the celery root until tender, about 10 minutes.

Rub a baking dish with the cut side of the garlic clove and discard the garlic. Then spread the butter in the dish.

Place half of the celery root in the buttered dish and sprinkle with half of the bread crumbs and cheese. Season with salt, pepper, and nutmeg. Repeat the layering.

Bake for 10 to 15 minutes, or until golden brown.

Serve hot.

SERVES 8 TO 12

Coal Creek Canyon Corn

16 to 24 ears of corn
salt
water

OPTIONAL:
butter
freshly ground black pepper

Soak unhusked corn in salted water to cover 3 to 4 hours. Remove the corn from the water and drain for 30 minutes.

Heat a charcoal grill. Place unhusked corn on the grill and roast, turning frequently, for 10 to 15 minutes until the husks are charred.

Remove the husks. Add butter and pepper, if desired, and serve.

The sugar in corn begins to convert to starch as soon as it is picked. This means that the longer you keep fresh corn, the less sweet it will be. Add a pinch of sugar to the water if boiling or steaming corn.

SERVES 8

Eggplant Romano

1 large eggplant, peeled and cut into 1-inch cubes
salt
½ cup butter
1 medium onion, chopped
3 tomatoes, peeled and chopped or 1 can (16 ounces) toma-
    toes, drained
2 tablespoons chopped fresh parsley
freshly ground black pepper to taste
2 eggs, lightly beaten
1 cup fine-dry Italian-style bread crumbs
½ cup grated Romano cheese

Preheat the oven to 350° F.
Cook the eggplant in salted water until tender. Drain
well and reserve.
Melt the butter in a sauté pan and cook the onion until
transparent. Add the tomatoes and cook for 5 minutes. Add
the parsley and season with salt and pepper.
Combine the eggplant and the onion-tomato mixture.
Add the eggs and bread crumbs and mix well. Place the
mixture in a buttered 9 x 13-inch casserole dish and bake for
30 minutes. Sprinkle the cheese on top and bake for 5 minutes
more. Serve hot.

SERVES 6

Thanksgiving Onions

6 cups thinly sliced onion rings (about 6 medium onions)
4 tablespoons butter
¼ cup all-purpose flour
2 cups milk
salt and freshly ground black pepper to taste
dash of hot pepper sauce
3 cups grated sharp Cheddar cheese (12 ounces)

Preheat the oven to 325° F.
Place the onion rings in a buttered 7 x 11-inch casserole.
Melt the butter in a small saucepan. Blend in the flour
and gradually stir in the milk. Cook until thickened and
season to taste with salt, pepper, and hot pepper sauce. Add
2 cups of the cheese and stir until the cheese melts.
Pour the sauce over the onion rings and top with the
remaining cheese. Bake, uncovered, for 1 hour. Serve hot.

SERVES 6

Sweet and Sour Onions

1 pound tiny onions, peeled
1 cup water
¼ cup wine vinegar
3 tablespoons olive oil
¼ cup granulated sugar
3 tablespoons tomato paste
½ cup raisins
bouquet garni (6 parsley sprigs, 1 teaspoon thyme, ½ bay
    leaf tied in cheesecloth)
salt and freshly ground black pepper to taste
¼ cup Madeira

Place all the ingredients, except the Madeira, in a sauce-pan and bring to a boil. Simmer, uncovered, for about 1 hour, or until the onions are tender. Most of the liquid should have evaporated, so the mixture will be moist but not runny. Add the Madeira. Continue cooking until the Madeira is hot. Discard the bouquet garni and transfer the onions to a serving bowl. Serve at room temperature.

SERVES 4 TO 6

Mushroom Soufflé

2 tablespoons butter
1 tablespoon vegetable oil
8 ounces mushrooms, thinly sliced
¼ cup sliced green onion
1 tablespoon lemon juice
¼ cup all-purpose flour
½ cup Madeira
½ cup heavy cream
½ teaspoon salt
¼ teaspoon freshly ground black pepper
⅛ teaspoon hot pepper sauce
5 eggs, separated

Preheat the oven to 400°F.

Heat the butter and oil in a heavy sauté pan. Add the mushrooms, onion, and lemon juice and sauté rapidly, stirring, until all the liquid has evaporated. Stir in the flour and blend well. Add the Madeira, cream, salt, pepper, and hot pepper sauce and cook until thickened, stirring constantly. Remove from the heat and beat in the egg yolks, one at a time.

In a small bowl, beat the egg whites until they hold stiff peaks. Gently but thoroughly, fold half of the whites into the sauce. Fold in the remaining whites just until blended.

Pour the mixture into a buttered 1½-quart soufflé dish. Run the point of a knife around the top of the soufflé within an inch of the rim of the dish. Place in the preheated oven and immediately lower the heat to 375° F. Bake for 35 minutes. Serve immediately.

Peas in Cream

SERVES 8

2 tablespoons butter
½ cup heavy cream
½ teaspoon dried mint
salt and freshly ground black pepper to taste
2 packages (10 ounces each) frozen tiny peas, defrosted

Combine the butter, cream, mint, salt, and pepper in a nonaluminum 3-quart saucepan and simmer for about 6 to 8 minutes, or until the liquid is slightly reduced and thickened. Stir in the peas and cook just until heated through. Do not overcook. Serve immediately.

Potatoes and Cream

SERVES 8 TO 10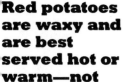

Red potatoes are waxy and are best served hot or warm—not chilled.

15 medium potatoes (about 4 pounds)
3 cups heavy cream
½ small onion, grated
1½ teaspoons salt
¼ teaspoon freshly ground white pepper
paprika
4 tablespoons butter

Cook the potatoes in their skins, then refrigerate overnight.

Preheat the oven to 375° F.

Peel the potatoes and grate on a coarse grater into a bowl. Add the cream, onion, salt, pepper, and paprika and mix well. Place the mixture in a buttered 9 x 13-inch casserole dish. Dot the top with the butter. Bake, uncovered, for 1 hour. Serve hot.

Potatoes and Bacon

6 large potatoes, peeled
½ cup unsalted butter
¼ cup olive oil
1 teaspoon dried rosemary, crushed
paprika
½ teaspoon salt
freshly ground black pepper to taste
½ pound bacon, blanched and chopped

Cook the potatoes in salted water to cover in a large saucepan until still slightly firm when pierced with a knife. Do not overcook.

Preheat the oven to 450° F.

When the potatoes are done, drain and cool, then cut into thick slices.

Thickly coat the bottom and sides of a 9 x 13-inch casserole dish with the butter. Layer the potatoes in the dish.

Drizzle the oil on top of the potatoes and sprinkle with the rosemary and paprika. Season with salt and pepper, then sprinkle the bacon on top.

Bake, turning often, until the potatoes are well browned and very crisp, about 45 minutes. Serve hot.

Sauerkraut

1 pound sauerkraut (bulk or plastic-packed, not canned)
3 strips bacon, diced
1 medium onion, chopped
½ cup water
1 large potato, peeled and grated
salt to taste

Rinse and drain the sauerkraut.

Cook the bacon in a large sauté pan for 1 to 2 minutes. Add the onion and sauté until the bacon is crisp and the onion is transparent. Add the sauerkraut and water. Simmer, covered, over low heat for 2½ to 3 hours, stirring occasionally.

Add the potato and season to taste with salt, if necessary. Simmer for 15 minutes. This can be refrigerated for up to 1 week in a covered container and served hot or cold.

SERVES 8

This filling
also works
well in
cooked,
drained
artichokes
(chokes
removed).

Cheese Soufflé in Tomatoes

8 medium tomatoes
½ teaspoon salt
4 tablespoons butter
1½ tablespoons all-purpose flour
½ cup milk
½ teaspoon dried oregano, basil, or tarragon
3 dashes hot pepper sauce
¾ cup grated Cheddar cheese (3 ounces)
3 large eggs, separated

Wash and dry the tomatoes. Cut a ½-inch slice off of the stem ends. Scoop out the pulp and reserve for another use or discard. The tomatoes should have about a ½-inch shell. Salt the inside of the tomatoes and invert on paper toweling to drain for 45 minutes to 1 hour.

Preheat the oven to 375° F.

Melt the butter in a saucepan and blend in the flour. Cook for at least 1 minute over medium heat. Add the milk and whisk constantly to produce a smooth white sauce. Remove from the heat and stir in the herbs, hot pepper sauce, and cheese. Beat in the egg yolks, one at a time.

Beat the egg whites until stiff. Add about one fourth of the whites to the cheese sauce and mix thoroughly. Fold in the remaining egg whites, but do not overblend.

Spoon the soufflé mixture into the tomatoes and mound on top. Place the tomatoes in a buttered baking dish and bake for 25 to 30 minutes, or until puffed and golden. Serve immediately.

SERVES 4

Tomatoes Provençal

24 firm red cherry tomatoes
2 tablespoons olive oil
1 teaspoon chopped garlic
2 tablespoons chopped fresh parsley

Wash and dry the tomatoes. Heat the oil in a sauté pan and sauté the garlic for 1 minute over medium heat. Add the tomatoes and sauté for 1 minute more, shaking the pan so that the tomatoes cook evenly. Add the parsley and stir. Serve immediately.

SERVES 6

Cold Tomato Cobb

6 firm medium tomatoes (preferably home grown)
½ cup mayonnaise
1 teaspoon curry powder
2 teaspoons lemon juice
½ teaspoon granulated sugar
1 tablespoon minced fresh parsley

OPTIONAL:
¼ cup chopped green onion

    Scald the tomatoes and plunge immediately into ice water. Peel the tomatoes and cut into large pieces. Place the tomatoes in a bowl.

    In a small bowl, combine the remaining ingredients. Pour the sauce over the tomatoes and mix gently. Chill thoroughly.

    Place the tomatoes in shallow bowls. Place the bowls in the freezer for 5 to 10 minutes to get icy cold. Serve immediately.

SERVES 8

Zucchini Tomato Bake

2 cups grated sharp Cheddar cheese (8 ounces)
3 cups small croutons
4 cups sliced zucchini
½ cup chopped onion
½ cup chopped green bell pepper
3 tomatoes, peeled, diced, and well drained
4 tablespoons butter, melted

    Preheat the oven to 350° F.

    Reserve ½ cup cheese and ½ cup of the croutons.

    Combine the remaining cheese and croutons, the zucchini, onion, green pepper, and tomatoes. Add the butter and mix well. Place the mixture in a buttered casserole dish and top with the reserved cheese and croutons. Bake, covered, for 1½ hours. Serve hot.

SERVES 8 TO 10

Wild rice is not a true rice, but a native American grain that is still hand-gathered. The best grades usually have long, dark grains.

Wild Rice Pilaf

1 cup wild rice
2 cups Chicken Stock (see page 56)
¾ cup dry vermouth
1½ cups sliced fresh mushrooms
1½ cups sliced celery
5 tablespoons butter
1 package (10 ounces) frozen artichoke hearts, thawed
¼ cup sliced green onion
2 tablespoons chopped pimiento
1 teaspoon finely shredded lemon zest
1 tablespoon lemon juice
¾ teaspoon salt
½ teaspoon dried thyme, crushed
¼ teaspoon freshly ground black pepper

GARNISH:
minced fresh parsley

Run cold water over the rice in a strainer for 1 to 2 minutes, lifting the rice with fingers to rinse thoroughly.

Combine the rice, chicken stock, and ½ cup of the vermouth in a 3-quart saucepan and bring to a boil. Reduce the heat, cover, and simmer for 30 minutes (the rice should be undercooked). Do not drain.

Preheat the oven to 325° F.

While the rice is cooking, sauté the mushrooms and celery in 4 tablespoons of the butter for 4 to 5 minutes, or until crisp-tender. Stir in the artichoke hearts, green onion, pimiento, lemon zest, lemon juice, salt, thyme, pepper, and the remaining 1 tablespoon butter and ¼ cup vermouth. Remove from the heat.

Combine the rice and mushroom mixture and mix well. Place in a buttered 2-quart casserole dish and bake, covered, for 45 minutes, or until heated through. Serve garnished with the parsley.

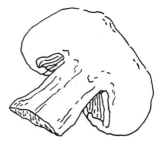

SERVES 6

Italian Rice

½ cup butter
1 cup Italian (Arborio) rice
1 cup peeled, seeded, and chopped fresh tomato
4 ounces mushrooms, sliced
½ cup chopped onion
2 cups Chicken Stock (see page 56)
½ cup red wine
1 teaspoon salt
⅛ teaspoon freshly ground black pepper
1 cup cooked green peas
¼ cup freshly grated Parmesan cheese

Heat the butter in a large skillet over medium heat and sauté the rice, tomato, mushrooms, and onion for 10 minutes, stirring occasionally. Add the chicken stock, wine, and seasonings. Mix well, cover, and simmer over low heat for 45 minutes, or until the rice is tender and all the liquid is absorbed.

Stir in the peas and heat through. Sprinkle with Parmesan cheese and serve immediately.

SERVES 4

Confetti Brown Rice

3 tablespoons vegetable oil
1 small onion, chopped
1 cup mixed dried fruit, chopped
⅔ cup mixed nuts, chopped
⅓ cup sesame seeds
¼ to ½ teaspoon ground cloves
½ teaspoon salt
1 cup raw brown rice, cooked
4 tablespoons butter, melted

Preheat the oven to 350° F.

Heat the oil in a skillet and sauté the onion, fruit, nuts, and sesame seeds until the onion is translucent, about 5 minutes.

Add the cloves and salt to the onion mixture and stir. Add the rice and mix well.

Place the rice in a small buttered casserole dish and pour the butter over all. Bake for 15 to 20 minutes to heat through. Serve immediately.

SERVES 6

Good Life Rice

2 tablespoons olive oil
1 small onion, chopped
2 stalks celery, chopped
1 carrot, peeled and chopped
1 tablespoon sesame seeds
2 tablespoons pumpkin seed
2 tablespoons sliced or slivered almonds
2 tablespoons sunflower seeds
2 cups brown rice
½ cup millet
¼ cup lentils or split peas, soaked
5 cups water
2 tablespoons miso
1 tablespoon soy sauce
2 bay leaves

Heat the oil in a large heavy saucepan over medium heat and sauté the onion, celery, and carrot for 3 to 4 minutes.

Add the remaining ingredients and stir until the miso is dissolved.

Reduce the heat, cover, and cook for 45 minutes. Remove from the heat and let stand for 10 minutes. Serve immediately.

SERVES 8 TO 10

White Turnip Pudding

Turnips are an excellent vegetable to serve with game hens, quail, pheasant, or turkey.

8 medium white turnips, peeled and sliced
½ cup chopped onion
½ cup heavy cream
2 tablespoons butter
salt and freshly ground black pepper
2 egg whites, stiffly beaten

Preheat the oven to 350° F.

Steam the turnips and onion over boiling water until tender. Purée in a blender or food processor.

Heat the cream in a heavy saucepan. Add the purée and butter and cook over low heat until the cream is absorbed. Cool. Season with salt and pepper.

Fold the beaten egg whites gently into the turnip purée and pour into a buttered 1½-quart baking dish. Bake until puffed and lightly browned, about 30 to 40 minutes. Serve immediately.

SERVES 6

Fennel has a large, bulbous root with feathery leaves. It has a distinctive anise flavor and can be prepared in most of the ways celery is.

Vegetable Pudding

3 tablespoons butter
5 ounces fennel bulb or celery
1 bay leaf, crushed
1 teaspoon salt
2 small zucchini, trimmed but unpeeled,
     cut into ½-inch pieces
1 small onion, diced
½ green bell pepper, seeded and diced
3½ ounces mushrooms, diced
½ teaspoon dried thyme
3 eggs
1 cup heavy cream
1½ teaspoons tomato paste
⅛ teaspoon freshly ground black pepper
2½ ounces Polish ham, diced
Tomato Sauce (recipe follows)

Preheat the oven to 350° F. and butter six 4-ounce ramekins, using 1 tablespoon of the butter.

Cut the fennel or celery into ½-inch pieces and cover with water in a saucepan. Add the bay leaf and ½ teaspoon of the salt and bring to a boil. Cook for 15 minutes, or until tender. Drain well and set aside in a large mixing bowl.

Melt the remaining 2 tablespoons butter in a large skillet over medium heat. Add the zucchini, onion, and green pepper. Cook for 3 minutes. Add the mushrooms and thyme and cook 3 minutes more, or until the vegetables are tender but not brown. Drain liquid from the pan and discard. Pat the vegetables dry with paper toweling and add them to the celery in the mixing bowl.

In a small bowl, combine the eggs, cream, tomato paste, pepper, and remaining ½ teaspoon salt. Mix well with a whisk until frothy, about 10 seconds. Add the egg mixture and ham to the vegetables and mix well.

Pour the batter into the buttered ramekins not quite to the top. Place the ramekins in a baking pan. Carefully pour hot water from a kettle into the baking pan until the water reaches two thirds up the sides of the ramekins. Place the baking pan on the center rack of the oven.

Bake for 40 minutes until puffed and brown, or until a knife inserted in the center comes out clean.

When baked, remove the ramekins from the water bath with rubber tongs or a slotted spoon or spatula. Let stand for 15 minutes before reversing on a platter. Serve immediately, with the tomato sauce.

TOMATO SAUCE:
2 shallots, peeled and minced
¾ cup dry vermouth
¼ cup minced fresh mint or 1 tablespoon dried
¼ cup water
1¼ cups peeled, seeded, and diced tomato
3 tablespoons butter
¼ teaspoon salt
⅛ teaspoon freshly ground black pepper
1 teaspoon granulated sugar

Place the shallots in a small saucepan. Add the vermouth, mint, and water and cook over high heat until the alcohol evaporates, about 2 minutes.

Add the tomatoes and cook 3 minutes more over high heat.

Reduce the heat and beat in the butter, a tablespoon at a time, with a whisk. Add the seasonings and sugar and allow the sauce to simmer for an additional 5 minutes. Serve hot.

SERVES 8

Yams with Rum Glaze

6 medium yams, cooked, peeled, and sliced
3 tablespoons cornstarch
¾ cup (packed) brown sugar
¼ teaspoon salt
1½ cups orange juice
⅓ cup seedless raisins
¼ cup chopped walnuts
1 teaspoon grated orange zest
½ cup dark rum
6 tablespoons butter

GARNISH:
1 orange, thinly sliced

Preheat the oven to 350° F.

Arrange the sliced yams in overlapping rows in a buttered 9 x 13-inch casserole dish.

Combine the cornstarch, brown sugar, and salt in a saucepan. Blend in the orange juice and bring to a boil, stirring. Remove from the heat, add the remaining ingredients and blend well. Return the pan to the heat and bring to a boil. Spoon the glaze over the yams.

Bake, uncovered, for 20 minutes, or until the yams are well glazed. Garnish with orange slices and serve immediately.

US SKI TEAM The traditional thrills of the Olympic men's downhill could hardly have matched the excitement of the training sessions for the 1948 race. Whole teams ran the St. Moritz downhill course simultaneously as part of their wax-testing program.

SERVES 10

Bourbon Apples with Cranberries

6 large tart apples, peeled and sliced
1 cup bourbon
12 ounces fresh cranberries
½ cup granulated sugar
½ cup raisins
1 tablespoon butter

Place the apple slices in a heavy saucepan with ½ cup of the bourbon. Cover and simmer over low heat, stirring often, for 15 minutes.

Add the cranberries, sugar, and raisins and cook 10 minutes longer, or until the cranberries pop.

Remove from the heat and stir in the butter and remaining ½ cup bourbon. Serve hot, cold, or at room temperature as an accompaniment to meat, or as a brunch dish.

SERVES 6 TO 8

An excellent accompaniment to ham.

Baked Pineapple

½ cup all-purpose flour
¾ cup granulated sugar
3 cups grated Longhorn cheese (12 ounces)
4 cups pineapple chunks, drained, juice reserved

Preheat the oven to 325° F.

Combine the flour, sugar, and cheese in a bowl.

Place a layer of half the pineapple in a buttered 2-quart casserole dish. Sprinkle with half the cheese-flour mixture. Repeat the layering.

Pour the reserved pineapple juice over all, using just enough to barely cover. Bake for 1 hour. Serve hot.

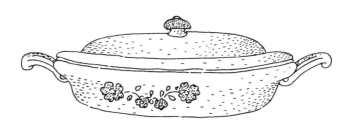

SERVES 6

A marvelous meat accompaniment— a great change from cranberries with turkey, and good with ham, chicken, or roasts.

Scalloped Rhubarb

3 cups dry bread cubes (crusts removed)
½ cup butter, melted
3 cups diced uncooked rhubarb
1 cup granulated sugar
⅓ cup water

Preheat the oven to 325° F.

Toss the bread cubes with the melted butter in a bowl. Add the rhubarb and sugar and mix gently. Place the mixture in a 7 x 11-inch casserole dish and pour ⅓ the water over it. Bake, uncovered, for 45 minutes.

SERVES 4

Fresh Tomato Sauce for Vegetables

⅓ cup mayonnaise, preferably homemade
1 teaspoon lemon juice
dash of salt
drop of hot pepper sauce
⅓ cup peeled, seeded, and diced tomato

Combine the mayonnaise, lemon juice, salt, and hot pepper sauce in a small saucepan. Cook, stirring, over low heat just until heated through. Remove from the heat and stir in tomatoes. Serve over vegetables, especially asparagus.

SERVES 4

Egg Cream Sauce for Vegetables

This is an excellent sauce over steamed vegetables, such as asparagus, broccoli, and cauliflower.

3 to 4 sieved hard-cooked egg yolks
¼ teaspoon granulated sugar
¼ teaspoon salt
¼ teaspoon vinegar
¼ teaspoon prepared mustard
½ cup heavy cream

Mix together the egg yolks, sugar, salt, vinegar, and mustard. This will have a paste-like consistency. Add the cream and whip until thick.

SERVES 4

Mediterranean Eggplant

1 medium-large eggplant
salt
¼ cup chopped onion
2 tablespoons chopped fresh parsley
1 teaspoon dried mint
vegetable oil
freshly ground black pepper to taste
3 tablespoons raisins
3 tablespoons chopped walnuts
2 tablespoons tomato purée
¼ teaspoon ground cinnamon
2 cups hot cooked rice

OPTIONAL:
2 tablespoons frozen apple juice concentrate, thawed

GARNISH:
chutney
plain yogurt
toasted sesame seeds

Slice the eggplant into ½-inch slices, sprinkle with salt and place in a colander to drain for 20 to 30 minutes. Rinse, dry, and cut into cubes. Steam for 5 to 10 minutes, or until barely tender.

Meanwhile, sauté the onion, parsley, and mint in the oil, in a Dutch oven, stirring often, until the onion is transparent. Stir in the pepper, raisins, walnuts, tomato purée, cinnamon, and apple juice concentrate, if desired. Cook, stirring often, over low heat for 3 to 5 minutes.

Stir in the hot cooked rice. If rice has cooled, heat together until piping hot. Add the reserved eggplant, stir gently, and heat through. Serve garnished with chutney, yogurt, and sesame seeds.

US SKI TEAM Steamboat Springs, Colorado, has been the home of many Olympic team members over the years. Among the most notable was Wallace "Buddy" Werner, one of the fastest American male racers ever. His win in the downhill and slalom and second-place finish in the giant slalom at the North American Championships in 1959, coupled with his victory at the challenging Hahnenkamm in Kitzbühel, Austria, the same year, readied him for the 1960 Olympics. Yet, two months before the games, he broke his leg and was unable to compete. He was ready for the 1964 games when he became another tragic statistic in the annals of ski history. He was killed attempting to outrun an avalanche in the Swiss Alps.

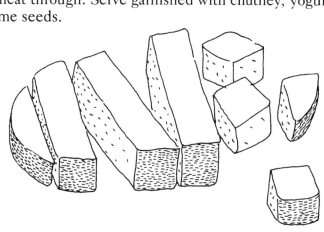

Steamboat Springs Stuffed Squash

SERVES 4

Good served with cranberry relish as a vegetarian holiday entrée.

2 medium acorn squash
3 tablespoons butter
1 small onion, chopped
2 cloves garlic, minced
¼ cup chopped walnuts
¼ cup chopped celery
¼ cup chopped green bell pepper
1 cup whole-wheat bread crumbs
½ teaspoon dried sage
½ teaspoon dried thyme
¼ cup sunflower seeds
1 tablespoon lemon juice
¼ cup raisins
salt and freshly ground black pepper to taste
¾ cup grated Cheddar cheese

Preheat the oven to 350° F.

Cut the squash in half lengthwise and remove the seeds. Place the squash, cut side down, in a large, shallow casserole dish. Add ½ inch of water and bake for 30 minutes, or until tender.

Meanwhile, melt the butter in a large skillet and sauté the onion, garlic, walnuts, and celery over low heat for 10 minutes. Add the remaining ingredients, except the cheese, and cook and stir for 6 to 7 minutes more, or until the green pepper is tender. Stir in the cheese and mix well.

Divide the stuffing among the squash cavities. Place the squash on a lightly oiled baking tray and bake for 20 to 25 minutes, covered.

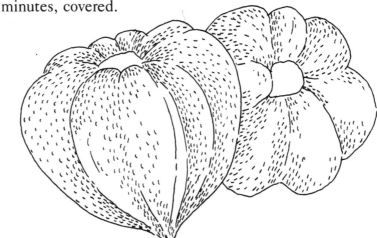

SERVES 4

Brown Rice and Vegetable Stir-Fry

3 tablespoons vegetable oil
1 cup sliced carrots
1 medium onion, sliced
1 clove garlic, minced
1 green bell pepper, seeded and cut into strips
2 cups broccoli florets
1 cup sliced mushrooms
2 cups bean sprouts
1 cup regular brown rice, cooked according to package
    directions
¼ cup soy sauce
salt and freshly ground black pepper to taste

Have all the ingredients ready before starting to cook.

Heat the oil in a wok or large skillet over high heat. Add the carrots and cook, stirring, for 1 minute. Add the onion, garlic, green pepper, and broccoli and cook, stirring, about 2 minutes longer. Add the mushrooms and cook for 1 minute. Add the bean sprouts and rice and cook, stirring, until heated thoroughly. Season with soy sauce, salt and pepper. Serve immediately.

Breads

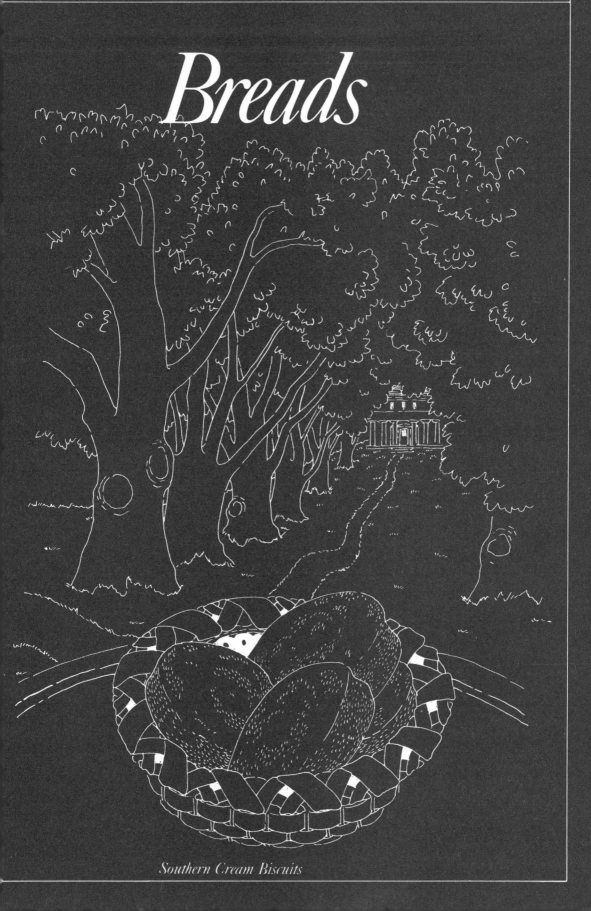

Southern Cream Biscuits

**MAKES 2
LOAVES**

Cracked-Wheat Bread

1 cup cracked wheat (bulgur)
3¼ cups water
⅓ cup honey
3 tablespoons butter
2 teaspoons salt
2 cups whole-wheat flour
2 packages active dry yeast
4 to 4½ cups all-purpose flour

Combine the cracked wheat and water in a medium saucepan. Bring to a boil, then reduce the heat, cover, and cook for 8 minutes. For a crunchier bread, heat the water and cracked wheat but do not cook it. Add the honey, butter, and salt. Cool to lukewarm (110° to 115° F.).

Combine the whole-wheat flour and yeast in a large mixing bowl. Add the warm cracked-wheat mixture and beat at low speed for 30 seconds, scraping the sides of the bowl constantly. Beat for 3 minutes at high speed. By hand, stir in enough of the all-purpose flour to make a moderately stiff dough.

Turn the dough out onto a lightly floured surface. Knead until smooth and elastic, 8 to 10 minutes. Shape into a ball and place in a lightly greased bowl, turning once to grease the surface. Cover and let rise in a warm place until doubled, about 45 to 60 minutes.

Punch the dough down and turn out onto a lightly floured surface.

Divide in half, cover, and let rest for about 10 minutes. Shape each half into a loaf and place in two greased 8½ x 4½ x 2½-inch loaf pans. Cover and let rise until doubled, about 30 minutes.

Preheat the oven to 400° F.

Bake for 30 to 35 minutes. If bread browns too quickly, cover loosely with foil. Remove from pans and cool on racks.

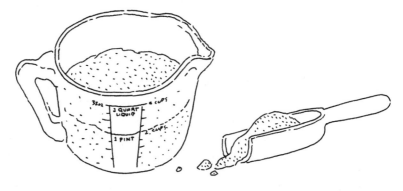

Water temperature is very important when using dry yeast. It should be 110° to 115° F. If the water is too hot, it will kill the yeast; if the water is too cold, it will not activate the yeast. (If you do not have a thermometer, it should be the same temperature as a baby's bath water.)

Sourdough Starter

1 package active dry yeast
2 cups warm water (115° F.)
2 cups all-purpose flour

___

In a nonmetallic bowl (glass or plastic), mix together the yeast, water, and flour. Cover with plastic wrap or cheese-cloth and let stand at room temperature for 48 hours, stirring twice a day. The mixture should bubble.

Remove as much starter as the recipe requires. To the remaining starter, add equal amounts of flour and water (1 cup flour and 1 cup water) and stir. Let this mixture stand at room temperature for a few hours, then cover tightly and refrigerate until needed. Before using, let the starter stand at room temperature for 4 to 5 hours, loosely covered.

If the starter is not used every week, then one half of it should be thrown out and more flour and water added—just as if you were using it for bread.

Open the lid of the glass or plastic container every few weeks as gasses can build up. *Never* store the starter at room temperature with a lid on the container, as it might explode.

Sourdough Bread

1 package active dry yeast
¼ cup lukewarm water
1 cup hot water
2 tablespoons granulated sugar
2 tablespoons butter
1½ cups Sourdough Starter (see above)
2 teaspoons salt
2 teaspoons white vinegar
4 to 5 cups unbleached white flour
1 tablespoon cornmeal
1 egg white
1 tablespoon cold water

___

Mix the yeast and warm water in a small bowl; stir to dissolve. Pour the hot water over the sugar and butter in a large mixing bowl and stir to blend. Cool the butter mixture to lukewarm and add the yeast mixture, starter, and salt. Add the vinegar and 2 cups of the flour and beat about 1 minute, or until well blended. Stir in enough of the remaining flour to make a very stiff dough. Turn the dough out on a board and knead for 8 to 10 minutes, or until the dough is smooth.

Place the dough in a large greased bowl, turning the dough to oil the surface. Cover and let rise 1 to 2 hours, or until doubled in bulk. Punch down the dough and let rise again for 30 minutes. Turn out on a board and divide in half. Shape into two long rolls. Place the loaves in bread pans that have been oiled and sprinkled with cornmeal. Cover the loaves and let rise until doubled, about 1½ hours.

Preheat the oven to 400° F.

Cut diagonal slashes in the loaves and brush with a mixture of beaten egg white and water. Bake for about 35 to 40 minutes, or until browned and hollow sounding when tapped. Cool before cutting.

MAKES 2 LOAVES

Faux French Bread

1 package active dry yeast
1 tablespoon honey
1 cup warm (110° to 115°) water
3 cups all-purpose flour
2 eggs
½ teaspoon salt
vegetable shortening
cornmeal

Combine the yeast, honey, and water in a small bowl and proof for 10 minutes.

Combine the flour, one of the eggs, salt, and yeast mixture in a food processor. Process until the dough forms a ball around the side and begins to thump, about 2 minutes or 50 thumps.

Place the dough in a greased bowl and let rise, covered, for 45 minutes.

Grease 2 French bread baguette pans and sprinkle with cornmeal.

Punch down the dough, divide into 2 portions and let rest for 10 minutes.

Roll each portion into a long loaf and place in prepared pans. Cover and let rise 45 minutes.

Preheat the oven to 400° F.

Brush the tops of the risen loaves with the remaining egg, beaten. Make diagonal slashes on the tops of the loaves. Bake for 20 minutes, or until browned. Remove to a rack to cool before slicing.

MAKES 1 LOAF

If using glass baking pans, reduce the oven temperature by 25° F.

Apple Rye Bread

cornmeal
1½ cups unbleached all-purpose flour
1 cup rye flour
1 package active dry yeast
½ teaspoon salt
2 tablespoons caraway seeds
¾ cup applesauce
2 tablespoons molasses
2 tablespoons butter
1 egg, lightly beaten

Grease a 5 x 9-inch loaf pan. Dust it with cornmeal.

Sift together the all-purpose flour, rye flour, yeast, and salt. Stir in the caraway seeds.

Heat the applesauce, molasses, and butter just until the butter melts, about 120° F. Add the applesauce mixture to the dry ingredients and stir until the dough forms a ball.

Knead the dough. Place in a greased bowl. Turn the dough over to grease the surface. Cover and let rise until doubled in bulk, from 45 minutes to 1 hour, 15 minutes. Punch down, shape into an oval loaf, put in the prepared pan and let rise again until doubled, from 45 minutes to 1 hour.

Preheat the oven to 375° F.

When the dough has doubled, brush with the beaten egg. Bake for 50 minutes. Remove from the pan and place on a wire rack to cool before slicing.

MAKES 2 RINGS

Monkey Bread

1 cup milk, scalded
1 cup mashed potatoes
⅔ cup vegetable shortening
1 teaspoon salt
⅔ cup granulated sugar
1 package active dry yeast
½ cup warm water (110° to 115° F.)
2 eggs, well beaten
5 to 6 cups all-purpose flour
vegetable oil
melted butter

Combine the milk, potatoes, shortening, salt, and sugar in a large bowl. Let stand until lukewarm.

Dissolve the yeast in the water and add to the potato mixture. Stir in the eggs. Add 1½ cups of the flour and beat well. Continue adding flour until the dough is stiff.

Turn the dough out on a floured board and knead thoroughly.

Place the dough in a greased bowl. Brush oil over the top and cover loosely. Let rise for 2½ hours, then chill in the refrigerator for 1 hour for easier handling.

About 1½ to 2 hours before serving, roll the dough into a ½ inch-thick rectangle. Cut into 2-inch diamonds. Pull each diamond at opposite ends to elongate. Dip in melted butter.

Arrange the diamonds in layers in two well-buttered 2-quart ring molds or Bundt pans. Put a second layer of dough pieces on top, overlapping them. Continue layering until all the dough is used. Cover and let rise until doubled.

Preheat oven to 400° F.

Bake the loaves for 30 minutes, or until done. Cool on racks before slicing.

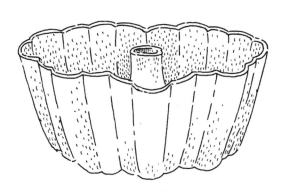

Back in the days of Iron Man ski racing, the U.S. team entered the 1936 King's Cup tournament in Sestriere, Italy—six downhills in six days, measuring up to ten miles. And, following the custom of the era, the courses received no special preparation. Competitors agreed that the most difficult race was a ten-miler run in breakable crust. The problem was that the crust tended to saw through their boot laces, leading to uncertain control.

**MAKES 2
LOAVES**

I Never Want to See Another Zucchini Bread

**The amount of
flour required
for this or any
bread recipe
will vary
because of
humidity
and the
composition of
the flour.**

1½ cups warm water
1 package dry yeast
1 cup Sourdough Starter, at room
    temperature, (see page 226)
6 cups unsifted all-purpose flour
2 teaspoons salt
2 teaspoons granulated sugar
1 cup zucchini, shredded and well drained
2 tablespoons chopped onion
½ teaspoon baking soda
coarse salt
garlic powder

Pour the warm water into a large mixing bowl and stir in the yeast. Let proof for 5 to 10 minutes. Add the starter, 4 cups of the flour, salt, and sugar. Stir vigorously for 3 minutes with a wooden spoon. Then stir in the zucchini and onion.

Knead the dough slightly until it forms a ball. Place the dough in a large greased bowl. Cover and let rise until doubled (about 3 hours, depending on the weather conditions). Punch down, cover, and let rise again.

Mix the baking soda with 1 cup of the remaining flour and stir into the dough. Turn out onto a floured board and knead, adding as much of the remaining cup of flour as the bread will take.

Shape into round loaves and place in greased ovenproof bowls. Cover and let rise for 45 to 50 minutes. Make slashes diagonally across the top with a sharp knife. Brush with water; sprinkle with coarse salt and garlic powder.

Preheat the oven to 400° F. Bake until the crust is medium brown, about 50 minutes. Cool before slicing.

**MAKES 16
PIECES**

Garlic Sticks

1⅓ cups warm water
1 tablespoon plus 2 teaspoons salt
1 tablespoon plus 2 teaspoons granulated sugar
1 egg, beaten
1 tablespoon vegetable oil, plus additional for coating
⅓ ounce cake yeast or ½ package dry yeast
4½ cups all-purpose flour
minced fresh garlic to taste
garlic powder to taste
salt to taste
dried oregano to taste
dried basil to taste
paprika to taste

Combine the water, salt, sugar, half the beaten egg (discard the rest), oil, and yeast in a large bowl. Stir to dissolve the sugar and proof the yeast.

Add half the flour and beat well. Add enough of the remaining flour to produce a smooth, but not sticky, dough. Knead the dough, expelling all the air.

Shape the dough into 2 balls and coat with oil. Cover and let rise in a warm (80° F.) place for 1 hour.

Grease a 9 x 13-inch baking pan. Pat each ball into a strip the length of the pan so that the strips are touching. Coat with oil and cover (at this point the dough will pull back from the sides of the pan).

Let rise for 1 hour, or until the dough is about 1 inch high. Restretch the dough to the edge of the pan.

Cut with a pizza cutter into about 4 x 1½-inch strips. Place the pan in a cold oven. Set oven temperature to 450° F. Bake for 25 minutes, or until golden brown. Watch to see that the bottom is not browning faster than the top.

Remove from the oven. Brush the top with oil and season to taste with garlic, garlic powder, salt, oregano, basil, and paprika. Serve warm or at room temperature.

**MAKES 2 LARGE
OR 4 SMALL
LOAVES**

Poppy Seed Bread

3 cups all-purpose flour
½ teaspoon salt
1½ teaspoons baking powder
2 tablespoons poppy seeds
2¾ cups granulated sugar
1½ cups vegetable oil
3 eggs
1½ teaspoons vanilla extract
2 teaspoons almond extract
1½ cups milk
¼ cup orange juice

Preheat the oven to 350° F.

Combine the flour, salt, baking powder, and poppy seeds in a large bowl. Set aside.

Cream together 2 cups of the sugar, oil, eggs, vanilla, and 1½ teaspoons of the almond extract in a medium bowl.

Add the dry ingredients to the sugar mixture alternately with the milk, ending with the dry ingredients.

Bake in 2 large greased loaf pans or four small greased loaf pans for 40 to 65 minutes, or until the bread tests done.

Combine the orange juice, remaining ¾ cup sugar, and remaining ½ teaspoon almond extract and drizzle this mixture over the top of the baked bread. Cool on a wire rack.

**MAKES 2 SMALL
LOAVES**

Honey Oatmeal Bread

1 cup boiling water
1 cup oatmeal
½ cup raisins
4 tablespoons butter, softened
2 cups firmly packed brown sugar
2 eggs
1 cup all-purpose flour
1 teaspoon ground cinnamon
1 teaspoon ground cloves
1 teaspoon baking soda
1 cup chopped pecans
½ cup confectioner's sugar

Preheat the oven to 350° F. Grease and flour 2 small loaf pans.

Pour the boiling water over the oatmeal and raisins in a medium bowl and set aside until cool, about 15 minutes.

Meanwhile, in a large bowl, cream together the butter and brown sugar, then beat in the eggs, one at a time. Blend in the flour, spices, and baking soda. Beat in the oatmeal-raisin mixture and fold in the pecans.

Pour the batter into the prepared loaf pans and bake for 40 to 50 minutes, or until a wooden pick inserted in the center comes out clean.

Cool on a rack for 10 minutes, then remove from the pans. Cool completely, then dust with confectioner's sugar.

Jack O'Lantern Bread

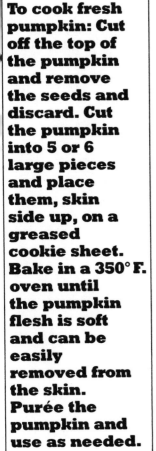

3 cups all-purpose flour
2 teaspoons baking soda
½ teaspoon baking powder
1 teaspoon ground cinnamon
1 teaspoon ground cloves
1 teaspoon salt
½ cup butter, softened
2½ cups granulated sugar
4 eggs
2½ cups freshly cooked pumpkin
½ cup chopped walnuts
½ cup chopped raisins

Preheat the oven to 350° F.

Butter and flour 2 standard or 4 small loaf pans.

Sift together the flour, baking soda, baking powder, cinnamon, cloves, and salt.

Cream the butter and sugar together. Beat in the eggs, one at a time. Stir in the pumpkin. Beat in the flour mixture, one third at a time. Stir in the walnuts and raisins.

Ladle the batter into the prepared pans. Bake for 50 to 60 minutes for the large pans, 30 to 40 minutes for the small loaf pans. Turn the loaves out onto a wire rack and cool to room temperature. Wrap and refrigerate overnight before slicing. This bread may be refrigerated for 2 weeks or it may be frozen.

MAKES 2 STANDARD LOAVES OR 4 SMALL LOAVES

To cook fresh pumpkin: Cut off the top of the pumpkin and remove the seeds and discard. Cut the pumpkin into 5 or 6 large pieces and place them, skin side up, on a greased cookie sheet. Bake in a 350° F. oven until the pumpkin flesh is soft and can be easily removed from the skin. Purée the pumpkin and use as needed.

MAKES 1 LOAF

Banana Lemon Tea Bread

⅔ cup butter
1 cup granulated sugar
2 eggs
3 ripe bananas, mashed
6 tablespoons fresh lemon juice
2 cups sifted all-purpose flour
1 teaspoon baking soda
1 teaspoon salt
1 tablespoon grated lemon zest
confectioner's sugar

Preheat the oven to 350° F.

Cream the butter and sugar together until light and fluffy. Beat in the eggs, one at a time, beating well after each addition. Blend in the bananas and lemon juice.

Stir together the flour, baking soda, and salt and add to the banana mixture. Stir in the lemon zest and mix just until blended.

Pour the batter into a greased standard loaf pan and bake for 1 hour.

Remove the baked loaf from the pan and cool. Sift confectioner's sugar over the top when completely cooled.

MAKES 2 LOAVES

Maui Pineapple Bread

1 cup vegetable oil
3 eggs, beaten
2 cups granulated sugar
2 teaspoons vanilla extract
2 cups grated zucchini
1 cup drained crushed pineapple
2 teaspoons baking soda
3 cups all-purpose flour
¾ teaspoon salt
1½ teaspoons baking powder
1 teaspoon ground cinnamon
1 teaspoon ground allspice
1 cup golden raisins
1 cup chopped pecans

Preheat the oven to 350° F.

Combine the oil, eggs, sugar, and vanilla in a large bowl and blend well. Add the zucchini and pineapple.

Mix the dry ingredients and spices together and add them to the zucchini mixture. Add the raisins and pecans and mix well.

Pour the mixture into 2 greased and floured standard loaf pans. Bake for 1 hour, or until the bread tests done. Cool in pans for 30 minutes. Turn out on a rack to cool completely. Wrap in plastic wrap and refrigerate for at least 1 day before serving.

Cranberry Bread

MAKES 1 LOAF

When fresh cranberries are available, purchase several packages and store them in the freezer for up to 4 months.

1½ cups all-purpose flour
½ teaspoon salt
½ teaspoon cream of tartar
¼ teaspoon baking soda
½ cup chopped pecans
1 cup granulated sugar
2 strips (3 x 1 inches each) lemon zest
½ cup unsalted butter, softened
2 eggs
¾ teaspoon vanilla extract
6 tablespoons plain yogurt
1½ cups fresh cranberries, washed

Preheat the oven to 350° F.

Sift together the flour, salt, cream of tartar, and baking soda. Stir in the pecans and set aside.

Place the sugar and lemon zest in a food processor or a blender and process until the zest is finely grated. Add the butter and process until creamy. Add the eggs, one at a time, through the feed tube and mix well. Add the vanilla and yogurt and mix well. Transfer the butter-yogurt mixture to a large bowl.

Place the cranberries in a processor and pulse on and off 3 or 4 times until coarsely chopped.

Add the cranberries to the dry ingredients and combine well.

Stir the flour-cranberry mixture into the butter-yogurt mixture and mix well.

Place the batter in a greased and floured loaf pan and bake 50 to 60 minutes, or until a wooden pick inserted in the center comes out clean.

Cool on a rack for 30 minutes, then remove from the pan and finish cooling on the rack. Wrap well and refrigerate for 24 hours before serving. The bread freezes well.

Strawberry Bread

3 cups plus 3 tablespoons all-purpose flour
1 teaspoon baking soda
1 teaspoon salt
3 teaspoons ground cinnamon
2 cups granulated sugar
2 packages (10 ounces each) frozen strawberries, thawed
4 eggs, well beaten
1¼ cups vegetable oil
1¼ cups chopped pecans

Preheat the oven to 350° F.

Mix the dry ingredients together in a large bowl. Make a well in the center and add the strawberries and eggs. Then add the oil and pecans. Mix thoroughly.

Pour the batter into 2 greased and floured standard loaf pans. Bake for 1 hour, or until the bread tests done. Cool on rack.

Sun Valley Hobo Bread

2½ cups boiling water
1 box (15 ounces) raisins
4 teaspoons baking soda
2 teaspoons grated orange zest
¾ cup (packed) brown sugar
1 cup granulated sugar
¼ cup vegetable oil
4 cups rye flour
½ teaspoon salt

Most quick breads are best made at least 24 hours before serving, then wrapped, and refrigerated. This allows the flavors to mellow, and also makes for easier slicing.

Combine the water, raisins, baking soda, and zest and let stand, covered, overnight.

Preheat the oven to 350° F.

Combine the raisin mixture with the remaining ingredients in a large bowl and beat well.

Grease and flour three 1-pound coffee cans or standard loaf pans. Pour the batter into the pans and bake on the lowest oven shelf for 1 hour and 15 minutes, or until the bread tests done.

If the top of the bread is browning too quickly, cover with foil.

SERVES 9

Butter Pecan–Apple Coffee Cake

⅓ cup butter
1 cup chopped pecans
½ cup (packed) brown sugar
2 tablespoons light corn syrup
1 teaspoon ground cinnamon
1 apple, peeled, cored, and thinly sliced
1 package active dry yeast
¾ cup warm water (110° to 115° F.)
¼ cup granulated sugar
1 teaspoon salt
1 egg
¼ cup vegetable shortening
2¼ cups all-purpose flour

Melt the butter in a 9-inch square flameproof baking pan; stir in the pecans. Heat until the butter is brown and the pecans are toasted. Remove from the heat and cool, then stir in the brown sugar, corn syrup, and cinnamon. Spread evenly in the pan. Arrange the apple slices over the butter-nut mixture and set aside.

Dissolve the yeast in the warm water in a large mixing bowl. Add the sugar, salt, egg, shortening, and 1¼ cups of the flour. Beat for 2 minutes on medium speed, scraping the bowl frequently.

Stir in the remaining flour and continue stirring until smooth.

Drop the batter by spoonsful onto the mixture in the baking pan. Cover and let rise in a warm place until double, about 1 hour.

Preheat the oven to 375° F.

Bake the coffee cake for 30 to 35 minutes until golden brown. Remove the cake from the oven and immediately invert the pan onto a serving plate. Let the baking pan remain on the coffee cake a minute so that the topping will drizzle down onto the cake. Remove pan and serve warm.

US SKI TEAM Weather forecasters may want to note that the winter of the 1932 Olympics was the warmest in the 147-year history of New York State weather records. Lake Placid was on the winter map again in 1950 as the location of the Nordic world championships. But the weather jinx struck again and the races were moved to Rumford, Maine, on 56 hours notice. Undismayed, Lake Placid pressed on. And sure enough, there was no snow again for the 1980 Olympics.

SERVES 6 TO 8

Cranberry Kuchen

1 egg beaten
½ cup granulated sugar
½ cup milk
2 tablespoons vegetable oil
1 cup sifted all-purpose flour
2 teaspoons baking powder
½ teaspoon salt
2 cups fresh cranberries, washed

CRUMB TOPPING:
¾ cup all-purpose flour
½ cup granulated sugar
½ cup chopped nuts
3 tablespoons butter

Preheat the oven to 375° F.

Beat together the egg, sugar, milk, and vegetable oil.

Sift the dry ingredients together and add to the egg mixture. Mix well. Turn the batter into a greased and floured 8-inch square pan.

Put the cranberries through a food processor or finely chop. Sprinkle the cranberries over the batter. Mix all the topping ingredients together and sprinkle over the batter.

Bake for 25 to 30 minutes. Serve warm.

MAKES 24
CROISSANTS

Danish Croissants with Lemon-Cream Cheese Filling

1 stick butter, softened
1 cup small-curd cottage cheese
1 cup all-purpose flour
¼ pound cream cheese
¼ cup granulated sugar
1 tablespoon grated lemon zest
confectioner's sugar

In a large bowl of an electric mixer, beat together the butter and cottage cheese until blended. Beat in the flour until blended.

Shape the dough into a 6-inch circle and wrap in floured waxed paper. Refrigerate for 1 hour.

Preheat the oven to 350° F.

Beat together the cream cheese, sugar, and lemon zest until blended.

Divide the dough into thirds. Roll each third out on a floured pastry cloth until the circle measures about 9 inches. Spread one third of the lemon–cream cheese filling over each circle of dough and cut the circle into 8 triangular wedges, as though the dough were a pie. Repeat. Roll each triangle from the wide end toward the center and curve slightly into a crescent. Sprinkle with a generous shake of confectioner's sugar.

Place the croissants on a lightly greased cookie sheet and bake for about 25 minutes, or until they are golden brown. Remove to a rack or double thicknesses of paper toweling to cool. Can be made in a food processor.

Brown Sugar Coffee Cake

SERVES 6 TO 8

2 cups (lightly packed) brown sugar
2 cups all-purpose flour
½ cup butter, softened
1 egg
1 teaspoon freshly grated nutmeg
1 teaspoon baking soda
1 cup sour cream
½ teaspoon ground cinnamon
½ cup chopped nuts

OPTIONAL:
heavy cream, whipped

Preheat the oven to 350° F.

Thoroughly mix together the brown sugar, flour, and butter in a medium bowl. Spread half of this mixture in a lightly greased 9-inch square pan.

Add the egg and nutmeg to the remaining brown sugar mixture.

Mix the baking soda into the sour cream and add to the brown sugar-egg mixture, stirring well. Spread this batter over the first mixture in the pan.

Sprinkle the cinnamon and nuts over the batter and bake for 40 minutes.

Serve as a coffee cake, or top with whipped cream and serve as dessert.

MAKES 4 DOZEN ◼

To use this recipe for cinnamon rolls, substitute cinnamon sugar for the orange-sugar mixture.

Orange Refrigerator Rolls

2 packages active dry yeast
½ cup warm water (110° to 115° F.)
2 cups milk, scalded and cooled
⅓ cup vegetable shortening
1½ cups granulated sugar
2 teaspoons salt
3 eggs, beaten
6 to 6½ cups all-purpose flour
grated zest of 4 oranges
½ cup butter, melted

Proof the yeast in warm water until foamy. Stir to dissolve.

Combine the milk, shortening, ½ cup of the sugar, and salt in a large bowl and stir until the shortening is melted and the sugar is dissolved. Add the yeast mixture, eggs, and 3 cups of the flour. Beat until well mixed.

Add enough of the remaining flour to make a stiff dough and knead well. Place in a bowl and refrigerate, covered, overnight.

Combine the orange zest and remaining 1 cup sugar in a small bowl.

Preheat the oven to 400° F.

Pull off a piece of dough the size of a small egg. Dip the dough in melted butter, then in the orange-sugar mixture. Stretch and tie the dough into a knot. Place in a greased muffin tin. Repeat with as much of the remaining dough as you wish to use. Refrigerate the remaining dough for up to 4 days.

Bake for 12 to 15 minutes, or until lightly browned. Serve warm.

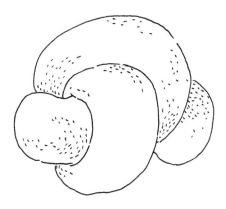

**MAKES 30
BISCUITS**

Southern Cream Biscuits

2½ cups all-purpose flour
2 tablespoons baking powder
1 teaspoon salt
½ cup butter, well chilled and cut into pieces
2 to 2¼ cups heavy cream

Preheat the oven to 425° F.

Sift the flour with the baking powder and salt into a large mixing bowl. Cut in the butter, using a pastry blender or 2 knives, until the mixture resembles coarse meal. Add 2 cups of the cream and blend to a soft dough, adding more cream if necessary.

Turn the dough out onto a lightly floured surface and roll to a thickness of ¾ inch. Cut into small squares or rounds. Bake on a lightly greased baking sheet until the biscuits are golden, about 15 minutes. Serve hot.

**MAKES 12
BISCUITS**

Sour Cream Biscuits

1 cup sour cream
2 tablespoons granulated sugar
1 tablespoon vegetable oil
1 egg, beaten
1½ cups all-purpose flour
½ teaspoon baking soda
2 teaspoons baking powder
½ teaspoon salt

Preheat the oven to 400° F.

Mix the sour cream, sugar, and oil together. Add the egg and mix well. Sift the dry ingredients together and mix into the sour cream mixture. Fill greased muffin tins three-fourths full and bake for 15 minutes. Serve hot.

US SKI TEAM During the 1976 Olympics at Innsbruck, Austria, U.S. Women's Ski Team member Cindy Nelson won the third-place bronze medal in the downhill—the only medal won by the U.S. women's team in 1976.

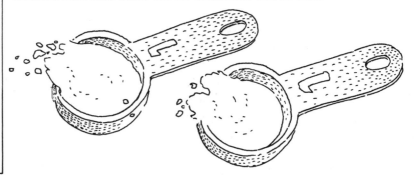

**MAKES 2 DOZEN
2-INCH BISCUITS**

Old Fashioned Buttermilk Biscuits

2 cups all-purpose flour
½ teaspoon salt
2 teaspoons baking powder
½ teaspoon baking soda
⅓ cup vegetable shortening
1 cup buttermilk
2 tablespoons butter, melted

Preheat the oven to 450° F.

Sift the flour, salt, baking powder, and baking soda into a medium bowl. Cut in the shortening. Add the buttermilk and stir just until moistened.

Turn the batter out onto a floured board and knead *very lightly*, just until the dough is smooth enough to pat or roll out ½ inch thick.

Cut out the biscuits with a biscuit cutter or small glass and dip the top of each biscuit in the melted butter. Turn the biscuits over and place on a large baking sheet.

Bake for 12 to 15 minutes. Serve hot.

MAKES 2 DOZEN

Gingerbread Muffins

1 cup granulated sugar
½ cup butter, softened
4 eggs
½ cup molasses
½ cup dark corn syrup
1 cup sour milk (1 cup milk plus 1 teaspoon vinegar; let
     stand 15 minutes)
1 cup sour cream
4 cups all-purpose flour
1 teaspoon baking soda
1 teaspoon ground ginger
1 teaspoon ground cinnamon
½ teaspoon ground allspice
pinch of salt
1 cup raisins
1 cup chopped nuts
cinnamon sugar

Preheat the oven to 425°. F.

Cream the sugar and butter together in a medium bowl. Beat in the eggs, one at a time. Blend in the molasses, corn syrup, sour milk, and sour cream.

In a large bowl, mix the dry ingredients together. Gradually blend the dry ingredients into the butter mixture, then stir in the raisins and nuts.

Spoon the batter into greased muffin tins, filling three-fourths full, and sprinkle with cinnamon sugar. Bake for 15 to 20 minutes. Batter keeps in refrigerator for 1 to 2 weeks.

MAKES 4 DOZEN LARGE MUFFINS OR 8 DOZEN SMALL MUFFINS

Six-Week Bran Muffins

2 cups Bran Buds cereal
2 cups boiling water
1 heaping cup vegetable shortening
2 cups granulated sugar
4 eggs
4 cups buttermilk
5 cups sifted all-purpose flour
5 teaspoons baking soda
1 teaspoon salt
4 cups All-Bran cereal

Preheat oven to 375° F.

Soak the Bran Buds in the boiling water in a medium bowl.

In a large bowl, cream the shortening with the sugar. Add the eggs, one at a time, beating well after each addition. Add the buttermilk and Bran Buds mixture and mix well.

Mix the flour, baking soda, and salt together and add to the Bran Buds mixture. Fold in the All-Bran and mix well.

At this point the mixture may be stored, covered, in the refrigerator for up to 6 weeks.

Fill greased muffin tins three-fourths full. Bake 10 minutes for small muffins, 15 minutes for large muffins, or until a wooden pick inserted in the center comes out clean.

**MAKES ABOUT
1½ DOZEN
MUFFINS**

Spice Muffins

1 cup butter or vegetable shortening
1 cup granulated sugar
3 eggs, separated
2½ cups sifted all-purpose flour
¼ teaspoon baking soda
3 teaspoons unsweetened cocoa powder
1 teaspoon ground ginger
1 teaspoon ground cinnamon
¼ teaspoon salt
1 cup water
1 cup chopped pecans
1 cup golden raisins, lightly floured

Preheat the oven to 400° F.

Cream the butter and sugar together. Add the egg yolks, one at a time, then beat the mixture until light.

Mix the flour, baking soda, and spices together. Add to the butter mixture alternately with the water. Beat the egg whites until stiff and fold in. Fold in the pecans and raisins.

Fill greased muffin tins three-fourths full with the batter and bake for approximately 20 minutes. Serve warm.

This batter may be stored in glass fruit jars for as long as a week. When using, do not stir batter.

U S
SKI TEAM The first officially supplied crash helmets for the U.S. team appeared in 1952. Gretchen Fraser, then women's manager, joined forces with Al Lindley of the 1936 team and persuaded the Dobbs Hat Company to provide the skiers with the plastic liner that went with the hard hats that horseback riders use. These were brimless affairs with considerable extra room in the top—the skiers were afraid that if they fell while wearing them, the helmet would be jammed down and cut off their ears.

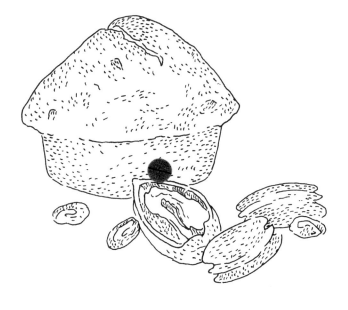

SERVES 10 TO 12

Rio Grande Corn Bread

1½ cups yellow cornmeal
1 cup milk
¾ teaspoon salt
½ cup bacon drippings
½ teaspoon baking soda
2 cups cream-style corn
½ pound grated mozzarella cheese
1 large onion, finely chopped
4 canned jalapeño peppers, chopped or 1 can (4 ounces)
    green chilies, diced, if milder flavor is desired.

Preheat the oven to 350° F.

Mix the first 6 ingredients together in a medium bowl.

Grease a 9-inch square baking pan. Pour half of the batter into the pan and sprinkle with the cheese, onion, and peppers. Top with the remaining batter.

Bake for 50 minutes. Serve warm.

MAKES 2 LOAVES

Boston Brown Bread

2 cups unsifted all-purpose flour
2 cups yellow cornmeal
2 teaspoons baking soda
1 teaspoon salt
1½ cups milk
1⅓ cups buttermilk
¾ cup dark molasses
¾ cup raisins

Grease two 1-pound coffee cans and set aside.

Sift together the flour, cornmeal, baking soda, and salt into a large bowl and set aside.

In another large bowl, mix together the milk, buttermilk, molasses, and raisins. Gradually add the sifted dry ingredients to the milk mixture and mix well with a spoon.

Turn the batter into the prepared coffee cans, filling each can two-thirds full.

Cover the cans tightly with aluminum foil. Place the cans in a large kettle with boiling water halfway up the sides of the cans. Steam for 2½ to 3 hours, adding water as necessary. Cool in cans and then turn upside down to unmold.

**MAKES 5
DOZEN RUSKS**

Royal Rusks

1 cup granulated sugar
1 cup butter, softened
2 eggs, beaten
1 cup sour cream
1 teaspoon almond extract
1 teaspoon baking soda
5½ to 6 cups all-purpose flour
dash of salt
1 cup chopped almonds

Preheat the oven to 375° F.

Cream the sugar and butter in a large bowl until light and fluffy. Add the eggs, sour cream, almond extract, baking soda, 3 cups of the flour, and the salt and beat until smooth. Add the almonds and enough of the remaining flour to make a stiff dough.

Divide the dough into 2 portions. Shape each portion into a long roll. Slightly flatten the tops with the palm of your hand.

Place the rolls on lightly greased baking sheets and bake for 20 to 25 minutes, or until browned. Cool.

When the rolls are cool, cut into ½ to ¾-inch slices. Place the slices on baking sheets and dry in a 225° to 250° F. oven for 2 hours, depending on the thickness of the slices. Cool.

**MAKES 6
POPOVERS**

Spectacular Popovers

1 cup Wondra flour (or any quick-mixing flour)
3 eggs, beaten
½ teaspoon salt
1 cup cold milk

Preheat the oven to 475° F. Grease 6 deep custard cups.

Combine all the ingredients in a medium mixing bowl and stir with a fork just until smooth. Do not overbeat.

Fill the custard cups half full. Bake for 20 minutes, then reduce the oven temperature to 375° F. and bake for 5 to 10 minutes longer, or until the popovers are a deep golden brown. Immediately remove from the cups and serve hot, with butter and jam. This recipe is for high altitudes. At lower altitudes, use 2 eggs and start the oven at 450° F. and then reduce it to 350° F.

SERVES 6 TO 8

Mississippi Spoon Bread

2 cups milk
½ cup white cornmeal
1 teaspoon granulated sugar
½ teaspoon baking powder
1 teaspoon salt
3 eggs, separated
4 tablespoons butter, melted

Preheat the oven to 350° F.

Scald the milk in a large saucepan. Gradually add the cornmeal, stirring vigorously. Cook over low heat until the mixture is the consistency of mush. Cool. Add the sugar, baking powder, salt, egg yolks, and butter.

Beat the egg whites in a small bowl until stiff. Fold the egg whites into the cornmeal mixture.

Pour the batter into a greased 2-quart casserole. Bake for 35 to 40 minutes. Serve immediately. This has the consistency of a soufflé and should be eaten with a fork.

MAKES 2 LOAVES

Beer Bread

3 cups self-rising flour
3 tablespoons granulated sugar
1 bottle (12 ounces) beer

Preheat the oven to 350° F.

Combine all the ingredients in a medium bowl and mix well. Turn the batter into 2 lightly greased standard loaf pans. Bake for about 1 hour. Turn out on a rack to cool. This bread is especially good toasted.

US SKI TEAM When Don Fraser went to the 1936 Olympics, he made the trip from Seattle to Europe on a Norwegian fruit boat, chipping rust and painting at a dollar a day to pay for the passage. It took 30 days to get there.

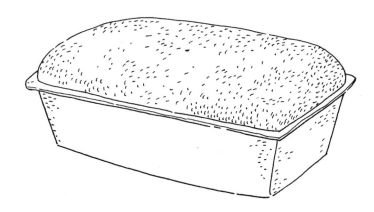

**MAKES 12
TORTILLAS**

Flour Tortillas

3 cups all-purpose flour
½ teaspoon salt
1½ teapoons baking powder
1 tablespoon vegetable shortening
1¼ cups very warm water

Blend the dry ingredients with the shortening using a pastry blender. Stir in 1 cup of the water. Add enough of the remaining ¼ cup water to moisten all the flour.

Knead the dough on a lightly floured board until smooth. Divide into 12 portions, roll into balls, and let rest for 15 minutes, covered.

Roll out and cook, one at a time, on a *hot*, ungreased cast-iron griddle until each tortilla bubbles up on the top side, about 1 minute. Turn the tortilla and cook 1 minute longer.

Place the finished tortillas in a plastic bag so the steam they create will keep them soft and pliable until used.

SERVES 10 TO 12

Pita Toasts

¾ cup butter, softened
2 tablespoons minced fresh parsley
1 tablespoon snipped chives
1 tablespoon lemon juice
1 clove garlic, crushed
¼ teaspoon salt
dash of freshly ground black pepper
6 pita loaves

Cream the butter. Beat in parsley, chives, lemon juice, garlic, salt, and pepper. Let stand at room temperature, covered, for at least 1 hour.

Preheat the oven to 450° F.

Halve the pita horizontally. Cut each half into 2 pieces and spread the inside part of each piece with the butter mixture.

Arrange the bread on a baking sheet in one layer. Bake for 3 to 5 minutes, or until lightly browned and crisp. Serve instead of garlic bread as a snack.

Make–Ahead
Favorites

Mount Rainier Apple Cake

SECTION CHAIRMEN
Mimi Nelson
Nancy Wiedel

TESTERS
Mary Bellamy
Judy Brubaker
Diane Choate
Jan Clymer
Donna Copeland
Beverly Fry
Bonnie Gray
Patty Liston
Joan Mackey
Maidie Mestek
Ginny O'Toole
Carol Reeves
Ida Seaberg
Joan Strande
Julie Turner
Geneva Vance

Vermont Pasties

SERVES 12

When rolling pastry, keep it as cold as possible. A marble slab or laminated kitchen countertop are preferred to a cloth or board. Heat causes the shortening to break down and therefore decreases flakiness.

3½ cups all-purpose flour
pinch of salt
1 cup vegetable shortening
about ¾ cup ice water
5 cups Beef Stock (see page 56)
1 teaspoon dried basil
2 teaspoons dried thyme
1 teaspoon dried dill weed
1 teaspoon dried rosemary
1 clove garlic, minced
¾ cup peeled, diced carrot
½ cup peeled, diced rutabaga
⅓ cup peeled, diced potato
⅓ cup peeled, diced parsnip
1 cup diced onion
¾ cup diced lean veal
¾ cup diced lean pork
salt and freshly ground black pepper to taste
1 egg, beaten

In a large bowl, combine the flour and salt and blend in the shortening thoroughly. The mixture should be crumbly. Slowly incorporate the ice water, mixing with a fork, using just enough water so the pastry sticks together. Gather the dough into a ball, wrap, and refrigerate for at least 30 minutes.

Pour the stock into a large pot. Add the herbs and garlic. Bring to a boil and boil for about 5 minutes. Add the vegetables and reduce the heat. Cover the pot and cook for about 4 to 5 minutes, or until the vegetables are just tender. Drain the vegetables and combine with the meat. Season the mixture to taste with salt and pepper.

On a floured board, roll out the dough ¼ inch thick. Cut into twelve 5-inch rounds.

Preheat the oven to 400° F. Line a large baking sheet with parchment paper or buttered waxed paper.

Place a portion of the vegetable-meat mixture on one half of each round. Brush the edges with water and fold the other half over the filling. Seal the edges by crimping them with a fork. Place on the prepared baking sheet. Repeat until all the rounds are filled. Prick the top of each pastie 2 or 3 times with a fork. Brush the top of each pastie with the beaten egg.

Bake the pasties for 15 minutes, then reduce the heat to 350° F. and bake for 30 minutes more, or until golden brown. Serve hot or at room temperature.

SERVES 10 TO 12

Fresh tomatoes for sandwiches should be sliced, seeded, and drained on paper toweling before using to avoid soggy bread.

Rib-Eye Sandwiches

½ cup coarsely cracked pepper
½ teaspoon crushed cardamom
1 rib-eye or eye of round steak (5 to 6 pounds)
1 tablespoon tomato paste
½ teaspoon garlic powder
1 teaspoon paprika
1 cup soy sauce
¾ cup vinegar

Mix the pepper and cardamom together and press into the meat. Place the meat in a shallow dish.

Make a paste of the tomato paste, garlic powder, and paprika. Add the soy sauce and vinegar and blend well. Pour the marinade over the meat and marinate for 2 to 3 days, refrigerated, turning occasionally.

Preheat the oven to 300° F.

Remove the meat from the marinade and drain. Wrap the meat in foil and roast in a shallow pan for 2 hours. Serve thinly sliced in small French rolls.

SERVES 8

Sandwich in the Round

1½ pounds round French bread
¼ cup olive oil
2 cloves garlic, minced
3 large tomatoes, sliced
½ pound assorted sliced luncheon meat
3 ounces sliced pepperoni or salami
¼ pound assorted sliced cheeses
6 ounces marinated artichoke hearts, drained
2¼ ounces sliced ripe olives, drained
2 to 3 large dill pickles, sliced lengthwise
1 mild red or white onion, sliced

OPTIONAL:
mayonnaise
2 ounces anchovy fillets, drained

Cut the bread in half horizontally. Hollow out the soft bread from the top and bottom halves, leaving a shell about ½ to ¾ inch thick (reserve soft bread for another use).

In a small bowl, combine the olive oil with the garlic. Brush the cut surfaces of the bread shells with the oil. Spread the shells with mayonnaise, if desired.

To assemble: layer one third of the tomato slices on the bottom bread crust, then top with alternate layers of meats, pepperoni, cheeses, half of the remaining tomatoes, artichoke hearts, olives, pickles, onion, and anchovies, if desired. Top with the remaining tomatoes and place the top crust on the filling, pressing down firmly. Seal the sandwich tightly in plastic wrap and foil. If made ahead, refrigerate. Just before serving, place the wrapped sandwich on a flat surface and press down firmly on top to flatten it. Unwrap and cut into wedges.

MAKES 2½ TO 3 DOZEN

Piroshki

1 cup butter, at room temperature
½ pound cream cheese, at room temperature
2 cups all-purpose flour
1 scant teaspoon baking powder
1 pound ground beef round
2 medium onions, chopped
1 clove garlic, minced
1½ tablespoons chopped fresh dill or 2 teaspoons dried
salt and freshly ground black pepper to taste
3 hard-cooked eggs, chopped

In a large bowl, beat together the butter and cream cheese until smooth. Add the flour and baking powder and blend until smooth. Form into 2 balls and wrap in plastic wrap. Refrigerate overnight. Remove 20 minutes before using.

Preheat the oven to 375° F.

Sauté the ground round, onions, and garlic in a skillet over medium heat until the meat is browned and the onion is limp, about 8 to 10 minutes. Drain well. Stir in the dill, salt, pepper, and egg and mix well.

Roll out the prepared dough on a floured board and cut into 3 to 4-inch circles. Place 1½ teaspoons filling in the center of each circle and fold the dough in half to form an oval shape. Brush the edges with water and seal.

Place the piroshki on baking sheets and bake for 15 to 20 minutes, or until golden brown. Serve hot or at room temperature. Wrap in newspaper to transport; foil will hold in heat but cause the pastry to get soggy.

Ever faithful to its editorial responsibilities. *The New York Times* carried advisory notes for people planning to attend the 1936 Olympics. For instance: "Slalom is downhill work on the long wooden runners. Poles are allowed as accessories or accelerators. The winner is the fellow who has the best score when the times and the downhill touring style is taken into account."

MAKES 15

Sausage-Stuffed Whole-Wheat Buns

Honey can often be substituted for sugar in baking (though not in most cake recipes). It gives a heavier but moister texture. It may, however, cause excessive browning. For 1¼ cups sugar, use 1 cup honey and decrease liquid by ¼ cup.

DOUGH:
1 package active dry yeast
1¼ cups water (110° to 115° F.)
2 tablespoons honey
2 tablespoons butter
1¼ cups whole-wheat flour
1¾ cups all-purpose flour

FILLING:
1 pound bulk hot Italian sausage
½ cup minced green onion
1½ pounds fresh spinach or 1 package (10 ounces) frozen chopped spinach, thawed
1 cup ricotta cheese
2 eggs, beaten
Worcestershire sauce to taste

Combine the yeast, water, and honey in a large bowl, and let proof for 5 minutes. Add the butter and half the flours and beat with a heavy-duty electric mixer or in a food processor. Add the remaining flour and beat until smooth, or knead in by hand. Place in a greased bowl and let rise until doubled, about 45 mintues.

Sauté the sausage and green onion in a large skillet until the sausage is browned and the onion is soft. Drain off grease. Stir in the spinach. Mix in the ricotta, 1 egg, and Worchestershire sauce and blend well. Reserve.

Preheat the oven to 375° F.

Punch down the dough. Roll out on a floured board to ¼ inch thick. Cut into 4-inch circles.

Place ⅓ cup filling in the center of each circle, bring the edges up to the center, and pinch together.

Place the buns on a lightly greased baking sheet and brush with the remaining egg. Bake for about 40 minutes, or until golden brown. Serve hot or at room temperature.

SERVES 6

Curried Shrimp and Rice in Pita

1½ cups cooked long-grain rice
1½ to 2 pounds medium shrimp, cooked, peeled, deveined, and chopped
2 tart green apples, peeled and diced
1 medium avocado, peeled and diced
½ cup salted cashews, chopped
⅓ cup chopped green onion
1 to 2 teaspoons curry powder
1 to 1½ cups mayonnaise
⅔ cup sour cream
salt and freshly ground black pepper to taste
pita bread
shredded lettuce

GARNISH:
¾ cup tomato, pear, or mango chutney

Combine the rice, shrimp, apple, avocado, cashews, and green onion in a large mixing bowl.

In another bowl, mix together the curry powder and mayonnaise and blend well. Add the sour cream and season to taste with salt and pepper.

Pour half of the curry sauce over the shrimp-rice mixture and fold until well moistened. Use more of the sauce as needed. Chill the filling for 3 to 4 hours.

Serve in pita bread with shredded lettuce and garnished with chutney.

There have been at least 20 family groups on the U.S. Alpine Ski Team. Ann and Brooks Dodge, Terry and Tyler Palmer, Chuck and Barbara Ferries, Susie and Pete Patterson, Cathy and Judy Nagle, Debbie and Holly Flanders, Dennis and Penny McCoy, Rick and Suzy Chaffee, Bill and Max Marolt, Eric and Sandra Paulsen, Wendy and Cathy Allen, Bill and Jim Barrier, Ken and Susie Corrock, John and Gere Teague, Katie and Robin Morning, and Richie and Julie Woodworth are among the pairs.

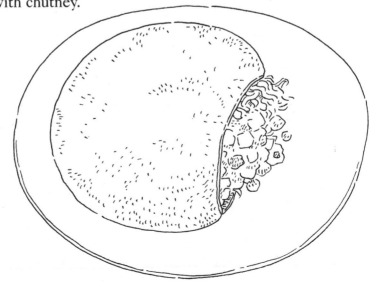

MAKES 8 5-INCH CALZONES

Italian Sausage Calzones

FILLING:
2 tablespoons olive oil
½ cup chopped onion
1 clove garlic, minced
1 pound bulk Italian sausage
1 can (15 ounces) tomato purée
pinch of dried oregano
pinch of dried basil
salt and freshly ground black pepper to taste
1 cup shredded mozzarella cheese

CALZONE DOUGH:
1 package active dry yeast
½ teaspoon sugar
1¼ cups water (110° to 115° F.)
¼ cup light olive oil
1½ teaspoons coarse salt
3 to 3¼ cups all-purpose flour

Heat the olive oil in a large skillet and sauté the onion and garlic. Add the sausage and cook, breaking up the meat, for 10 minutes. Drain. Add the tomato purée, oregano, basil, salt and pepper and simmer for 10 minutes. Cool and reserve the filling.

In a large bowl, dissolve the yeast and sugar in the water. Let stand until the mixture is foamy, about 5 minutes. Stir in the olive oil and salt. Add the flour gradually, stirring constantly, until the mixture cleans the sides of the bowl.

Turn the dough out onto a lightly floured board. Knead the dough, adding flour as necessary to prevent sticking, until smooth and elastic, about 10 minutes.

Wash and dry the bowl, then oil the bowl lightly.

Place the dough in the bowl. Let the dough rise, covered, in a warm place until doubled in bulk, about 1½ hours.

Preheat the oven to 425° F.

Punch the dough down. Divide the dough into 8 equal portions. On a lightly floured surface, roll out each portion into a 5-inch circle.

Mound the filling on one side of each circle, dividing filling evenly among the circles. Sprinkle the cheese over the filling. Fold each dough circle in half to enclose the filling, forming a half-moon shape. Pinch the edges to seal and crimp.

Arrange the calzones 2 inches apart on a lightly oiled baking sheet. Let stand, covered, for 15 minutes.

Bake for 20 minutes, or until golden brown and puffed.

SERVES 10 TO 12

Marinated Vegetables

1¼ to 1½ cups vegetable oil
½ cup red wine vinegar
3 tablespoons tarragon vinegar
3 tablespoons finely minced onion
1 teaspoon granulated sugar
1 teaspoon dry mustard
1½ teaspoons salt
½ teaspoon freshly ground black pepper
½ to 1 teaspoon dried basil
24 whole cherry tomatoes
1½ pounds fresh mushrooms, sliced
1 large green bell pepper, seeded and thinly sliced
1 head cauliflower, cut into bite-sized pieces
1 head broccoli, cut into bite-sized pieces
3 stalks celery, diagonally sliced
1 zucchini or yellow squash, unpeeled and sliced

Combine the oil, vinegars, onion, sugar, and seasonings in a small bowl. Mix well with a whisk.

Combine all the vegetables in a large bowl. Then pour the dressing over. Marinate, refrigerated, in the dressing for at least 5 hours.

SERVES 6

Mediterranean Rice Salad

For a super-fast vegetable salad, add a natural prepared salad dressing to cut-up vegetables. Adjust seasoning with herbs, sugar or lemon juice, and salt and pepper.

4 cups cooked rice
1 cup cooked peas
1 cup chopped celery
½ cup grated carrot
¼ cup chopped green bell pepper
¼ cup sliced radish
¼ cup chopped green onion
¼ cup pimiento-stuffed green olives
⅔ cup Green Onion-Lemon Vinaigrette (see page 107)
1½ cups cooked ham, cut into julienne

Combine the rice with the vegetables and olives and toss with the vinaigrette. Chill well. Just before serving, add the ham and toss again.

SERVES 8 TO 10 ■

Antipasto Salad

1 tablespoon salt
1 tablespoon vegetable oil
8 ounces corkscrew or curly pasta
½ cup olive or vegetable oil
¼ cup lemon juice
1 teaspoon salt
¼ teaspoon freshly ground black pepper
⅛ teaspoon crushed red pepper
1 clove garlic, crushed
1 tablespoon snipped fresh basil or 1 teaspoon dried
1 small green bell pepper, seeded and sliced into strips
1 small red bell pepper, seeded and sliced into strips, or 1 jar (4 ounces) whole pimientos, drained and sliced into strips
4 to 6 medium mushrooms, washed and sliced
4 ounces provolone cheese, cubed
1 can (1 pound) garbanzo beans, drained
4 ounces salami, sliced (and slices cut into quarters)
¼ cup small ripe pitted olives
2 tablespoons chopped fresh parsley

Bring 3 quarts water, the salt, and 1 tablespoon vegetable oil to a rapid boil in a large kettle. Add the pasta and bring back to a boil. Cook, uncovered, stirring occasionally with a long fork to prevent sticking, just until tender, about 7 to 8 minutes. Do not overcook. Drain well; do not rinse.

Combine the ½ cup oil, lemon juice, salt, black and red peppers, garlic, and basil in a small bowl. Whisk together until the dressing is well blended, about 1 minute. Or combine all the dressing ingredients in a small screw-top jar and shake well.

Place the cooked pasta in a large bowl. Add the dressing and toss to combine. Cool, unrefrigerated, to room temperature.

To the pasta mixture, add the green and red pepper, mushrooms, cheese, garbanzo beans, salami, olives, and parsley; toss lightly to combine. Place the salad in a serving bowl and refrigerate, covered, for at least 1 hour. At serving time, retoss the salad.

US SKI TEAM Team skier Pinky Robinson lost his pants during the Harriman Cup downhill, a designated tryout race for the 1952 Olympic team. He pulled them up, lost them again, and pulled them up again before the end of the race. Pinky was generally considered a slalom specialist, but he placed seventh in this downhill before winning the slalom. Specialists among the coaching ranks suggested that this unusually good downhill showing was due to the lower than usual position that Pinky adopted to avoid further embarrassment.

Tabouli

1 cup cracked wheat (bulgur)
2 cups boiling water
1 cup minced fresh parsley
½ cup chopped green onion with tops
¼ cup chopped fresh mint
¾ cup olive oil
½ cup lemon juice
3 large tomatoes, seeded and diced
2 teaspoons salt
freshly ground black pepper to taste

Soak the cracked wheat in the boiling water for 30 to 45 minutes. Drain the cracked wheat, then squeeze dry in a kitchen towel.

Put the cracked wheat in a large bowl and add the parsley, green onion, mint, oil, and lemon juice. Mix well. Refrigerate for 4 hours or overnight.

Mix the salad to reblend the dressing. Add the tomatoes and season to taste with salt and pepper.

MAKES 1 CUP

Spread this pâté on a bagel or hard roll, freeze, and send it to work the next day for an elegant brown bag lunch.

Quick Picnic Pâté

1 to 1¼ cups cooked meat (leftover beef, pork, turkey, or chicken)
4 ounces unsalted butter, softened
juice of 2 lemons (6 tablespoons)
½ to 1 red onion, finely minced
2 teaspoons drained capers
1 can (2 ounces) anchovy fillets, drained
1 teaspoon Worcestershire sauce
1 teaspoon dried thyme or basil
freshly ground black pepper to taste

OPTIONAL:
olives
other herbs
sautéed mushrooms

Put the meat into a food processor and grind (or put through a meat grinder using finest blade 2 times). Add the remaining ingredients and process until mixture is the consistency desired.

Pack into a small crock and refrigerate, covered, at least 2 hours or until ready to serve.

Serve with crackers and/or sliced French bread, Dijon mustard, and cornichons.

SERVES 6 TO 8

Crustless Corn and Chili Quiche

1½ cups corn kernels, cut off the cob
1 cup heavy cream
5 medium eggs, beaten
1 cup grated Monterey Jack cheese
1 or 2 cans (4 ounces each) chopped green chilies
salt and freshly ground black pepper to taste

GARNISH:
sour cream
chopped green onion
chopped tomato

Preheat the oven to 350° F.
Butter a 2-quart quiche pan or shallow casserole dish.

Combine the corn, cream, eggs, cheese, chilies, and salt and pepper in a bowl. Pour the mixture into the prepared pan.

Cover the quiche with a round of buttered waxed paper and set into a large pan containing ½ inch of hot water.

Bake until set, about 45 to 50 minutes.

At serving time, garnish the quiche with sour cream, green onion, and tomato and cut into wedges. Good served warm or at room temperature.

SERVES 8

Picnic Spinach Torte

½ to 1 pound bulk pork sausage
2 medium onions, chopped
1 to 2 slices French bread
¼ cup milk
1½ pounds fresh spinach
1 cup freshly grated Parmesan cheese
3 eggs, beaten
1 teaspoon salt
½ teaspoon freshly ground black pepper
½ teaspoon ground sage
½ teaspoon freshly grated nutmeg

Preheat the oven to 350° F.

Crumble the pork sausage into a skillet over medium-high heat. Cook, stirring, until the pink color is gone. Add the onions and cook, stirring, until the onions are golden and the pork is browned, about 10 minutes. Set aside to cool.

Force the meat-onion mixture through the medium blade of a food mill or mince in a food processor. Place the meat mixture in a large bowl and set aside.

Tear the bread into pieces and process in a food processor or blender to make ⅓ cup of crumbs. Add the crumbs and milk to the meat.

Wash the spinach and remove the stems. Steam the spinach, covered, with just the water that clings to the leaves, until limp, about 3 minutes. Drain well and chop.

Add the spinach to the meat mixture. Stir in the cheese, eggs, salt, pepper, sage, and nutmeg.

Spoon the mixture into a buttered 9-inch springform pan or a buttered 5 x 9-inch loaf pan. Bake, uncovered, for 50 minutes, or until set. Cool, cover, and chill.

Bring to room temperature before serving in wedges or slices with a variety of mustards and crusty bread.

US SKI TEAM Five World Cup slaloms have been won by the narrowest possible margin—0:00.01 second. American women won two of them: Kiki Cutter held that edge over Ingrid Lafforgue in 1969, and Abbi Fisher did it against Perrine Pelen in 1978. Oddly enough, Perrine was in three of the five races, twice as winner.

SERVES 6 TO 8

Bermuda Tart

3 large red Bermuda onions, sliced
4 tablespoons butter
1 cup sour cream
6 tablespoons dry sherry
3 eggs, lightly beaten
salt and freshly ground black pepper to taste
¼ teaspoon hot pepper sauce
⅛ teaspoon freshly grated nutmeg
⅛ teaspoon dried thyme
⅛ teaspoon ground cloves
1 unbaked 9-inch pie shell
5 slices lean bacon, cut into squares and blanched in boiling
    water for 3 minutes

Preheat the oven to 375° F.

In a sauté pan, sauté the onions in butter over low heat for 15 minutes, or until very soft and golden.

Mix the sour cream, sherry, eggs, and seasonings in a bowl.

Arrange the sautéed onions in the unbaked pie shell, pour the sour cream mixture over, and top with blanched bacon squares.

Bake for 40 minutes, or until set. Serve hot or at room temperature.

SERVES 6 TO 8

Barbecued Teriyaki Chicken

1 recipe Marinade II (see page 113)
1½ to 2 cups canned crushed pineapple, undrained
18 chicken legs, thighs, or breast halves

Preheat the oven to 400° F.

Combine the marinade and pineapple in 2 shallow glass casseroles. Place the chicken pieces in the dishes. Bake for 40 minutes.

Remove the casseroles from the oven, turn the chicken pieces over, and refrigerate, covered, for 4 hours or overnight.

Remove the chicken from the refrigerator. Heat a charcoal grill.

Cook the chicken over medium-hot coals for 6 to 7 minutes per side, brushing frequently with the marinade. Excellent served cold.

Sesame Chicken Breasts

SERVES 4 TO 6 ●

For a picnic with panache, serve Filled Snow Peas (page 28), Iced Papaya Soup (page 44), Sesame Chicken Breasts, Artichoke-Rice Salad (page 100), Faux French Bread (page 227), and Tarte Tatin (page 270).

1 egg
1 tablespoon milk
½ cup bread crumbs
½ cup sesame seeds
1 tablespoon finely chopped fresh parsley
1 teaspoon salt
½ teaspoon freshly ground black pepper
3 whole chicken breasts, skinned and halved
lemon juice
2 tablespoons vegetable oil
2 tablespoons butter

GARNISH:
lemon wedges

Beat the egg and milk together in a small bowl.

In a plastic bag, combine the bread crumbs, sesame seeds, parsley, salt, and pepper.

Sprinkle the chicken breasts with lemon juice. Dip each breast into the beaten egg, then shake in the crumb mixture to coat. Place the breaded breasts on a plate and refrigerate for 10 to 15 minutes.

In a large skillet, heat the oil and butter over medium-high heat. Brown the breasts for 1 or 2 minutes on each side. Continue to cook for 4 to 5 minutes on each side. Remove the breasts to a heated platter and garnish with lemon wedges.

SERVES 10

Filet of Beef Stuffed with Spinach

1 beef tenderloin (5 pounds)
1 cup butter, softened
2 cloves garlic, minced
1 pound fresh spinach, cooked and drained
3 eggs, beaten
1 cup fresh bread crumbs
1 pound bacon slices, cut in half

Preheat the oven to 400° F.

Trim the fat from the tenderloin. Make a lengthwise cut down the center of the meat, cutting to within ½ inch of the other side. Pound with a meat mallet to flatten to a rough rectangle.

Combine the butter and garlic in a bowl. Spread over the meat. In bowl, combine the spinach, eggs, and bread crumbs and mix well. Spoon onto the butter mixture on the meat. Roll the meat up from the long side and fasten with picks or tie with string. Place the bacon slices over the meat.

Place the meat on a rack in a shallow roasting pan, tucking ends of bacon underneath. Roast 50 minutes for rare. Serve hot or at cool room temperature.

MAKES 48

Pineapple Cookies

These cookies freeze well and are even better after being frozen.

½ cup butter
½ cup granulated sugar
½ cup (packed) brown sugar
1 egg, beaten
1 cup crushed pineapple, drained
½ cup chopped pecans
2 cups all-purpose flour
½ teaspoon baking soda
¼ teaspoon salt
1 teaspoon baking powder

Preheat the oven to 375° F.

Cream the butter and sugars. Add the egg, pineapple, and nuts. Combine the dry ingredients, then add to the pineapple mixture and mix well.

Drop the dough by rounded teaspoonsful onto a greased cookie sheet and bake for 10 to 12 minutes.

SERVES 8 TO 10

Poppy Seed Pound Cake

1 cup butter
3 cups granulated sugar
6 eggs
3 cups all-purpose flour
1 cup heavy cream
¼ cup poppy seeds
1 tablespoon vanilla extract

With an electric mixer, cream the butter and sugar in a large bowl. Add 1 egg at a time, beating well after each addition. Beat thoroughly after adding all the eggs, about 3 minutes more. Gently fold in the flour alternately with the cream. Add the poppy seeds and vanilla.

Pour into a large greased and floured tube pan or Bundt pan. Place in a cold oven. Turn the heat to 325° F. Bake for 1¼ to 1½ hours, or until the cake tests done. Cool.

Serve plain, toasted, or with custard sauce.

MAKES 32

Chocolate Nut Chewies

⅔ cup butter, softened
1 pound brown sugar
3 eggs
1 teaspoon vanilla extract
2 cups all-purpose flour (add 2 tablespoons in high altitude)
1 teaspoon baking powder
½ teaspoon salt
1 cup chopped pecans
1 package (6 ounces) chocolate chips (about 1 cup)

Preheat the oven to 350° F.

Cream the butter and brown sugar together until light and fluffy. Add the eggs, one at a time, and beat until well blended. Add the vanilla.

Add the flour, baking powder, and salt. Beat well. Fold in the nuts and chocolate chips.

Place in a greased and floured 9x13-inch baking pan. Bake for 30 to 35 minutes. When cool, cut into squares.

US SKI TEAM At the 1948 Olympics, Gretchen Fraser was starting number 1 in the second heat of the slalom. Just before "go," the timing communications failed and she stood in the start gate, for 18 minutes without moving a muscle. When the wiring was restored, she pushed off and won the gold medal.

SERVES 8

Mount Rainier Apple Cake

4 tablespoons butter
1 cup granulated sugar
1 egg, beaten
3 apples (Golden Delicious preferred), peeled and chopped
1 cup all-purpose flour
1 teaspoon baking soda
½ teaspoon ground cinnamon
¼ teaspoon ground cloves
¼ teaspoon freshly grated nutmeg
¼ teaspoon salt
½ cup chopped walnuts

FROSTING:
2 tablespoons butter, softened
1 cup confectioner's sugar
½ teaspoon vanilla extract
1 to 2 tablespoons apple juice

Preheat the oven to 350° F.

Cream the butter and sugar. Add the egg and beat well. Add the remaining ingredients and mix until blended.

Pour the batter into a greased and floured 8-inch square pan and bake for 45 minutes, or until the cake tests done.

Meanwhile, make the frosting. In a small bowl, beat together the butter, sugar, and vanilla and enough apple juice to produce a spreading consistency.

Frost the cake while still warm.

Desserts

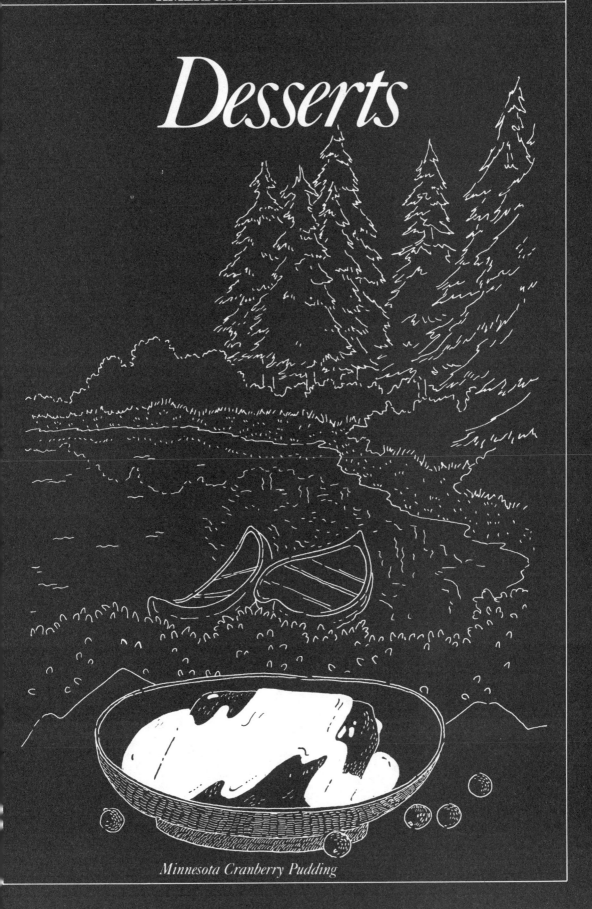

Minnesota Cranberry Pudding

SECTION CHAIRMAN
Mary Bell

TESTERS
Jeanine Armstrong
Mary Benson
Linda Branish
Jane Davis
Sally Gart
Peggy Gutrich
Bev Howell
Mary Krugman
Mary Melland
Eileen Meurer
Mary Otten
Jeanne Ross
Lyn Schmausser
Rosemary Thomas
Ali Zinn

SERVES 10

Filled pastry shells do not freeze well because the pastry can absorb the liquids and become soggy. Empty pastry shells, however, do freeze well.

Fresh Peach Tart

French Pastry (recipe follows)
¾ cup ground, blanched almonds
4 to 5 fresh peaches, peeled and sliced into twelfths
½ cup granulated sugar
1 tablespoon fresh lemon juice
½ cup Apricot Glaze (recipe follows)

Preheat the oven to 400° F.

Prepare the pastry and roll out to a 13 to 14-inch circle between sheets of waxed paper.

Line a 10 to 11-inch ceramic quiche dish with the pastry. Crimp edges with a fork. Sprinkle the pastry with the almonds and press gently but firmly into the pastry. Refrigerate while preparing the filling. At this point, the pastry may be wrapped in plastic and chilled as long as overnight.

In a large bowl, mix the peaches gently with the sugar and lemon juice, using a rubber spatula.

Arrange the peaches in the pastry in overlapping, concentric circles, beginning at the outside and working toward the center.

Place the tart on the lowest shelf of the oven. Bake for 15 minutes. Reduce the heat to 375° F. and bake for 25 minutes longer.

Remove from the oven and brush with the apricot glaze while still hot. This tart is best served within 1 to 2 hours after baking.

FRENCH PASTRY:
12 tablespoons cold butter, cut into small cubes
1½ cups all-purpose flour
2 tablespoons granulated sugar
2 to 3 tablespoons ice water

Place the butter, flour, and sugar in a food processor with the steel blade. Process while adding the water gradually. Add only enough water so that the dough holds together in a ball.

Gather the dough into a ball, wrap in waxed paper, and chill for 30 minutes or longer.

APRICOT GLAZE:
½ cup sieved apricot jam
2 tablespoons Cognac, kirsch, brandy, or applejack.

Heat the jam to the boiling point in a saucepan. Stir in the flavoring. Use the glaze while it is hot.

Tarte Tatin (Upside-Down Apple Tart)

SERVES 6 TO 8

¾ cup butter, softened
1 cup Vanilla Sugar (see left)
5 to 6 pounds Golden Delicious apples
Sweet Short Pastry (see page 283)

To make Vanilla Sugar, place a 3-inch or longer vanilla bean into a covered container filled with 3 to 4 cups granulated sugar. Let stand 2 to 3 days. As sugar is used, refill. When the bean is hard and dry, replace it.

Spread the butter over the sides and bottom of a 9 to 10-inch skillet with sloping sides or a tatin pan; sprinkle with the vanilla sugar.

Peel the apples, halve and core them, then arrange them standing upright in overlapping circles around the edge of the pan and flat in the center to fill the mold tightly. (This arrangement will be the top of the tart.)

Cook the apples on a burner over medium-low heat for 60 to 90 minutes, or until the sugar has carmelized and the syrup that bubbles up the side of the apples is golden. (After 10 minutes cooking time, 1 to 2 more apple halves may be added to keep the shape tight.) Let cool thoroughly. (This may be done ahead; cover tightly with plastic wrap.)

Prepare pastry dough. Chill for 30 minutes to 1 hour.

Preheat the oven to 350° F.

When the apples have cooled sufficiently, roll out the pastry dough into a circle the size of the skillet. Place it over the apples, allowing the edges to fall against the inside edge of the skillet. Bake the tart for 40 to 50 minutes, or until the pastry is crisp and brown.

Let the tart cool for 15 to 30 minutes. Reverse onto a serving platter. If any apples stick to the base of the pan, remove them with a knife and reposition them into the tart.

Peach Kuchen

**MAKES
1 9 TO 10-INCH
PIE SHELL**

1½ cups all-purpose flour
½ teaspoon salt
½ cup cold butter, cut into pieces
2 tablespoons plus ⅓ cup sour cream
3 large egg yolks
1 cup granulated sugar
1 to 1½ pounds fresh ripe peaches (about 6 medium), peeled, pitted, and thickly sliced

Preheat the oven to 375° F.

In a food processor, using the metal blade, process 1¼ cups of the flour, ¼ teaspoon salt, and butter until crumbly. Add the 2 tablespoons sour cream and let the machine run until the dough just forms a ball, about 4 to 6 seconds.

With fingers, press the dough into a tart or pie pan to cover the bottom and sides of the pan evenly. Bake for 20 minutes, or until lightly browned. Let cool while making the filling.

Lower the oven temperature to 350° F.

In a food processor, using the metal blade, process the egg yolks, the ⅓ cup sour cream, remaining ¼ cup flour, the sugar, and ¼ teaspoon salt for 5 seconds. Scrape down the sides of the bowl and process about 10 seconds.

Pour half the custard mixture into the prepared crust. Arrange the peaches in concentric circles on top of the custard. Pour the remaining custard over the peaches.

Bake for 40 to 50 minutes, or until custard is set and top lightly browned. Allow to cool for 10 minutes before serving. Serve warm or at room temperature.

Almond-Apple Crunch

SERVES 12

1¼ cups all-purpose flour
1½ cups granulated sugar
¾ cup butter, softened
½ cup almond paste
soft, fine bread crumbs
6 tart apples, thinly sliced
juice of 1 lemon
pinch of salt
½ teaspoon ground cinnamon
pinch of ground cloves
pinch of freshly grated nutmeg

Combine the flour, 1 cup sugar, butter, and almond paste in a bowl and chill for 2 hours.

Preheat the oven to 350° F.

Butter a 9 x 13-inch baking dish and coat with bread crumbs.

In a large bowl, mix the apples, the remaining ½ cup sugar, lemon juice, salt, and spices. Place the apple mixture in the baking dish, then crumble the almond paste mixture over the apples.

Bake for 45 minutes, or until the top is golden brown.

SERVES 8 TO 10 ■ # Star-Spangled Strawberry Shortcake

2 cups all-purpose flour
4 teaspoons baking powder
2 tablespoons plus ⅓ cup granulated sugar
½ teaspoon salt
⅓ cup vegetable shortening
1 extra-large egg
⅓ cup heavy cream
6 tablespoons butter, melted and slightly cooled
6 cups strawberries, washed and hulled

GARNISH:
heavy cream, whipped
light cream
OPTIONAL:
3 tablespoons light cream

Preheat the oven to 425° F.

In a large bowl, mix the flour, baking powder, 2 tablespoons sugar, and salt together with a fork. Cut in the shortening with a pastry blender until very fine crumbs form.

Break the egg into a medium bowl, add the heavy cream, and beat lightly with a fork. Add the melted butter. Add the egg-cream mixture to the flour mixture and stir with a fork. If still too dry, add up to 3 tablespoons light cream. The dough should be moist enough to form a ball.

Butter a 9-inch layer cake pan. Pat the dough into the pan, but make no attempt to smooth out the top. Bake for 15 to 20 minutes, or until lightly browned. Cool on a cake rack for 5 minutes.

Place the cake rack on top of the cake pan and reverse it. Place a serving plate on top of the dough and reverse again.

Slice the strawberries and combine with the remaining sugar, according to sweetness of the berries. Top the dough with berries. Cut into pie-shaped wedges. Top with whipped cream or light cream and serve.

Apple Crumb Pie

SERVES 6 TO 8

Pies can be frozen before baking. Do not thaw, but increase baking time by 15 to 20 minutes.

1 9-inch unbaked pie shell
1 cup granulated sugar
1 teaspoon ground cinnamon
6 to 8 large McIntosh apples (or Granny Smith apples if a tarter flavor is desired)
½ cup all-purpose flour
⅓ cup butter, softened

Preheat the oven to 375° F.

Mix ½ cup of the sugar with the cinnamon.

Peel, core, and thinly slice the apples. Arrange the apples in layers in the pie shell, sprinkling with the cinnamon-sugar mixture as you layer. Mound the apples quite high in the pie shell, as they will cook down.

In a small mixing bowl, combine the flour and remaining ½ cup sugar and cut in the butter until crumbly. Pat this mixture by large spoonsful evenly over the apples, forming a crust. Seal at the edges.

Bake for 50 to 60 minutes, or until golden brown.

White Pass Apple Pie

SERVES 8

5 cups peeled and sliced apples (Jonathan or Golden Delicious)
pastry for 2 crust 9-inch pie (see Never-Fail Pie Crust, page 283)
1 tablespoon lemon juice
½ to ¾ cup granulated sugar
2 tablespoons all-purpose flour
1 teaspoon ground cinnamon
1½ tablespoons butter
milk
cinnamon sugar

Preheat the oven to 400° F.

Place the apples in a pastry-lined pie plate.

Combine the lemon juice, sugar, flour, and cinnamon and pour over the apples. Dot with the butter.

Cover with the top crust. Brush the top crust with milk and sprinkle with cinnamon sugar. Bake for 45 minutes, or until the apples test done.

DESSERTS: PIES

SERVES 6

This is not a classic meringue pie, but a quick and easy combination of custard and meringue.

Rhubarb Meringue Pie

1 cup granulated sugar
1 egg
dash of salt
1 tablespoon all-purpose flour
¼ teaspoon freshly grated nutmeg
3 tablespoons butter, melted
2 cups diced rhubarb
1 8-inch unbaked pie shell

Preheat the oven to 350° F.

In a large bowl, combine the sugar and egg and beat well.

Add the salt, flour, and nutmeg and blend. Add the butter and rhubarb and mix well. Pour into the prepared pie shell and bake for 1 hour.

SERVES 8

Pumpkin Chiffon Pie

1 envelope unflavored gelatin
½ cup milk
⅔ cup (packed) brown sugar
½ teaspoon salt
½ teaspoon ground cinnamon
½ teaspoon freshly grated nutmeg
½ teaspoon ground ginger
1¼ cups mashed cooked pumpkin
3 eggs, separated and at room temperature
½ cup granulated sugar
1 9-inch pie shell, baked

GARNISH:
heavy cream, whipped

Soften the gelatin in milk in a large saucepan. Add the brown sugar, salt, cinnamon, nutmeg, ginger, pumpkin, and egg yolks and beat well. Cook and stir until gelatin is dissolved and mixture boils.

Remove from the heat and place the pan in cold water until the mixture mounds slightly when dropped from a spoon.

Beat the egg whites until soft peaks form. Add the sugar, a little at a time, and beat until stiff. Fold the meringue mixture into the pumpkin mixture. Pour into the prepared pie shell. Chill for 2 hours. Top with whipped cream.

SERVES 10 TO 12 ⬤

Lemon Drop Ice Cream

5 cups milk
2¼ cups granulated sugar
2 eggs, separated
3 cups heavy cream
zest of 3 lemons, minced
⅔ cup fresh lemon juice
1½ cups crushed lemon drops

Scald the milk in a large saucepan. Add the sugar and stir until well dissolved.

Beat the egg yolks in a small bowl. Remove ¼ cup of the hot milk and add to the egg yolks. Beat well, then return the egg mixture to the saucepan. Cook and stir for 2 minutes. Remove from the heat and cool.

Add the cream, lemon zest, and lemon juice to the cooled mixture. Fold in the egg whites, stiffly beaten, and lemon drops and turn mixture into a gallon freezer can. Complete the procedure as indicated on freezer instructions.

SERVES 6 ⬤

Cranberry Sherbet

1 envelope unflavored gelatin
½ cup cold water
¾ cup boiling water
1 cup granulated sugar
2 cups cranberry juice
¼ cup lemon juice

Soften the gelatin in cold water in a heatproof bowl. Add the boiling water and stir until the gelatin is dissolved.

Dissolve the sugar in the cranberry and lemon juices and add to the gelatin. Pour into a shallow pan and freeze until firm.

Turn the sherbet out into a chilled bowl and beat with an electric mixer until smooth or process in a food processor. Return the sherbet to the pan and refreeze until firm. Just before serving, beat or process again. Serve immediately.

US SKI TEAM Ralph Miller, a team skier in the 1950s, liked to go barefoot inside his boots on race day. He had reasoned this out carefully. Bare skin had the best grip on leather; therefore, he wouldn't need to lace his boots so tightly, which would allow better blood circulation, warmer feet, better control, and more resistance to injury. Few doctors of today would argue with him.

SERVES 8

Grapefruit Sherbet

3 cups fresh grapefruit juice
1½ cups granulated sugar
2 teaspoons grated grapefruit zest
¼ cup orange juice
1 cup heavy cream

Blend all the ingredients and pour into a shallow pan and freeze until mushy. Beat with an electric mixer or food processor until smooth. Refreeze until firm. Let stand at room temperature for 5 minutes before serving.

MAKES 1 QUART

Pineapple Sherbet

4 cups buttermilk
1½ cups granulated sugar
1 can (8 ounces) crushed pineapple
1 tablespoon vanilla extract
1 teaspoon almond extract

Combine all ingredients and blend well. Place in a shallow pan and freeze until firm.

At least 3 hours before serving, remove from the freezer and break into pieces. Process the sherbet in a food processor or blender until smooth. Refreeze until serving time. Let stand at room temperature for 5 minutes before serving.

US SKI TEAM The American uniforms didn't fit as well as some of the skiers would have liked at the 1956 Olympics. Dodie Post, the manager of the women's team, decided to go public with her objections, so she cut her ski pants off at the knees.

Fresh Strawberry Sherbet

If frozen in the freezer, the sherbet should be placed in a metal container (an 8-inch layer cake pan is good) for fast freezing. After it is frozen, it should be partially thawed, then beaten in a food processor using the steel blade. Sherbets that have become crystalline in the freezer should be partially thawed, then reprocessed in the food processor or beaten thoroughly with a wooden spoon and refrozen.

⅔ cup granulated sugar
⅔ cup water
2½ pints strawberries, puréed and chilled
2 tablespoons Grand Marnier
2 tablespoons lemon juice
grated zest of 1 lemon

GARNISH:
kiwi slices or sliced strawberries
Raspberry-Strawberry Sauce (recipe follows)

Combine the sugar and water in a small saucepan over medium-high heat and stir until the sugar is dissolved. Just before the syrup comes to a boil, remove from the heat. Cool and chill.

Combine the strawberries, Grand Marnier, lemon juice, and lemon zest and blend well. Add the syrup to the strawberries.

Freeze in an ice cream maker or freezer. Garnish with kiwi slices or strawberries and serve with Raspberry-Strawberry Sauce.

RASPBERRY-STRAWBERRY SAUCE:
1 pint strawberries, hulled
1 package (10 ounces) frozen raspberries, thawed
1 tablespoon Grand Marnier or framboise

Combine all the ingredients and purée. Transfer to a serving dish and chill. May be strained, if you prefer.

MAKES 3 DOZEN

Chocolate Peanut Butter Balls

2 cups creamy peanut butter
1 cup butter, softened
1 pound confectioner's sugar
2 cups Rice Krispies cereal
1 teaspoon vanilla extract
melted chocolate

Combine the peanut butter, butter, confectioner's sugar, cereal, and vanilla in a large mixing bowl.

Roll the dough into small, bite-sized balls. Dip the balls in melted chocolate. Place on tray or cookie sheet for 20 minutes to harden.

MAKES 4 TO 5 DOZEN

Christmas Shortbreads

1 cup butter, softened
¾ cup confectioner's sugar
1 teaspoon vanilla extract
1¾ cups all-purpose flour
6 squares (1 ounce each) semisweet chocolate
1 teaspoon vegetable shortening
1½ cups chopped pecans

In a large mixing bowl, cream the butter, sugar, and vanilla together. Add the flour and mix well.

Form the dough into a long roll, about 18 inches. Wrap in waxed paper and chill for several hours or overnight.

Preheat the oven to 300° F.

Cut the roll into ¼-inch slices, then cut the rounds in half, forming half circles. Bake on ungreased baking sheets for 16 to 20 minutes. Cookies should be dry but not browned. Cool.

Melt the chocolate and shortening over hot, not boiling, water. Dip the tip of the cookies into the chocolate, then into the pecans. Cool on baking sheets in the refrigerator until the chocolate is set. Store in the refrigerator.

US SKI TEAM **Two families have put three children on the alpine team: Buddy, Skeeter, and Loris Werner; Steve, Sheila, and Tamara McKinney are the triple placings. One family sent four children onto the team— Barbara Anne, Marilyn, Linda, and Bob made it a clean sweep for their generation of Cochrans. Bowing to the obvious, their father was appointed coach.**

**MAKES 20
COOKIES**

Melting Moments

1 cup butter
5½ tablespoons confectioner's sugar
¾ cup cornstarch
1 cup all-purpose flour
Glaze (recipe follows)

Preheat the oven to 350° F.

In a large bowl, cream the butter with the confectioner's sugar, then add the cornstarch and flour.

Shape the dough into balls the size of a walnut and place on greased cookie sheets. Flatten the balls with the bottom of a wet glass.

Bake for 8 minutes, or until just slightly brown on the edges. While cookies are still warm, top with glaze.

GLAZE:
1 cup confectioner's sugar
1 tablespoon butter, melted
1 tablespoon lemon juice
1 tablespoon orange juice

In a mixing bowl, combine the confectioner's sugar with the butter, lemon juice, and orange juice. Beat well.

MAKES 40

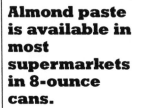

**Almond paste
is available in
most
supermarkets
in 8-ounce
cans.**

Almond Macaroons

½ pound (1 cup) almond paste
1 cup confectioner's sugar
3 large egg whites, at room temperature
dash of salt
½ teaspoon vanilla extract
granulated sugar

Preheat the oven to 300° F.

Chop the almond paste, add the sugar, and work with the fingers until blended.

Add the egg whites, one at a time, blending well after each addition. Use only enough egg white to make a soft dough that will hold its shape when dropped from a spoon. Add the salt and vanilla.

Drop dough the size of a quarter onto greased and floured cookie sheets. Sprinkle each cookie with granulated sugar and bake for 20 minutes.

MAKES 20 BARS

Trail Bars

1 large egg, beaten
1 teaspoon vanilla extract
½ cup (packed) brown sugar
½ cup maple syrup
1 cup butter
1 cup all-purpose flour
⅔ cup rolled oats
3 cups granola cereal with raisins and dates
1 can (14 ounces) condensed milk

Preheat the oven to 350° F.

Combine the egg, vanilla, brown sugar, syrup, and butter in a large bowl and beat with a wooden spoon until creamy. Stir in the remaining ingredients and mix well.

Spread the batter in an ungreased 11 x 17-inch jelly roll pan. Bake for 30 minutes. Cool and cut into bars.

MAKES 16

Brownies

½ cup butter
2 ounces unsweetened chocolate
2 eggs
1 cup granulated sugar
½ cup all-purpose flour
1 teaspoon vanilla extract

OPTIONAL:
1 cup chopped nuts
confectioner's sugar

Preheat the oven to 325° F.

Melt the butter and chocolate in a saucepan over low heat. Cool.

Beat the eggs until light and fluffy. Add the sugar and beat well. Blend in the chocolate mixture. Add the flour, vanilla, and nuts, if desired.

Pour the batter into a greased and floured 8-inch square pan. Bake for 30 minutes. Cool. Sprinkle with confectioner's sugar if desired and cut into squares.

US SKI TEAM **Margins were bigger in the heroic age. Toni Matt beat Dick Durrance by 1:00.1 in the 1939 Mt. Washington Inferno, but Matt's 6:29.1 cut the old record *in half*! Durrance, member of the 1936 Olympic team, had set that record. Matt was on the 1950 U.S. team at the world championships.**

MAKES 24

Caramel Bars

¾ cup butter, melted
1 cup all-purpose flour
1 cup oatmeal
¾ cup (packed) brown sugar
1 teaspoon baking soda
32 caramels
3 tablespoons butter
3 tablespoons cream
1 package (6 ounces) chocolate chips (about 1 cup)
½ cup chopped nuts

Preheat the oven to 350° F.

In a small mixing bowl, combine the butter, flour, oatmeal, brown sugar, and baking soda and mix well. Put three-fourths of the butter mixture in a 9 x 13-inch pan, pressing evenly over the bottom of the pan. Bake for 10 minutes.

Meanwhile, in a saucepan, combine the caramels, butter, and cream and heat, stirring, until the caramels are melted.

Pour the caramel mixture over the crust and sprinkle with chocolate chips and nuts. Top with the remaining butter-oatmeal mixture. Bake for 15 minutes more. Cool and cut into bars.

MAKES 40 TO
50 BALLS

This is a high-energy snack for hiking and back-packing.

Power Balls

1 cup peanut butter
½ cup dry milk
1½ cups granola
½ cup wheat germ
½ cup honey
⅔ cup coconut

Combine all the ingredients in a large bowl and mix well. Shape into 1-inch balls. Store in the refrigerator.

MAKES 3 DOZEN

Fresh Apple Cookies

2 cups all-purpose flour
1 teaspoon baking soda
½ cup butter, softened
1⅓ cups (packed) brown sugar
½ teaspoon salt
1 teaspoon ground cinnamon
1 teaspoon ground cloves
½ teaspoon freshly grated nutmeg
1 egg, beaten
¼ cup apple juice or milk
1 cup chopped apples
½ to 1 cup chopped nuts
1 cup chopped raisins
Vanilla Glaze (recipe follows)

Preheat the oven to 375°F.

Sift the flour and baking soda together in a medium mixing bowl.

In a large bowl, cream together the butter, brown sugar, salt, cinnamon, cloves, nutmeg, and egg. Add half the flour to the butter mixture and blend well. Mix in half the juice or milk.

Add the apples, nuts, and raisins to the remaining flour. Add this apple mixture to the butter mixture. Stir in the remaining juice or milk.

Drop the dough by teaspoonsful onto greased cookie sheets. Bake for 8 to 9 minutes, or until cookies are firm. While cookies are hot, spread with Vanilla Glaze.

VANILLA GLAZE:
1 cup confectioner's sugar
1 tablespoon butter, softened
¼ teaspoon vanilla extract
¼ teaspoon salt
1½ tablespoons light cream or milk

Blend all the ingredients together in a mixing bowl and mix until smooth.

US SKI TEAM There are certain athletes who bring more to their sport by simply putting on a uniform than the sport can ever return. Cindy Nelson is one of these athletes. Beginning her twelfth year with the team, she has distinguished herself as one of the very best this country has produced. Continuing to compete in all three disciplines, Cindy equaled the best downhill finish for an American woman in either an Olympics or world championship with her silver-medal performance at the world championships in Schladming, Austria, in 1982. She and teammate Holly Flanders combined efforts in a historic one-two sweep in Arosa, Switzerland, World Cup competition, marking the first time American women have swept the top two places in a World Cup race since 1971.

**MAKES
1 9 TO 10-INCH
PIE SHELL**

Sweet Short Pastry

2 cups all-purpose flour
2 tablespoons granulated sugar
1 teaspoon salt
½ cup unsalted butter, chilled
4 tablespoons vegetable shortening, chilled
4 to 5 tablespoons ice water

Place the flour in a bowl with the sugar and salt. Cut the butter and shortening into pieces and mix into the flour until crumbly. Add just enough water to form a ball. It should not be sticky.

Remove from the bowl and knead quickly into a smooth ball. Wrap in plastic wrap and chill for 1 hour.

**MAKES 2 9-INCH
PIE SHELLS**

**For a flaky
crust, do not
use too much
flour when
rolling out
pastry.**

Never-Fail Pie Crust

1 teaspoon salt
3 cups all-purpose flour
1¼ cups vegetable shortening
1 egg, well beaten
5 tablespoons ice water
1 tablespoon white vinegar

In a large bowl, sift together the salt and flour. Cut in the shortening.

In a small bowl, combine the egg, ice water, and vinegar. Pour this egg mixture into the flour mixture all at once. Blend just until flour is moistened. If the dough is too sticky, add just enough flour for easy handling. Chill for 1 hour before rolling out on a lightly floured board.

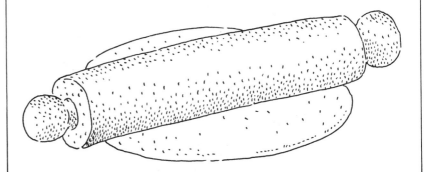

Red Oak Meringue Torte

SERVES 12

6 egg whites, at room temperature
½ teaspoon cream of tartar
2 cups granulated sugar
2 teaspoons vanilla extract
¾ cup chopped pecans
2 cups saltine crackers, coarsely broken
1½ to 2 cups heavy cream, whipped

GARNISH:
fresh strawberries sweetened to taste with Vanilla Sugar (see
    page 270)

Preheat the oven to 350° F.

Beat the egg whites until frothy in a large bowl. Add the cream of tartar and beat until stiff. Add the sugar and vanilla gradually. Fold in the nuts and crackers.

Spread in a greased 10-inch springform pan. Bake for 50 to 60 minutes. Remove from the oven and cool slightly. Do not remove the sides of the pan until ready to serve. Push down the outside edges of the torte to level the top (the center will sink).

When cooled completely, frost the top of the torte with the whipped cream at least 4 hours before serving. Serve with fresh berries on top.

Chocolate Nut Torte

SERVES 12

6 large eggs, separated
1 cup granulated sugar
1 bar (8 ounces) German's sweet chocolate, grated
⅓ cup plus 2 tablespoons all-purpose flour
3 teaspoons baking powder

FILLING:
¼ cup milk, scalded
1 cup ground walnuts (4 ounces)
1 cup unsalted butter
1 cup confectioner's sugar
1 teaspoon vanilla extract

FROSTING:
1 cup unsalted butter
1 bar (8 ounces) German's sweet chocolate
1 tablespoon vanilla extract

Preheat the oven to 375° F.

In a medium bowl, beat the egg yolks with the sugar until thick and lemon colored. In another bowl, beat the egg whites until stiff. Fold the beaten egg whites into the egg yolks. Add the chocolate.

Sift the flour and baking powder together, then fold into the egg white mixture.

Bake for 20 to 25 minutes in three 8-inch greased and floured cake pans. Remove to racks to cool.

To make the filling, pour the milk over the nuts and let stand until cool. Cream the butter and sugar together. Add the milk and nuts and blend in the vanilla.

Melt all the frosting ingredients together over low heat until smooth. Let cool in the refrigerator until thickened, about 30 minutes. If the frosting becomes too hard, reheat slightly.

When the cake is cool, spread filling between the layers and spread the torte with frosting.

Mocha Tortoni

SERVES 8

Great for a group. Can be made in larger quantities. The cherry garnish is festive for holiday entertaining.

1 egg white, at room temperature
1 tablespoon instant coffee
⅛ teaspoon salt
⅓ cup granulated sugar
1 cup heavy cream
1 teaspoon vanilla extract
¼ teaspoon almond extract
¼ teaspoon brandy extract
¼ cup almonds, toasted and slivered

GARNISH:
cherries with stem attached
slivered almonds

In a small bowl, combine the egg white, coffee, and salt and beat until stiff but not dry. Add 2 tablespoons of the sugar and beat until stiff and satiny.

In a chilled bowl, combine the cream, remaining sugar, the vanilla, almond and brandy extracts and beat until stiff. Fold in the egg-white mixture and almonds.

Place the mixture in small sherbet bowls, parfait glasses, or pot de crème cups. Freeze until firm. Remove from the freezer 30 minutes before serving.

To serve, garnish with maraschino cherries and slivered almonds.

SERVES 12

Carefully separate eggs when making meringue. Even a speck of yolk will inhibit the full volume of beaten whites.

Walnut Torte

6 eggs, separated and at room temperature
1½ cups granulated sugar
2 tablespoons all-purpose flour
2 teaspoons baking powder
¼ teaspoon salt
3 cups finely chopped walnuts
2 cups heavy cream
5 to 6 tablespoons confectioner's sugar
1 teaspoon vanilla extract

GARNISH:
chocolate curls
walnut halves

Preheat the oven to 350° F.

Beat the egg yolks until thick and lemon colored. Gradually beat in half of the sugar.

In another bowl, mix together the flour, baking powder, and salt. Blend in the walnuts.

Beat the egg whites until stiff and add to the flour mixture. Gradually beat in the remaining sugar. Carefully fold the egg yolk mixture into the flour mixture.

Pour the batter into two 9-inch round layer pans lined with buttered waxed paper. Bake for 25 to 30 minutes, or until no impression shows when the cake is touched lightly with finger. Cool.

Whip the cream until stiff. Fold in the confectioner's sugar and vanilla.

Spread the whipped cream between the layers and over the top and sides. Garnish with chocolate curls and walnut halves.

SERVES 12

Pewaukee Pistachio Cake

6 eggs, separated and at room temperature
1½ tablespoons water
1 teaspoon vanilla extract
1½ tablespoons orange juice
1 tablespoon grated orange zest
1 cup granulated sugar
1¼ cups plus 1 tablespoon sifted cake flour
½ teaspoon salt
½ teaspoon cream of tartar

FILLING:
¾ cup granulated sugar
juice and zest of 1 orange
3 tablespoons all-purpose flour
1 egg, beaten
1 cup heavy cream, whipped

FROSTING:
1 egg yolk
2 cups confectioner's sugar
4 tablespoons butter, softened
1 tablespoon light cream
2 tablespoons orange juice

GARNISH:
½ cup chopped pistachio nuts

Preheat the oven to 350° F.

In a large mixing bowl, combine the egg yolks, water, vanilla, orange juice, and orange zest. Beat at high speed, gradually adding the sugar. Continue beating until the batter is thick, about 2 to 3 minutes, scraping the bowl frequently. Add the flour and salt and beat for 1 minute on low speed, scraping frequently.

In a separate bowl, beat the egg whites and cream of tartar together until stiff, but not dry, peaks form. Add the beaten egg whites by thirds to the batter. Fold about 10 strokes after the first two additions and about 15 strokes after the third addition.

Pour the batter into an ungreased 8-inch tube pan. Bake for 40 to 50 minutes. Remove from the oven and cool in the inverted pan.

To make the filling, combine the sugar, orange juice and zest, flour, and egg in the top of a double boiler. Beat well. Cook, stirring constantly, until very thick. Cool. Fold the whipped cream into the sugar mixture.

Cream all the frosting ingredients together until of desired spreading consistency.

When cool, cut the cake into 3 layers and spread filling between the layers, then frost. Sprinkle with pistachio nuts.

US SKI TEAM Three generations of the same family have raced with the U.S. Ski Team—a record few, if any, sports organizations in the world can match. Sel Hannah was a member of the team in the 1930s; his daughter, Joan Hannah, raced for the United States through the 1960s, placing third in the 1962 world championship giant slalom; and Sel's granddaughter Eva Pfosi is a member of the current team.

**SERVES
8 TO 10**

Christmas Log

3 eggs
1 cup granulated sugar
⅓ cup water
1 teaspoon vanilla extract
1 cup cake flour, sifted
¼ cup unsweetened cocoa powder
1 teaspoon baking powder
¼ teaspoon salt
confectioner's sugar

COFFEE CREAM FILLING:
1 cup heavy cream
1 tablespoon instant coffee
½ cup confectioner's sugar

CHOCOLATE BUTTER FROSTING:
4 tablespoons butter
2 squares (1 ounce each) unsweetened chocolate
2 cups confectioner's sugar
¼ cup milk
½ teaspoon vanilla extract

Preheat the oven to 375° F.

Grease a jelly-roll pan and line with waxed paper cut ½ inch smaller than the pan. Grease the paper.

In a large bowl, beat the eggs until thick and lemon colored. Beat in the sugar, 1 tablespoon at a time, until thick. Stir in the water and vanilla.

Sift together the cake flour, cocoa, baking powder, and salt. Fold this flour mixture into the egg mixture. Spread evenly in the prepared pan.

Bake until the center springs back, about 12 to 15 minutes.

With a sharp knife, cut around the cake ¼ inch from the edge of the pan. Invert the pan onto a clean towel dusted with confectioner's sugar; pull off the paper. Starting at the long side, roll up the cake jelly-roll fashion. Wrap in the towel and cool completely on a wire rack.

Combine all the filling ingredients and beat until stiff.

To make the frosting, melt together the butter and chocolate in a saucepan. Cool slightly. In a large bowl, combine the confectioner's sugar, milk, and vanilla. Add the chocolate mixture and beat until smooth.

Unroll the cake carefully and spread with filling. Reroll. Spread the cake with frosting. Then use fork tines to make a design resembling bark. Chill until serving time.

 The teams of today have lost touch with some of the more unusual insights that guided racers in the 1950s. Some U.S. team members tried to remember not to wash their socks before a big race, reasoning that a dirty sock made better contact with the inside of their leather boots than a slippery-clean one. Others maintained that hot water softened their muscles, so they wouldn't take baths or showers all week before a big race.

Amaretto Chiffon Cheesecake

SERVES 8

Pure vanilla extract, unlike artificial vanilla extract, holds its flavor well even when frozen.

CRUST:
1¾ cups fine graham cracker crumbs (about 20 crackers)
¼ cup minced walnuts
½ teaspoon ground cinnamon
½ cup butter, melted

FILLING:
3 eggs, beaten
2 packages (8 ounces each) cream cheese, softened
1 cup granulated sugar
¼ teaspoon salt
1 teaspoon vanilla extract
1 tablespoon Amaretto
½ teaspoon almond extract
3 cups sour cream

NOUGATINE:
½ cup almonds, sliced
½ cup granulated sugar
2 tablespoons water

Thoroughly mix together all the crust ingredients in a bowl. Press onto the bottom and sides of a 9-inch springform pan. The crust should be about 1¾ inches high on the sides.

Preheat the oven to 375° F.

Combine the eggs, cream cheese, sugar, salt, vanilla, Amaretto, and almond extract in a large bowl and blend well. Beat until smooth, about 2 minutes, with an electric mixer. Blend in the sour cream.

Pour the filling into the crust and bake for 35 minutes, or just until set. Cool. Chill thoroughly, about 4 to 5 hours or overnight.

Make the nougatine. Preheat the oven heat to 350° F. On a baking sheet, toast the almonds for 6 to 8 minutes in the oven. Combine the sugar and water in a saucepan and cook until the sugar carmelizes. Stir in the nuts. Remove from the heat and pour onto a buttered baking sheet. When cooled, break in small pieces. When the cheesecake is chilled, sprinkle with the nougatine.

SERVES 12

Chocolate Fudge Cake

3 squares (1 ounce each) unsweetened chocolate
2¼ cups sifted cake flour
2 teaspoons baking soda
½ teaspoon salt
½ cup butter
2¼ cups (firmly packed) light brown sugar
3 eggs
1½ teaspoons vanilla extract
1 cup sour cream
1 cup boiling water

CHOCOLATE FUDGE FROSTING:
3 squares (1 ounce each) unsweetened chocolate
½ cup butter
1 pound confectioner's sugar
½ cup milk
2 teaspoons vanilla extract

Preheat the oven to 375° F.

Grease and flour two 9-inch cake pans.

In a small bowl, over hot, but not boiling water, melt the chocolate. Cool.

Sift the flour, baking soda, and salt onto waxed paper.

In a large bowl, beat the butter until soft. Add the brown sugar and eggs and beat with an electric mixer for 5 minutes at high speed until light and fluffy. Beat in the vanilla and melted chocolate. Stir in the dry ingredients alternately with the sour cream, beating well with a wooden spoon after each addition until smooth. Stir in the boiling water (batter will be thin).

Pour into the prepared pans. Bake for 25 minutes, or until center springs back when touched lightly.

Cool on racks for 10 minutes. Loosen the edges with a knife. Turn out onto wire racks and cool completely.

To make the frosting, combine the chocolate and butter in a small heavy saucepan. Place over low heat and stir until just melted. Remove from the heat. Combine the confectioner's sugar, milk, and vanilla in a medium bowl. Stir until smooth. Add the chocolate mixture. Set the bowl in a pan of ice water and beat with a spoon until the frosting is thick enough to spread and hold its shape.

When the cake is cool, frost with Chocolate Fudge Frosting.

 **A member of the 1972, 1976, 1980, and 1984 Olympic teams, and the 1974, 1978, and 1982 world championship teams, Cindy Nelson has won six national titles, three each in slalom and downhill. When she's not competing or training, "Nellie" retreats to Vail, Colorado, where her own form of relaxation is preparing special culinary treats. Cindy says "I take a chunk of Tobler chocolate and melt it slowly in the microwave or on the stove, add a few drops of cold milk and serve it over vanilla ice cream."**

Flourless Chocolate Cake

SERVES 14 TO 16

10 ounces unsweetened chocolate, cut into pieces
1 cup unsalted butter
11 extra-large egg yolks, at room temperature
1⅓ cups granulated sugar
1 tablespoon Grand Marnier
8 extra-large egg whites, at room temperature

OPTIONAL:
1 tablespoon vanilla extract
1 tablespoon Kahlúa
2 teaspoons grated lemon zest
  or a combination of these flavorings

Preheat the oven to 325° F. Butter a 9-inch springform pan and dust the pan with sugar. Set aside.

In the top of a double boiler, melt the chocolate and butter and let cool.

In a large bowl, beat the egg yolks until they are thick and lemon colored. Add 1 cup sugar, a little at a time, beating until the mixture makes a ribbon when the beaters are held up. Beat in the Grand Marnier or other flavoring.

In a large bowl, beat the egg whites until they hold soft peaks. Add the remaining sugar, a little at a time, and beat until stiff.

Blend one fourth of the yolk mixture into the chocolate mixture. Fold in the remaining yolks. Blend in half the meringue mixture. Fold in the remaining meringue.

Spoon two thirds of the chocolate mixture into the prepared pan. Reserve the remaining mixture, covered, at room temperature.

Bake the cake for 40 to 50 minutes, or until it tests done. Remove from the oven and run a knife around the inside of the pan to loosen the cake. Cool for 30 minutes.

Remove the sides of the pan and continue cooling. Place the cake on a serving platter and frost with the reserved chocolate mixture. Refrigerate for 4 hours or overnight.

**SERVES
12 TO 14**

Cheesecake Supreme

Try a dessert buffet as a fun way of entertaining large groups, especially families. Set out 6 or 7 cakes, tarts, and trays of cookies, and serve with ice cold milk, coffee, and tea. Add fortified wines such as Sherry, Lillet, and Port, if desired.

CRUST:
1 cup sifted all-purpose flour
¼ cup granulated sugar
1 teaspoon grated lemon zest
½ cup butter, softened
1 egg yolk, lightly beaten
¼ teaspoon vanilla extract

FILLING:
5 packages (8 ounces each) cream cheese, at room temperature
½ teaspoon vanilla extract
grated zest of 1 lemon
3 tablespoons lemon juice
1¾ cups granulated sugar
3 tablespoons all-purpose flour
¼ teaspoon salt
1 cup eggs (4 to 5 eggs)
2 egg yolks
¼ cup heavy cream

OPTIONAL:
fresh fruit flavored with Vanilla Sugar (see page 270)

Preheat the oven to 400° F.

Combine the flour, sugar, and lemon zest in a bowl. Cut in the butter until the mixture is crumbly. Add the egg yolk and vanilla. Blend thoroughly.

Pat one third of the dough on the bottom of a 9-inch springform pan with sides removed. Bake for 8 minutes, or until golden. Cool.

Attach the sides to the pan, butter, and then pat the remaining dough onto the sides to a height of 1¾ inches.

Increase the oven to 450° F.

In a large bowl, beat the cream cheese until light and fluffy. And the vanilla, lemon zest, and lemon juice.

In a small bowl, mix together the sugar, flour, and salt. Add to the cheese mixture. Add the eggs and egg yolks, a tablespoon at a time, beating after each addition. Gently stir in the cream.

Pour the batter into the crust-lined pan. Bake for 12 minutes; then reduce the heat to 300° F. and continue baking for 55 minutes, or until the center tests done. Remove from the oven.

Cool for 30 minutes, then loosen the sides of the cake with a spatula. Remove the sides of the pan after 1 hour. Cool for 2 hours longer.

Serve with fresh fruit flavored with vanilla sugar, if desired.

SERVES 12 TO 16 ■

Carrot Cake

2 cups granulated sugar
1½ cups vegetable oil
4 medium eggs
2 cups all-purpose flour
2 teaspoons baking soda
2 teaspoons ground cinnamon
1 teaspoon salt
1½ tablespoons vanilla extract
3 cups grated carrots
1 cup chopped pecans

CREAM CHEESE FROSTING:
8 ounces cream cheese, softened
½ cup butter
1 pound confectioner's sugar
1 teaspoon vanilla extract
1 cup chopped pecans
1 can (5 ounces) crushed pineapple, drained

Preheat the oven to 350° F.

Combine the sugar, oil, and eggs in a large bowl and blend well.

Thoroughly mix together the dry ingredients.

Add the vanilla and dry ingredients to the egg mixture. Stir in the carrots and nuts. Pour the batter into 3 greased and floured 9-inch layer cake pans. Bake for 30 to 35 minutes, or until the cake tests done. Let cool on racks.

To make the frosting, cream together the cream cheese and butter. Beat in the confectioner's sugar and vanilla. Stir in the pecans and pineapple.

When the cake is cool, frost. This cake can also be baked in a 9 x 13-inch pan for 40 to 45 minutes. Use half the frosting recipe.

US SKI TEAM Food for the 1932 Olympics was provided by the ladies of the Episcopal Church, the Masonic Lodge, and the Lake Placid Ladies Club. Together, they cooked 6,650 meals a day. Cross-country racers should note that the feeding stations for the 1932 Olympics had 12-item menus that included bananas, raw eggs, rye bread, and beefsteak.

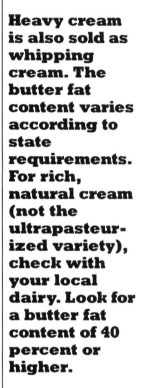

SERVES 10 TO 12

Heavy cream is also sold as whipping cream. The butter fat content varies according to state requirements. For rich, natural cream (not the ultrapasteurized variety), check with your local dairy. Look for a butter fat content of 40 percent or higher.

Pavlova

4 egg whites, at room temperature
⅛ teaspoon salt
1 cup granulated sugar
1 tablespoon cornstarch
1 teaspoon white wine vinegar
1 teaspoon vanilla extract
2 cups heavy cream, whipped
fresh fruit of your choice (kiwi, peaches, apricots, nectarines)
Raspberry Sauce for Pavlova (recipe follows)

Preheat the oven to 400° F.

In a mixing bowl, beat the egg whites and salt together until frothy, using high speed of an electric mixer. Gradually add all but 1 tablespoon of the sugar, 1 tablespoon every minute, to the egg whites.

Mix the last tablespoon of sugar with the cornstarch and add to the egg whites with the vinegar and vanilla. Beat until stiff peaks form.

Cover a baking sheet with parchment or brown paper.

Shape the meringue into a 7 to 9-inch circle, mounding slightly, on the paper-covered baking sheet. Place in the preheated oven, then immediately reduce the oven temperature to 250° F. Bake for 1½ hours, or until lightly browned and dry on the surface. Remove the meringue from the oven (meringue will crack). Cool completely. If desired, wrap the meringue airtight and store up to 24 hours at room temperature.

Before serving, swirl the whipped cream over the meringue, covering it completely. Garnish with fruit. Accompany with Raspberry Sauce to be spooned over each serving.

RASPBERRY SAUCE FOR PAVLOVA
1 tablespoon cornstarch
½ cup granulated sugar
dash of salt
½ cup water
2 teaspoons lemon juice
¼ teaspoon vanilla extract
1 package (10 ounces) frozen raspberries or 1½ to 2 cups
    fresh raspberries, slightly crushed

In a saucepan, blend together the cornstarch, sugar, and salt. Stir in the water, lemon juice, and vanilla. Add the berries. Cook, stirring, until sauce thickens. Cool, cover, and chill overnight, if desired.

SERVES 4

Rum Pudding

1 envelope unflavored gelatin
⅔ cup light cream
¼ teaspoon salt
3 egg yolks, beaten
6 tablespoons granulated sugar
1 cup heavy cream, whipped
3 tablespoons rum
Raspberry Sauce (recipe follows)

Soften the gelatin in the cream in a small saucepan. Then heat just until the gelatin is dissolved. Cool.

In a large bowl, combine the salt, egg yolks, and sugar and beat until thick and lemon colored. Fold in the gelatin-cream mixture and the whipped cream. Stir in the rum.

Pour into dishes and chill. Serve with Raspberry Sauce.

RASPBERRY SAUCE:
1 package (10 ounces) frozen raspberries
¼ cup granulated sugar
2 teaspoons cornstarch
⅓ cup cold water

Force the raspberries through a sieve to remove the seeds.

Combine the sugar, cornstarch, and water in a saucepan and mix well. Add the sieved berries and cook, stirring, until the sauce is thick. Chill.

SERVES 8 TO 10

Swedish Cream

1 tablespoon unflavored gelatin
1 tablespoon cold water
2 cups heavy cream
1 cup granulated sugar
2 cups sour cream
1 teaspoon vanilla extract
2 cups fresh fruit (raspberries, strawberries, blueberries, etc.), washed, stemmed, and very lightly mashed

Soften the gelatin in the cold water in a saucepan. Stir the cream and sugar into the softened gelatin and heat until the gelatin is dissolved.

Remove from the heat and add the sour cream and vanilla, whipping until smooth. Pour into small glasses, leaving ½ inch room at the top. Chill. To serve, top with fresh fruit.

SERVES 4

This can be prepared in less than 10 minutes.

Chocolate Mousse

1 cup heavy cream
½ cup granulated sugar
¼ cup water
6 ounces semisweet chocolate
2 large eggs
½ teaspoon instant coffee

OPTIONAL:
2 tablespoons Grand Marnier or brandy

Whip the cream until thick. Set aside.

Heat the sugar and water in a saucepan until sugar is dissolved and the mixture comes to a boil. Stir in the chocolate.

In a food processor, process the eggs and coffee for several seconds. With the machine running, pour in the chocolate syrup slowly and process until smooth. Add the Grand Marnier or brandy, if desired. Spoon the cream into the workbowl and pulse just until blended.

Pour into serving dishes (wine goblets work well) and refrigerate. This mousse will be very thin at first but thickens after several hours in the refrigerator.

SERVES 4

Blueberries in Lemon Mousse

4 egg yolks, at room temperature
½ cup granulated sugar
5 tablespoons lemon juice
2 teaspoons grated lemon zest
2 egg whites, at room temperature
½ cup heavy cream, whipped
1 cup fresh blueberries

Beat the egg yolks in a bowl until thick and lemon colored, about 4 minutes. Beat in the sugar, lemon juice, and lemon zest. Cook the mixture in the top of a double boiler, beating until thick, about 6 to 7 minutes. Cool.

In a small bowl, beat the egg whites until stiff. Fold the egg whites and whipped cream into the custard. Carefully fold in the blueberries.

Pour into a sugared 1-quart soufflé dish or individual serving dishes. Refrigerate 4 hours, or until serving time. This is easy to double.

Minnesota Cranberry Pudding

SERVES 8 TO 10

1⅓ cups sifted all-purpose flour
¼ cup molasses
¼ cup light corn syrup
⅓ cup hot water
2 teaspoons baking soda
dash of salt
2 cups fresh cranberries, chopped
¼ cup chopped nuts
Brandy Butter Sauce (recipe follows)

Preheat the oven to 325° F.

Combine all the ingredients in a large bowl and mix well.

Place the batter in a loaf pan. Cover the pan with foil and place in a pan of water in the oven to steam for 1½ hours.

Serve with Brandy Butter Sauce.

BRANDY BUTTER SAUCE:
1 cup granulated sugar
1 tablespoon all-purpose flour
½ cup heavy cream
½ cup butter
2 tablespoons brandy

Place all the ingredients, except the brandy, in the top of a double boiler and cook over simmering water for 20 minutes, or up to 2 hours. Add brandy 10 minutes before serving and heat through.

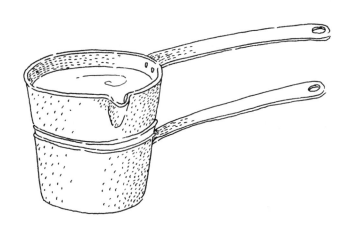

Lemon Cake-Top Pudding

SERVES 6

Eggs separate best when cold. Both egg whites and yolks attain greater volume when beaten at room temperature.

3 tablespoons butter
1 cup granulated sugar
4 eggs, separated and at room temperature
3 tablespoons all-purpose flour
¼ teaspoon salt
⅓ cup lemon juice
2 teaspoons grated lemon zest
1 cup milk
¼ cup chopped toasted almonds

Preheat the oven to 350° F.

In a large bowl, cream together the butter and sugar until light and fluffy. Add the egg yolks, one at a time, and beat well. Add the flour, salt, lemon juice, and lemon zest. Mix well. Add the milk and almonds and blend.

Beat the egg whites until stiff and fold into the pudding mixture.

Pour into a buttered 5 x 9-inch loaf pan or a 2-quart casserole. Place in a pan of hot water and bake for 30 minutes, or until lightly browned.

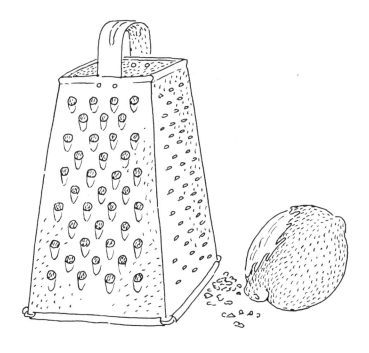

Fresh Cranberry Torte

SERVES 8 TO 10

1¼ cups graham cracker crumbs
½ cup chopped pecans
1¾ cups granulated sugar
½ cup unsalted butter, melted
1½ cups ground fresh cranberries
2 egg whites
1 tablespoon frozen orange juice concentrate, thawed
1 teaspoon vanilla extract
⅛ teaspoon salt
1 cup heavy cream

CRANBERRY GLAZE:
½ cup granulated sugar
1 tablespoon cornstarch
¾ cup fresh cranberries
¾ cup water

Preheat the oven to 375° F.

In a medium bowl, combine the cracker crumbs, pecans, and ¾ cup of sugar. Add the butter, mix well, and press into the bottom and sides of an 8-inch springform pan. Bake the crust for 6 minutes, or until lightly browned. Cool.

Combine the berries and remaining 1 cup sugar in a large mixing bowl. Let stand for 5 minutes. Add the egg whites, orange juice, vanilla, and salt. Beat on low speed until frothy. Then beat on high speed for 5 to 8 minutes, or until stiff peaks form.

Whip the cream to soft peaks in a small mixing bowl. Fold the cream into the cranberry mixture. Pour the mixture into the prepared crust. Freeze until firm, at least 4 hours.

To make the glaze, stir together the sugar and cornstarch in a saucepan. Stir in the cranberries and water. Cook and stir until bubbly. Continue to cook, stirring occasionally, just until the cranberry skins pop. Cool to room temperature. Do not chill, or the sauce may crystallize and become cloudy.

Remove the torte from the pan, place on a serving plate, and spoon the glaze on top.

SERVES 10

The Best Mud Pie

4 ounces chocolate wafer cookies
7 tablespoons butter
1½ quarts coffee ice cream, softened
⅓ cup unsweetened cocoa powder
⅔ cup granulated sugar
1⅓ cups heavy cream
1 teaspoon vanilla extract

GARNISH:
2 squares (1 ounce each) semisweet chocolate

Preheat the oven to 375 ° F.

In a blender container or food processor, crush the chocolate wafers to fine crumbs.

Melt 4 tablespoons of the butter in a small saucepan over low heat. Add the crumbs and mix well.

With hands, press the crumb mixture onto the bottom and sides of a 9-inch pie plate. Bake for 10 minutes. Cool crust completely on a wire rack.

Carefully spread the ice cream onto the cooled crust. Freeze until firm, about 1½ hours.

In a 2-quart saucepan over medium heat, cook and stir the cocoa, sugar, ⅓ cup of the cream, and remaining 3 tablespoons butter until the mixture is boiling. Remove from the heat. Stir in the vanilla. Cool the mixture slightly. Pour the chocolate mixture over the ice cream and return the pie to the freezer. Freeze until firm, at least 1 hour.

With the palm of your hands, slightly soften the chocolate squares. Make chocolate curls with a vegetable peeler.

When ready to serve, beat the remaining cream in a small bowl until soft peaks form. Spread the whipped cream over the pie. Garnish with the chocolate curls.

SERVES 6 TO 8

Frozen Amaretto Soufflé

1½ cups coarsely crumbled almond macaroon cookies
6 egg yolks
2 whole eggs
¾ cup granulated sugar
¼ cup Amaretto
2 cups heavy cream, whipped

GARNISH:
additional whipped cream

Preheat the oven to 300° F. Prepare a 1-quart soufflé dish with a 2½-inch buttered foil collar.

Spread the cookie crumbs in a shallow baking pan and toast for 20 minutes, stirring once. Cool.

In a large bowl, combine the egg yolks, eggs, and sugar. Beat on high speed until thick and fluffy and the sugar is dissolved, about 6 minutes. Continue beating, gradually adding the liqueur. By hand, fold in the whipped cream and 1 cup of the macaroon crumbs.

Gently spoon the soufflé into the prepared soufflé dish and freeze at least 4 to 6 hours.

Serve topped with additional whipped cream and remaining ½ cup cookie crumbs.

Ice Cream and Chocolate Squares

SERVES 12

Use peppermint stick ice cream during the holidays for a festive touch.

1 package (7½ ounces) vanilla wafers, crushed into crumbs
¾ cup butter, melted
2 squares (1 ounce each) unsweetened chocolate, melted
2 cups confectioner's sugar
3 eggs, separated and at room temperature
1 teaspoon vanilla extract
pinch of salt
1 cup chopped nuts
1 quart vanilla ice cream, softened

Combine the crumbs with ¼ cup of the melted butter and pat into the bottom of a 7 x 11-inch casserole dish, reserving ¼ cup of crumbs for the top.

Combine the chocolate, sugar, and remaining ½ cup melted butter in a saucepan and beat well. Add the egg yolks, one at a time, and beat well. Cook, stirring, over low heat until thick. Remove from heat. Add vanilla and salt. Cool.

Beat the egg whites until stiff and fold into the chocolate mixture.

Pour the chocolate mixture on top of the crumbs. Sprinkle with the chopped nuts. Spread ice cream evenly in the dish. Top with reserved crumbs. Freeze 4 hours or overnight.

SERVES 4

Alta Chocolate Soufflé with Vanilla Sauce

This soufflé works well up to 7,000 feet.

3 squares (1 ounce each) chocolate, melted
½ cup granulated sugar
4 eggs, separated
2 tablespoons butter
2 teaspoons all-purpose flour
pinch of salt
1 cup scalded milk
1 teaspoon vanilla extract
Vanilla Sauce (recipe follows)

Preheat the oven to 350 ° F.

Place the melted chocolate in a large bowl. Add ¼ cup of the sugar and mix well.

In a small bowl, beat together the egg yolks and remaining ¼ cup sugar until thick and lemon colored. Set aside.

Melt the butter in a double boiler. Add the flour and salt. Add the scalded milk to the butter and flour in the double boiler. Cook and stir over hot water until the mixture begins to thicken. Add the egg yolks to the milk mixture. Cook, stirring, until the mixture is thickened and pulls away from the sides of the pan.

Add this custard to the melted chocolate mixture and blend well. Add the vanilla and cover the mixture with waxed paper to prevent a crust from forming. Set aside.

When the chocolate mixture has cooled, add the egg whites, stiffly beaten, to the mixture and fold in gently.

Pour the mixture into buttered soufflé dishes. Set in a pan containing ½ inch of hot water. Bake for 40 minutes.

Serve immediately with Vanilla Sauce.

VANILLA SAUCE:
1 cup heavy cream
1 tablespoon granulated sugar
1 teaspoon vanilla extract
1 cup vanilla ice cream, softened

Whip the cream with the sugar and vanilla until stiff. Fold the whipped cream into the ice cream. Refrigerate until ready to serve. Can be made 2 hours before serving.

SERVES 6 TO 8

Hot Chocolate Ring with Whipped Cream

6 tablespoons unsweetened cocoa powder
1 cup granulated sugar
1 cup all-purpose flour
1 teaspoon baking powder
¼ teaspoon salt
¾ cup milk
3 tablespoons vegetable oil
1 teaspoon vanilla extract
1 egg
heavy cream, whipped or ice cream

Preheat the oven to 350 ° F.

Combine the cocoa, sugar, flour, baking powder, and salt in a large bowl.

In another bowl, mix the milk, oil, vanilla, and egg and beat well. Pour the milk mixture into the dry ingredients and beat well.

Pour into a buttered 7-inch ring mold and bake for 25 minutes. Unmold and serve hot, with the center filled with whipped cream or ice cream.

MAKES 4 CUPS

Blackhawk Hot-Fudge Sauce

Sweetened cocoa powder may be substituted for unsweetened for a lighter, sweeter sauce.

1 cup butter
2 squares (1 ounce each) semisweet chocolate
1½ cups granulated sugar
½ cup unsweetened cocoa powder
1 cup heavy cream
2 teaspoons vanilla extract

Melt the butter and chocolate in a saucepan. Add the sugar, cocoa, and cream. Bring to a boil, then add the vanilla. Remove from the heat and blend well.

Refrigerate in a covered container and heat before using.

SERVES 6

Sauce for Fresh Fruit

1 cup sour cream
1 tablespoon granulated sugar or Vanilla Sugar (see page 00).
½ teaspoon vanilla extract

GARNISH:
brown sugar

Mix the sour cream, sugar, and vanilla in a small bowl.
Serve with fresh strawberries, peaches, or grapes in dessert dishes. Sprinkle brown sugar over the top.

SERVES 8

Apricot Crêpes

16 prepared Sweet Crêpes (see page 83)
8 ounces cream cheese, softened
¼ cup butter, softened
2 tablespoons granulated sugar
1 teaspoon vanilla extract
1 teaspoon grated lemon zest

APRICOT SAUCE:
1 jar (10 ounces) apricot preserves
⅓ cup orange juice
2 tablespoons butter
1 tablespoon lemon juice
1½ teaspoons grated lemon zest
2 tablespoons Grand Marnier

Preheat the oven to 350 ° F.
Cream the cream cheese, butter, sugar, vanilla, and lemon zest together in a medium bowl.
Spread 1 to 2 tablespoonsful on each crêpe and fold into quarters.
Place the crêpes in a buttered 9x13-inch baking pan and heat in the oven for 10 minutes.
Meanwhile, combine all the sauce ingredients, except the Grand Marnier, in a saucepan and simmer for 5 minutes, watching carefully so that sauce does not burn. Add the Grand Marnier and stir to blend.
Spoon the hot sauce over the crêpes and serve.

Appendix

Contributors

These groups were responsible for testing recipes from all sections of America's Best.

CHARLOTTE KALINNA,
Coordinator of Snowmass Testers
EMMY LOU BRANDT
MARY ANN FERRUGGIA
NANCY GENSCH
RITA HUNTER
LISA MITCHELL
NUN MOSIMAN
LINDA SIMPKINS
JOANNE STUMPF
DIANE THOMPSON

JEANNE MYERS,
Coordinator of Aspen Testers
JANNY ANDERSON
MARDI EDEL
SUSAN HARVEY
CHERIE JORDAN
MARTHA MADSEN
HELGA MARQUSEE
WILMA MARTENS
CONNIE NOSTDAHL
MERBIE PAYNE
BRUNHILDA SCHLOFFER
ANN SCHREIBER
SARA THOMSON
ANNE THUILLIER
SUE WINDEMULLER

BETTY PHILLIPS,
Section Chairman
IRENE BRYANT
FELICE T. COTTLE
COLLEEN DARNALL
ELIZABETH ELLIS
JACKIE MEISSNER
SANDY MOELLER
MARILYN WILSON
NANCY WOLFE

Many thanks for the recipes contributed by the following restaurants, food shops, cooking schools, and chefs.

THE ALTA LODGE,
PAUL RADDON
SAM ARNOLD,
FOOD EXPERT
THE BAKER'S RACK,
D. L. CARVER
BERNARD'S,
BERNARD JACOUPY,
ROLAND GIBERT
BESANT'S,
DOUG BESANT
MARIAN BURROS,
NEW YORK TIMES
BUTCHER SHOP
RESTAURANT,
W. GARDNER
CAFÉ KANDAHAR,
STEVE KNOWLTON
CASINO DE MONTREUX,
MONTREUX,
SWITZERLAND
CHEZ VILLARET
THE CLASSIC COOK,
GEORGE M. SMITH

COLUMBINE CAFÉ
FARLEY'S RESTAURANT
FIRST SEASON
RESTAURANT,
CHEF MICHAEL MAUS
FOOD FOR THOUGHT,
ANN KENNEDY
FRENCH ROOM,
ROLAND PASSOT
GOURMET UNLIMITED,
FRANK SZYMANSKI
GWYN'S HIGH ALPINE
RESTAURANT,
GWYN GORDON
H. BRINKER
THE HOMESTEADER,
PATTI KEENAN
HOTEL EDELWEISS,
DADOU MAYER
INSIGHT,
GREG GRASS
JULIE AND PETER'S
CREATIVE CATERING
KITCHEN KORNER,
CARLA WOOD
KROWN KITCHENS,
LYNN C. CONNOR
LA VARENNE COOKING
SCHOOL, PARIS
LITTLE PEPINA'S,
RICK BLICK
NONESUCH COOKING
SCHOOL,
RHODA GORDON,
JEANINE MARTINEZ
MOLLY NG,
COOKING INSTRUCTOR
OLD WARSAW,
JEAN LAFFONT
THE PICNIC GOURMET,
JOAN HEMINGWAY,
CONNIE MARICICH
THE PLUM TREE CAFÉ,
KEVIN DOWLING
POWDER HOUSE DINING
AND SPIRITS,
LAWRENCE HOPKINS
RED FOX SKI LODGE,
PENNY WASHBURN
SNOWMASS CLUB,
HUBERT SEBANC
SOUPY SALES
TAILLEVENT,
PARIS
THE TYROLEAN INN,
PEPI LANGEGGER
WARM SPRINGS
RESTAURANT,
BERT BENDER

Many thanks for the recipes contributed by the following individuals from all fifty states.

BETH ABERNATHIE
ALLISON ADAMS
B. J. ADAMS
CAROL ADELMAN
PAUL AHLQUIST
SUSAN AHLQUIST
BONNIE AHRENT
INEZ AIMEE
EILEEN ALBERT
REBA ALLBRITTON
CATHY ALLEN
KATHY ALLEN

LUCILE ALLEN
MARY WALTERS ALLEN
ROZ ALTENBERG
MORTON AMSTER
BETH ANCTIL
ARLOWENE ANDERSON
DIANE ANDERSON
JANNY ANDERSON
DR. ROBIN ANDERSON
RUTH ANN ANDERSON
LORRAINE ARKIND
DOLLIE C. ARMSTRONG
HELEN ARTZ
PETER ASHLEY
CINDY ASPLUND
BARBARA BAAN
MARION SCOTT BAIN
KIM BALLOU
ALICE BARNARD
PATTY BARNARD
ANITA BARNETT
FRED & BARBARA BARR
MOOSE BARROWS
JIM BARTELS
SUSAN BARTON
GENEAN BAUG
EDIE BAUGH
EMMY BAUM
DIXIE BAYDEN
RENE BEACH
JUDY BEATY
SUE BEAUREGARD
PICKIE BEGGS
EVELYN BEIDLEMAN
MARGARET BEKINS
MARY BELL
PATSY BENEDICT
JEANETTE BENOIT
MARY BENSON
JEAN BERNEY
TERRY BIDDINGER
ELIZABETH BIEBER
REGINA BIEDERMAN
DIANE BINTNER
PAULA BISCARD
CAROLE BLACKBURN
ELEANOR J. BLISS
BODIL BLOCH
MRS. JOHN BLUE
ANNIE BLUM
ESTHER BOAT
JILL BOAT
JANE M. BOLLANT
EVE BOLLARD
DONNA BOLOTIN
NONNIE BOLTON
NORMA BONE
JACK BOOKER
TED BOONSTRA
JUNE BOSWICK
ALICE BOSWORTH
BABA BOSWORTH
KAREN BOWEN
HEIDI BOWES
MARIE BOWES
JUDY BOYES
JULIE BOYKO
BARBARA BOYLES
YVONNE BOYLES
DANA BRACHT
LISLE BRADLEY
JUDITH BRADSHAW
RANADA BRAUN
SUSAN BRAWNER
BEVERLEE BRAZIL
BARBARA BRECKENRIDGE
DONNA BREDFELDT
MARSHA BRENDLINGER
SALLY BRIDSES
DOROTHY BRIMNER
JO BRINKERHOFF

HELEN BRISSON
PEGGY & CLINT BRODAY
ANGELA BROWNE
JUDY BRUBAKER
BONNIE BRUCKER
IRENE BRYANT
SHEILA BUGDANOWITZ
DEBBIE BUNCHMAN
JANIS BUNCHMAN
SHARON BUNNETT
SALLY BURBANK
LYNN BURFORD
CAROL BUSBY
MARILYN BUSH
CAROLE BUTCHER
FERN BUTCHER
ALLENE BUTTRILL
GORDON BUTZ
SHARYL BYERLY
SHIRLEY CAMENSON
CAROL J. CAMPBELL
MARY CAMPBELL
JOANN CANNON
JOANNE CARDONE
NANCY CAREY
PAT CAREY
NANCY CARIANI
BONNIE CARLAZZI
DEBBY CARLSON
DONNA J. CARLSON
NANCY CARLSON
STACY CARLSON
BONNIE CARLOZZI
JULIA CARNAHAN
BOBBIE CARSON
SANDRA CARSON
PAT CARTER
RACHEL CARTER
CORALIE CASTLE
SALLY CHAPMAN
THE HONORABLE DICK
CHENEY
JANE CHESLEY
VIRGINIA CHICO
DIANE CHOATE
MRS. SAMUEL
CHRISTENSEN
CONNIE CIANCIO
GINA CIULLA
ANITA CLARK
GERI CLARK
JACKIE CLARK
AGGIE CLARKE
SALLY CLAYES
PAT CLAYTON
SALLY CLAYTON
J. CLEMMER
SYLVIA COHEN
ANNE COLBURN
SALLY COLE
LORRAINE COLEMAN
HARRIET COOK
SHIRLEY COON
CHRISTIN COOPER
LINDA COOPER
ROBERTA COPLAND
LORRAINE CORYELL
PAT COTSWORTH
REBECCA COX
CIRO COZZOLINO
DONNA CRAIG
MEG CRAMER
LEE OMA CRAWFORD
MARVIN CRAWFORD
MARGO CROSBY
JEANNE CROSS
OTIS CROSS
CHER CUNNINGHAM
JERRY CUNNINGHAM
JIM CUPAROSO
SUE DANFORD

CONTRIBUTORS

NIKKI DANKER
PHYLLIS DANNER
FRIEDA DANSBERGER
PAT DARLEY
LADY DASHWOOD
SIR FRANCIS DASHWOOD
ELLEN DAUS
SALLY DAVIDSON
BRIGIT ANN DAVIS
JEAN DAVIS
LIBBY DAVIS
DOROTHEA DAVISON
KIT DAYTON
JAN DEBOER
MARILYN DEBOER
PAUL DEBOER
AUDREY ELLISON DEBOW
GUS DELAPP
MRS. JOHN DELAURO
IVANETTE DENNIS
ANNIE DENVER
LINDA DESMARIS
SHEILA DEVORE
MARIE DEWANE
BARBARA E. DEVRIES
CINDY DETTLEBACH
JUDY DIERS
CAROLYN DIFFENBAUGH
MARTHA ANN DOBBINS
GERALDINE DOMARECK
MARY DORRA
WILLIAM A. DOUGLAS
PATRICIA DOUGLASS
NANCY G. DOYLE
MAUREEN DOZE
ANN DRAKE
DEBBIE DUGGAN
JOAN R. DUNCAN
VIRGINIA DUNKLEE
SERGIA DUNLAP
JEANNE DUVAL
JEAN EASLEY
GLORY A. EBNER
MARDI EDEL
MARIA EGEMEYER
JERI EIGNER
MARY EISEMAN
MAXINE ELLIOTT
ELIZABETH ELLIS
BETH ELLS
ANN EMERY
MAHRI ERIKSSON
NANCY ERSKINE
BUNTY EVANS
HELEN EVANS
JANICE EVANS
DOLORES EYLER
PEGGY FANCIER
SHERRY FARNY
MARTHA FEAGIN
S. FEATHERMAN
DEBORAH FELDMAN
MO FENNELLY
BETH FERGUS
SHARON FERLIC
HELENE FERNANDEZ
MARY ANNE FERRUGGIA
BARBIE FIEST
CHARLENE FIJI
SHIRLEE FINNEY
MARY CAROLINE FINNOFF
DIANE FISHER
KAREN FISHER
MARILYN FLANAGAN
HAZEL FORD
HEATHER FOX
KATIE FOX
MARCIA FOX
SANDY FRAM
ROBERTA FRASER
DEE FRAZIER
JAYNE FREEMAN
ELEANOR FRIED
WENDY FRIED
FLORRIE FUNK
RENEE FUNK
DR. JACK GAISFORD
DIANE GALLAGHER
SARAH GALLAGHER

MARILYN GAMBLE
ELAINE GARCIA
W. GARDNER
NANCY GART
SALLY GART
SARA GARTON
MARTY GASCHE
JOE GEIER
NANCY GENSCH
HELEN GERBER
JANET GIBAS
LAVINIA GIBBS
ERIK GIESE
MARY GIESE
LINDA GILLES
PATSY GILLHAM
MARINA GILNER
SUSIE GOLDBERG
RITA GOMEZ
NANCY GOODING
VIVIAN GOODNOUGH
ALICE GOOSSEN
ANN GORDON
NATALIE GOSS
DONNA GOSSELIN
DIXIE GRABOS
LAURIE BURROWS GRAD
PETER GRAVES
ROBIN GRAVES
PAM GRAY
SAMMIE GRAY
MARY GRECO
PAUL GREEN
PEGGY GREENBERG
BOB GREENE
MARY ANN GREENE
HELEN B. GREENLEAF
VIRGINIA GRILLO
MARGO GROSS
DEANNA GROSSMAN
JODY GROVES
MRS. GERALD H. GRUBER
VAL GUALTIERI
DORIS GUENTHER
KAREN GULLEY
BARBARA GUMP
JEAN GUNN
PEGGY GUNNESS
ROSE MARIE GUNSAULS
DICK GUNTREN
JEANNE HABER
JANE HAILEY
DORIS HALEY
MR. & MRS. JOHN HALL
JACKIE HALLETT
TERRY HALLETT
SALLY HAMBRECHT
MURIEL K. HAMMER
MARJORIE R. HAMMOND
NANCY HANBY
BETTINA H. HANEMAN
JANEY HANLEY
DEBORAH GRANT HANNA
CHARISSA HANNIGAN
HELEN HANNIGAN
MARY S. HANSEN
FERN HARBAGE
LINDA HARDEE
ELAINE HARFST
GORDON HARFST
MRS. BUTCH HARPER
JAN HARRINGTON
RHONNDA HARTMAN
SUSAN W. HARVEY
JEFF HASTINGS
SUSAN HASTINGS
GRETCHEN B. HATCH
MARJORIE HAY
CAROLYN HAYES
GLENDA HEALD
JODY HECHT
KAREN HEIMEL
MARY JO HEINEY
JOYCE HELM
DR. ROBERT HENDERSON
WINCIE HENDRICKS
SALLY HENKEL
FRED HERBSTZUBER
BARBARA HERDMAN

MARGARET HESS
SUSAN HESTOG
JEANINE HETTINGA
ROZ HEWEY
WALLY HEWSON
JUDY HEYN
CATHERINE HINZE
MALLORY HIRNER
GERRY HITCHENS
CAROLYN HOCK
JEAN C. HODGKINS
MONICA HOFF
RUTH HOFF
DONALEE HOGSTROM
CHARLENE HOLES
ROSALEE HOLLAND
HOBY HOOKER
LARRY HOPKINS
JANE ANN HORNBERGER
NANCY HOREY
MICHELE HOVEY
ELIZABETH HUDNUTT
MICHELE HUGHES
ROBBIE HUGHES
NANCY HUNT
SHIRLEY HUNT
BARB HURLBUTT
DONNA IACONO
PEGGY IMBROGNO
BUNKIE INKRET
BARBARA ISAKSON
JOY JACKSON
KATHY JACOBS
DAVEDA JACOBSON
KATHLEEN JAKUBOWSKI
SUNNY JANKE
GLENN JANSS
JAYNE JENNINGS
DORA JENSEN
MARILYN JOHANNESMAN
MARGARET JOHNS
GWYN JOHNSON
EVELYN JOHNSON
ROLAND JOHNSON
DAVID JONES
IRENE JONES
LYNNSAY JONES
RUTH KAIDING
MARY KAISER
JUDY KALAN
MARY KALB
MORTON KALB
CHARLOTTE KALINNA
MILDRED KANE
KAREN KASHINSKI
HANK KASHIWA
JACQUELYN KASTER
KERRY KASTER
ELLIE KATZ
BLYTHE KAUFMANN
MAUREEN KEEFNER
BARBARA KEENAN
PAMELA SHEDDAN KEESE
PHYLLIS KEIM
SHIRLEY KELLER
JANIE KELLY
JUDY L. KELLY
LORNA KENDALL
NINA D. KENION
LESLIE KENNEDY
NESSA KENNEDY
PATTY KENT
RUTH KEVAN
BILLY KIDD
ALISON OWEN KIESEL
PHYLLIS KIMBERLIN
SUE KINTZELE
JOYCE KITTEL
HELEN KALIN
    KLANDERUD
FLORENCE KLEIN
DANNA KLEWIN
MRS. J. M. KLUNGLE
MARIE KNAPP
JAN KOCH
CHRISTINE KOSMALSKI
VERONICA KRAEGLER
EDITH L. KRALIK
CAROLE KRAMER

DR. HARRY KRETZLER, SR.
NANCY KUHL
NANCY KUMAR
NARENDER KUMAR
HOWARD KUSHNER
DEBBIE LACEY
IRENE LANDRUM
CINDY LARKIN
JONY LARROWE
MARJORIE LARSON
TAIMI LAUBA
MARY LYNN LAWLER
TEDDY LEATHERWOOD
MARIBETH LEGG
JACKIE LEIDHOLT
KATHLEEN LEIDHOLT
PUDDY LEIDHOLT
FRANK LEONARD
NANCY LEONARD
MARY LEONARDI
SUSAN K. LERRA
JACKIE LEWIN
ALICE LEWIS
PENNY LEWIS
TOM LICHTY
VAL LIECHTY
SHIRLEY LIKLY
PATTY LISTON
CAROLYN LITTLEFIELD
LEONA LITTLEFIELD
MARILYN LITTLEJOHN
WILFRED LLOYD
MARSHA LOCKHART
SALLY LOEVNER
FORTUNEE LORANT
SALLY LOWE
CONNIE LUNDBY
HEIDI LUHRS
JOEL LYON
KATHLEEN LYONS
PATTY MACK
MARTHA MADSEN
ANN T. MAGNUSON
NANCY MAGOON
MARY MAHRE
KITTY MAKLEY
RAE MALCOLM
BARBARA A. MALLETTE
NANCY MALMSTEN
RUTH FRANCES
    MANGELSDORF
LINDA MANLEY
SARAH MARCELLIANO
MARIA MARICICH
STELLA MARKER
JOAN MARKEY
CONSTANCE MARLA
BRENDA MARLOW
MARY MARTIN
SUSAN MARTIN
VICKI MARQUESEE-SCOTT
LINDA MARSH
SARA JANE MARVIN
JOAN MASAITIS
DOROTHY MASBURN
CHARLOTTE PEARSON
    MASHYNA
GINGER MASHYNA
SUE MASON
JEANNE MASTRANDREA
ALEEN MATHEWS
LIZ MATTESON
BARBARA MATTHES
COZETTE MATTHEWS
THERESA MATTISON
BEVERLY A. MAUL
KAY MAYNARD
JEAN MAYTAG
BOB MCALLEN
LAURIE MCBRIDE
BARBARA MCCOY
NANCY MCCREADY
GEORGIA MCDANIEL
MARGIE L. MCDONALD
JOHN B. MCGINTY, M.D.
KAY MCGRATH
LINDA MCGREGOR
KATHY MCINERNY
HELEN MCINTYRE

CONTRIBUTORS

JAN MCMILLAN
LYNNE MCMURTRY
SUNNY MEEKER
LIZ MEHRTERS
WENDY MEISTER
MARY MELLAND
MARJORIE MENDEZ
MARY MESSMER
ERLA MESSNER
EILEEN MEURER
MARY MEURER
JEANNE MYERS
HELEN MIAZGA
BARBARA MICHAEL
JACKIE MILLER
SUSIE MILLER
MRS. WILLIAM L. MILLER
CLAUDETTE MILLS
PEGGY MINK
MARILYN MOHATT
JEAN ANN MOHLER
MARIAN MOHR
LILY MOMENT
BETTY MOORE
KATHY MOORE
VIRGINIA MORRIS
MIMI MORTON
ELSIE MUEHLSTEIN
RUTH MULARZ
ANN MULFORD
JEAN MUMAW
KATHYE MURPHY
MIKE MURPHY
FRANCES NABER
BETSY NAUMER
JODY NAYLOR
JOANNE NAWROCKI
MIMI NELSON
RUTH KNIGHT NELSON
CAROLE NELSON
CHAR NELSON
MARTY NEMECEK
JOAN NEWLIN
KAREN NEWTON
DOROTHY NIELAND
SALLY NIES
MRS. EMERSON NIXON
MARY BETH NORRIS
MITZI NORTON
CHRISTINE NUSS
DOROTHEA NUTE
ONEITA NYDEGGER
CLAIRE-ANN OAKLEY
CHERIE OATES
CAROL OBRECHT
MRS. ROBERT O'CONNOR
ANN O'DONNELL
NADINE OFTEDAHL
PEG OLSON
PEG OSTROM
ALLENE OUTMAN
URSULA PACHUKI
JEAN PAFFROTH
MARISSE PAGE
DORIS PANSZA
MARILYN PARK
JANE PARK
ANNE-LISE PARKER
COLLEEN PARROTT
HEATHER PARROTT
JUDY PARROTT
KRISTEN PARROTT
PEGGY PARROTT
TRACI PARROTT
ELLEN PARSLEY
JUNE PAUL
PATTI PAUL
NATHALEE PAULSEN
CHERYL PAULTER
PAULINE PEDERSEN
CONNIE PEDERSON
BRONYA KESTER PEREIRA
FRANCI PERKINS
SHIRLEY PERKINS
THERESA PERKINS
BECKY PERRY
LUCY PETERSON

FRANCINE PETRUCCI
LOUISE & CLARK PHIPPEN
DEB PIKE
RUSTY POULTER
HELEN POWELL
GEORGE ANN PRATT
JASON PRESCOTT
HEIDI PREUSS
ELIZABETH PUCKETT
SUE PURDY
AGNETTA PUUDU
RUDD PYLES-KNUTZEN
JANE RADU
LOIS RAINER
INGEBORG RATCLIFF
RUTHIE RATHER
R. E. RENKERT
GYPSY RICHARDS
JEANETTE RIECK
GERT RINNEBERG
CHARLOTTE RISING
VIKKI RISSMANN
PAT RIVERA
DOROTHY ROBERTS
HELEN ROBINETTE
JUDY ROBINS
M. ROBINSON
CAROL ROBSHAW
ANN ROEMER
LOIS ROMANO
JANE ROMBERG
BARBARA M. ROSA
ALENE ROSEBROUGH
MAXINE ROSENFELD
ELIZABETH
   ROSTERMUNDT
DOROTHY ROTHMAN
ELEDRA ROULIER
GLORIA ROUSE
LINDA ROUSE
ANN ROWAN
PEGGY ROWLAND
MAGGIE RUDIGOZ
LOUISE RUMAED
DIANE RUMSEY
JEAN A. RUSSELL
JOHNALL RUSSELL
DONNA RUST
ROBERTA RUTLEDGE
DIANE ANDERSON
   RUTTER
DOROTHY RUXTON
KRIS RYALL
ANN RYDEN
DEB RYGG
JILL SABOL
PHYLLIS SAER
SOPHIE SAKSO
KATHLEEN SANTA MARIA
MIRIAM SCANLON
RITA SCANNELL
DIANN SCARAVILLI
MARY M. SCHAEFER
MURIEL MACK SCHAPIRO
LU ANN SCHELL
DIANE SCHLIEBE
BRUNHILDA
   SCHLOFFER
DEE ANN SCHMAUSSER
KAREN SCHMIDT
DEE SCHRANZ
ANN B. SCHREIBER
LYNN SCHRIVER
LORI SCHWARZ
ROSE SCORDINO
CATHY SCOTT
DORIS SCOTT
JUDY SCOTT
DR. WYLIE SCOTT
JULIA SECOR
JEANNIE SELTON
CHUCK SEMPLE
ADELE SENFT
PATTI SERNYAK
DIANA SHAFROTH
ANDREA SHANNON
ERIC SHANNON

BETTY SHAW
PAT SHAW
DENA SHPALL
NANCY SHUELL
DR. THOMAS
   SIDEBOTHAM, JR.
MICHELE SIFUENTES
CHARLOTTE SILK
DR. FRANKLIN SIM
BECKY SINNING
PENELOPE SITWELL
RERESBY SITWELL
NANCY SLATTER
ELSIE SLAY
KAREN SLUSS
CAROL SMITH
GEORGE M. SMITH
JEAN SMITH
JULIE SMITH
MARTHA SMITH
MARY BEA SMITH
DR. LAWRENCE SNOW
LAURA SNYDER
KATHY SOURBEER
VI SOUTHARD
ELNA SPANGLER
DOROTHY SPAULDING
POLLY SPAULDING
JACQUELINE SPIKEY
LYNN SPILLER
ARLENE SPINELLI
DEE ANN SPIVAK
RUTH STAMBAUGH
DR. ROBERT STANTON
JOY STAPLETON
DELLA STARK
BETSY HARNETT
   STARODOJ
GAY STEADMAN
MARY STEENHOEK
BETTY STEPHAN
CAROLYN STEPHENS
CAROL JUNE STEVENS
LENORE STODDART
FRANCES STONE
EMILKA Z. STOOPS
DR. JAMES STRAIT
JOAN STRANDE
EMILY
   STRAUSSBERGER
K. K. SULLIVAN
LOUISE SUMMERS
SUZIE SWALES
NANCY SWANSON
KRISTI SWEENEY
CHARLIE SWINEHART
MARIE TACHÉ
DR. EDWARD TAPPER
JOSEPHINE TAYLOR
JOYCE TAYLOR
DAN TEMPLETON
DORCAS TERRIEN
JEAN THAYER
IDA THEYS
JOYCE THOFSON
ROSEMARY THOMAS
SARA THOMSON
TONI THOMSON
ANNE THUILLIER
MAURICE THUILLIER
R.MILLS TITTLE
MARIAN TOLLES
LAURA TOMLINSON
JUDITH E. TOUBES
LOUISE TOWNSEND
LIBBY TREVOR
LUCILE TRUEBLOOD
DR. MARTIN TRIEB
MARCY TURK
ROXIE TURK
GAYE GULLOS
JULIE TURNER
SUE TURNBULL
DAVID TYNER
GRETL UHL
DOROTHY ULLOM
TERI UYEHARA

RUTH VALDECK
SANDIE VALENTINE
RUBY VANDENBUSCHE
LINDA VAN DOORNINCK
DR. LARRY VAN
   GENDEREN
MARY ELLEN VAN RIPER
JAN VAN TASSEL
LINDA VARGO
JOAN VERNER
GINNY VICTOR
LINDA VIGOR
LINDA VITTI
LORNA WADDINGTON
LORI WADSWORTH
KAY WAGONER
JANET WALKER
PAM WALL
BECKY WALLACE
NANCY WALTON
CRAIG WARD
JENNIFER WARD
MARY JO WARD
SUZY WARD
VALERIE WARNER
PENNY WASHBURN
DR. RANDY WATSON
MARY LOIS WATTS
DR. JAMES WEAVER
JUDY WEBB
KARYL WEBB
MARY WEBSTER
MRS. ROBERT WEEKS
DONNA WEIDMANN
JANET WEINER
DOROTHY WEISS
BUDDY WERNER
LORIS WERNER
SKEETER WERNER
LAURIE WESTON
SUE WHALLON
B. J. WHEELER
LESLIE WHITAKER
ALLASON WHITE
JULIE WHITE
SANDRA P. WHITE
RUTH WHITMORE
RUTH WHYTE
NANCY WICKES
NANCY WIEDEL
SVEN WIIK
SHARON WILKINSON
THOMAS WILKINSON
CAROL WILEY
ANN WILLIAMS
BARBARA WILLIAMS
LYNDA WILLIAMS
SUE WINDEMULLER
SUSAN WINGET
ALICE WINTER
GERY SUE WINTERS
SUSAN WITTE
JACKIE WOGAN
BETTY WOLF
JUDY WOLF
LISA WOLF
MARY WOLF
ROSIE WOLFE
ELIZABETH D.
   WOOLSEY
MARY WOOTEN
LORENE WORKMAN
GORDON L. WREN
WELCH WRIGHT
DEAN "SKINNY"
   WRITER
CAROLYN WUTHRICH
MOLLY WYKOFF
MIMI YEN
BARBARA YOUNG
BONNIE YOUNG
JUDY ZANIN
ALI ZINN
GRANDMOTHER ZINN
CELIA ZISFEIN
REED ZUEHLKE
CAROL ZUNDEL

Index

A

al dente, about, 188
Almond-Apple Crunch, 271
Almond Brie, 24
Almond Macaroons, 279
Alta Chocolate Soufflé with Vanilla Sauce, 302
Amana Pork Chop Casserole, 123
Amaretto Chiffon Cheesecake, 289
Amaretto Soufflé, Frozen, 300
Anchovies, Spaghetti alla Puttanesca, 188
anchovies, Springfield Dip, 30
Anchovy Pâté, Quick Picnic, 260
Anchovy Puffs, 32
Antipasto Salad, 258
Appetizers
  anchovy Pâté, Quick Picnic, 260
  anchovy Puffs, 32
  Anchovy, Springfield Dip, 30
  Avocado Mold with Caviar, 29
  Bacon-Wrapped Scallops, 25
  beef-filled pastries, Atlantic City Puffs, 21
  Brie, Almond, 24
  Caviar-Stuffed New Potatoes, 17
  cheese and onion in phyllo pastry, French Onion Tart, 32
  Chicken Liver Mousseline with Apples, 27
  Chicken Wings, Sesame, 26
  Chili Dip, Oklahoma, 21
  Crab Bites, Kanapali, 26
  cream cheese with vegetables, Confetti Dip, 31
  Egg Rolls, San Francisco, 18
  Eggs, Ham Mousse Stuffed, 28
  Garlic Sticks, 231
  meat-filled pastries, Pork Dim Sum, 18
  Mexican Layered Dip, 23

Mushrooms, Gorgonzola-Stuffed, 27
Mussels, Cheesy, with Herbs, 16
Mussels, chilled, with spinach and basil sauce, Verde, 17
Pecans, Candied, 33
Pepperoni Puff, 24
Pita Toasts, 248
Poppy Seed Bacon Bread, 23
pork in gyoza skins, Pot Stickers, 20
Salsa Dip, Fresh, 31
Shrimp and Avocado with Carnival Sauce, 15
shrimp and cream cheese, Summer Spread, 30
shrimp and scallop, Seattle Seafood Melange, 16
Snow Peas, Filled, 28
Tortillas, Cheese-Filled, 28
Vegetables, Marinated, 257
wontons filled with crab and cheese, Crab Rangoon, 25
Wontons filled with Pork and Shrimp, 22
Apple(s)
  Cake, Mount Rainier, 266
  Cookies, Fresh, 282
  with Cranberries, Bourbon, 218
  Crumb Pie, 273
  Crunch, Almond-, 271
  Pie, White Pass, 273
  Potato Salad, Dilled, 99
  Rye Bread, 228
  Sausage Ring, 81
  Tart, Upside-Down, Tarte Tatin, 270
Apricot Carrots, 204
Apricot Crêpes, 304
Apricot Shrimp, Stir-Fry, 165
Artichoke-Rice Salad, 100
Artichoke and Spinach à la Crème, 201
Asiago cheese, about, 127
Asparagus and Ham Crepes, 82
Asparagus with Hazelnut-Butter Sauce, 201
Atlantic City Puffs, 21
Avocado with Carnival Sauce, Shrimp and, 15

Avocado, Green Chile Aspic with, 102
Avocado Mold with Caviar, 29
Avocado Soup, 44

B

Bacon-Wrapped Scallops, 25
Baked Pineapple, 218
Banana Lemon Tea Bread, 234
Barbecued Teriyaki Chicken, 262
Basic Chicken Sauté, 141
Basic Ribs, 124
Basil sauce, Pesto, 178
Basil Sauce, Tomato, 179
Beans, Green, with eggs and parsley, Polonaise, 202
Beans, Lima, in casserole with carrots and onion, Fermière, 202
Beef
  Brisket, Oklahoma Barbecued, 115
  Corned, in Foil, 116
  Filet of, Stuffed with Spinach, 264
  ground, in casserole with beans, One-Pot Dinner, 115
  ground, in casserole, Zucchini Italiano, 116
  Rib-Eye Sandwiches, 252
  shredded, in tortillas, Chimichangas, 117
  Steak, Italian Style, 118
  stew, Goulash, Hungarian, 118
Beef Stew Provençal, 48
  Stock, 56
  and Tomato Sauté, 119
Beer Bread, 247
Bermuda Tart, 262
Biscuits, Buttermilk, Old-Fashioned, 242
Biscuits, Sour Cream, 241
Biscuits, Southern Cream, 241
Black Bean Soup, 52
Blackhawk Hot Fudge Sauce, 303
Blintzes, Cheese, 71
Blueberries in Lemon Mousse, 296
Boston Brown Bread, 245
Bouillabaisse, see Ciop-

pino, 173
Bourbon Apples with Cranberries, 218
Bread(s)
  Quick
    Banana Lemon Tea, 234
    Beer, 247
    Biscuits, Buttermilk, Old-Fashioned, 242
    Biscuits, Sour Cream, 241
    Biscuits, Southern Cream, 241
    Blintzes, Cheese, 71
    Brown, Boston, 245
    Coffee Cake, Brown Sugar, 239
    coffee cake, Cranberry Kuchen, 238
    corn, Mississippi Spoon, 247
    Corn, Rio Grande, 245
    Cranberry, 235
    Crêpe Batter, Savory, 83
    Crêpe Batter, Sweet, 83
    Crêpes, Asparagus and Ham, 82
    Danish Croissants with Lemon Cream Cheese Filling, 238
    French Toast, with Grand Marnier, Elegant, 80
    French Toast, Skiers, 79
    French Toast, Stuffed with cream cheese and pecans, 78
    Muffins, Bran, Six-Week, 243
    Muffins, Gingerbread, 242
    Muffins, Spice, 244
    Oatmeal, Honey, 232
    Pancake, baked, German Apple, 77
    Pancakes, Cottage Cheese, 77
    Pancakes, Potato, with Sour Cream and Lingonberries, 78
    pineapple, Maui, 234
    Pita Toasts, 248
    Popovers, Spectacular, 246
    Poppy Seed, 232
    Poppy Seed Bacon, 23
    pumpkin, Jack

INDEX

O'Lantern, 233
raisin-rye, Sun Valley Hobo, 236
Rusks, Royal, 246
Strawberry, 236
Tortillas, Flour, 248
Waffles, Whole-Wheat Oatmeal, 80
Yeast
  Calzones, Italian Sausage, 256
  Coffee Cake, Butter Pecan-Apple, 237
  Cracked-Wheat, 225
  French, Faux, 227
  Garlic Sticks, 231
  Orange Refrigerator Rolls, 240
  potato, Monkey, 229
  Rye, Apple, 228
  Sourdough, 226
  sourdough, I Never Want to See Another Zucchini, 230
  Sourdough Starter, 226
  Whole-Wheat Buns, Sausage-Stuffed, 254
Brie and Bacon Pasta, 198
Brisket, Oklahoma Barbecued, 115
Broccoli, Molded, 203
Broccoli, with pasta, Mostaccioli, 188
Broiled Fish with Dijon Sauce, 159
Brown Bread, Boston, 245
Brown Rice and Vegetable Stir-Fry, 222
Brown Sugar Coffee Cake, 239
Brownies, 280

C
Cabbage, in casserole with bacon, ham, and green pepper, Scalloped, 204
Sauerkraut, 210
Soup, Ham and, 51
Cakes
  Apple, Mount Rainier, 266
  Carrot, 292, 293
  chocolate, Christmas Log, 288
  Chocolate Fudge, 290
  Flourless Chocolate, 291
  Pistachio, Pewaukee, 286
  Pound, Poppy Seed, 265
  Walnut Torte, 286
Candied Pecans, 33
Canelloni with Chicken, Cheese, and Mushroom Filling, 195

Capellini with Chesapeake Oysters, 186
Caramel Bars, 281
Carrot(s)
  Apricot, 204
  Cake, 293
  Dilled, 205
  Soufflé, 205
Casseroles
  Artichoke and Spinach à la Crème, 201
  beef, ground, with beans, One-Pot Dinner, 115
  beef, ground, Zucchini Italiano, 116
  Cabbage, with bacon, ham and green pepper, Scalloped, 204
  Celery Root with Cheese and Bread Crumbs, 206
  Chicken and Artichoke, 152
  Chicken, Ham, and Shrimp, 153
  Corn and Chili Quiche, Crustless, 260
  Crab-Zucchini, 172
  Eggplant, with tomatoes and cheese, Romano, 207
  eggs with Canadian bacon and mushrooms, Fancy Egg Scramble, 67
  eggs with sausage, and cheese, Country Brunch, 71
  Lima Beans Fermière, 202
  Onions with cheese, Thanksgiving, 207
  Oysters, Chesapeake, with Capellini, 186
  Pasta Shells, Stuffed, 197
  potato and sausage, Dutch Potatoes, 84
  turkey with tomatoes and rice, Turkey Risotto, 156
  Zucchini Tomato Bake, 212
Caviar, Avocado Mold with, 29
Caviar-Stuffed New Potatoes, 17
Celery, Leek, and Potato Soup, 42
Celery Root with Cheese and Bread Crumbs, 206
Cheese
  Blintzes, 71
  Brie, Almond, 24
  feta with phyllo pastry, Cheese Burek, 75
  Filled Tortellini, 196

Filled Tortillas, 28
Fondue, Swiss, 76
Mold, with grapes and pecans, Snow Cap, 103
and spinach pie, Copper Mountain Quiche, 74
Soufflé in Tomatoes, 211
Cheesecake, Amaretto Chiffon, 289
Cheesecake Supreme, 292
Cheesy Chowder, 43
Cheesy Mussels with Herbs, 16
Cheesy Noodles and Chives, 189
Chicken
  and Artichoke Casserole, 152
  Barbecued Teriyaki, 262
  breasts, boned, in cheese sauce, Quick Saucy, 139
  breasts, boned, in cream sauce with tomato and avocado, Suprèmes de Volaille aux Tomates, 138
  breasts, boned and stuffed with chilies and cheese, Monterey, 137
  breasts with capers and Parmesan, Piccata, 138
  Breasts, Crab-Stuffed, 140
  Breasts, Sesame, 263
  in casserole with sausage and ham, Chicken Sausage Jambalaya, 150
  Cheese and Mushroom, filling for Canneloni, 195
  with Cognac, Herbed, 143
  Curried Baked, 144
  and Gravy, Southern Fried, 144
  Ham, and Shrimp Casserole, 153
  with Italian sausage in tomato sauce, alla Roma, 149
  Lemon, 142
  Liver Mousseline with Apples, 27
  Piccata, 138
  to poach, 152
  Primavera, Cold Pasta and, 183
  Roast with Mushrooms and Cream, 148
  Salad, Macadamia Nut and, 90

Salad, Peachtree Pecan and, 91
alla Roma, 149
Salad Pie, 90
Sausage Jambalaya, 150
Sauté, Basic, 141
Sherried, 142
Soup, Curried, 39
and Spinach Enchiladas, 151
Stock, 56
Stew, 47
Stir-Fry with Cashews in Chili Sauce, 146
Stir-Fry Orange, 147
Walnut Soup, 37
Wings, Sesame, 26
Chiles, about, 117
Chili, Cowboy, 50
Chili with Green Chilies, Spicy, 49
Chili powder, about, 174
Chilled Cucumber Soup, 45
Chimichangas, 117
Chinatown Shrimp, 167
Christmas Log, 288
Christmas Shortbreads, 278
Chocolate
  Brownies, 280
  cake, Christmas Log, 288
  Cake, Flourless, 291
  Fudge Cake, 290
  Mousse, 296
  Nut Chewies, 265
  Peanut Butter Balls, 278
  Pie, The Best Mud, 300
  Ring with Whipped Cream, 303
  Sauce, Blackhawk Hot Fudge, 303
  Soufflé with Vanilla Sauce, 302
  -Strawberry Omelet, 84
  Squares, Ice Cream and, 301
Cioppino (West Coast Bouillabaisse), 173
Clam Chowder, 60
Clam Sauce, quick, 181
Clam Sauce, Shrimp or, 181
Coal Creek Canyon Corn, 206
Coffee as stock, about, 129
Coffee Cake, Brown Sugar, 239
Coffee Cake, Butter Pecan-Apple, 237
Coffee Cake, Cranberry Kuchen, 238
Cold Fettucine with Shrimp, 182
Cold Pasta and Chicken

Primavera, 183
Cold Tomato Cobb, 212
Cole Slaw, with bell pepper, Santa Fe, 96
Condiments
  Butter, Pistachio, 162
  Horseradish Mousse, 114
  Tomato Conserve, 130
Confetti Brown Rice, 214
Confetti Dip, 31
Cookies and Bars
  Apple Cookies, Fresh, 282
  Brownies, 280
  Caramel Bars, 281
  Chocolate Nut Chewies, 265
  Chocolate Peanut Butter Balls, 278
  cornstarch cookies, Melting Moments, 279
  granola bars, Trail, 280
  granola cookies, Power Balls, 281
  Macaroons, Almond, 279
  Pineapple, 264
  Shortbread, Christmas, 278
Copper Mountain Quiche, 74
Corn Bread, Rio Grande, 245
Corn and Chili Quiche, Crustless, 260
Corn Chowder, 43
Corn, whole ears grilled, Coal Creek Canyon, 206
Corned Beef in Foil, 116
Cottage Cheese Pancakes, 77
Country Brunch, 71
Cowboy Chili, 50
Crab
  Chowder, 62
  Rangoon, 25
  Soup, Cuttyhunk, 61
  -Stuffed Chicken Breasts, 140
  Zucchini Casserole, 172
Crabmeat Salad, Creamy, 92
Cracked-Wheat Bread, 225
Cranberry
  Bread, 235
  Kuchen, 238
  Pudding, Minnesota, 297
  Sherbet, 275
  Torte, Fresh, 299
Creamy Crabmeat Salad, 92
Creamy Mustard Dressing, 106
Creamy Mustard Sauce, 112

Crème Fraîche, 108
Crêpe Batter, Savory, 83
Crêpe Batter, Sweet, 83
Crêpes, Apricot, 304
Crêpes, Asparagus and Ham, 82
Crustless Corn and Chili Quiche, 260
Cucumber Bisque, Cold Shrimp and, 46
Cucumber Soup, Chilled, 45
Cucumber soup, Gazpacho Blanco, 45
Curried Baked Chicken, 144
Curried Chicken Soup, 39
Curried Figs, 66
Curried Shrimp and Rice in Pita, 255
Cuttyhunk Crab Soup, 61

D
Danish Croissants with Lemon-Cream Cheese Filling, 238
Deluxe Vegetarian Omelet, 68
Desserts and Sweets
  Almond-Apple Crunch, 271
  Almond Brie, 24
  Cheesecake, Amaretto Chiffon, 289
  Cheesecake Supreme, 292
  cakes, see Cakes
  chocolate, see Chocolate
  cookies, see Cookies and Bars
  Crêpes, Apricot, 304
  Flourless Chocolate Cake, 291
  fruit, see also Fruit(s)
  Fudge Sauce, Blackhawk Hot, 303
  Ice Cream and Chocolate Squares, 301
  Ice Cream, Lemon Drop, 275
  Ice Cream, Mocha Tortoni, 285
  Ice Cream, Pie, The Best Mud, 300
  meringue and fruit with whipped cream, Pavlova, 294
  Meringue Torte, Red Oak, 284
  Mousse
    Amaretto, Frozen Soufflé, 300
    Chocolate, 296
    frozen, Cranberry Torte, 299
    Lemon, Blueberries in, 296
  Omelet, Chocolate-

Strawberry, 84
Pecans, Candied, 33
pies, see Pies
Pudding
  Cranberry, Minnesota, 297
  Lemon Cake-Top, 298
  Rice, Shaker Heights, 85
  Rum, 295
  sour cream and vanilla, Swedish Cream, 295
Sauce for Fresh Fruit, 304
Sherbets
  Cranberry, 275
  Grapefruit, 276
  Pineapple, 276
  Strawberry, Fresh, 277
Soufflé, Chocolate, Alta, with Vanilla Sauce, 302
Soufflé, orange, Harvey Wallbanger, 86
Strawberry Shortcake, Star-Spangled, 272
Dilled Apple Potato Salad, 99
Dilled Carrots, 205
Duck with Raspberry Sauce, 155
Dutch Potatoes, 84

E
Easy Puff Pastry, 73
Egg(s)
  casserole with Canadian bacon and mushrooms, Fancy Egg Scramble, 67
  casserole with picante sauce and cheese, Yampa Valley Mexican Eggs, 68
  casserole with sausage, peppers, and cheese, Country Brunch, 71
  Cream Sauce for Vegetables, 219
  Ham Mousse Stuffed, 28
  Omelet
    Chocolate-Strawberry, 84
    fillings for, 68
    with Italian sausage and potatoes, Italian Sausage Frittata, 70
    Vegetarian Deluxe, 68
  in puff pastry with ham, spinach, and cheese, Tourte Milanaise, 72
  scrambled with peppers, onion, bacon,

and tomatoes, Ranch Eggs, 69
Soufflé
  Carrot, 205
  Cheese, in Tomatoes, 211
  Chocolate with Vanilla Sauce, 302
  Mushroom, 208
  orange, Harvey Wallbanger, 86
  alla Spaghetti, 190
Eggplant Romano, 207
Egg Rolls, San Francisco, 18
Elegant French Toast, 80
Elk
  medaillons in red wine and brandy with mushrooms and hazelnuts, Silver Bow, 133
  Roasted, with Lingonberry Sauce, 132
Enchiladas, Chicken and Spinach, 151

F
Fancy Egg Scramble, 67
Fargo Pheasant Stew, 154
Faux French Bread, 227
Fennel, about, 216
Fettuccine à la Crème, 192
Fettuccine with Gorgonzola, 191
Fettuccine Florentine, 189
Figs, Curried, 66
Filet of Beef Stuffed with Spinach, 264
Filled Snow Peas, 28
Fillet of Fish Florentine, 159
Fillings for omelets, 68
Fish, about buying, 173
Fish, about cooking, 159
Fish Chowder, 60
Fish and Seafood
  anchovy, Spaghetti alla Puttanesca, 188
  Chowder, 60
  Cioppino (West Coast Boulliabaise), 173
  Clam Chowder, 60
  Clam Sauce, Shrimp or, 181
  Crab
    Bites, Kanapali, 26
    with cheese in wontons, Rangoon, 25
    Chowder, 62
    Salad, Creamy, 92
    Soup, Cuttyhunk, 61
    -Zucchini Casserole, 172
  Fillets, Broiled with Dijon Sauce, 159
  Fillets, Florentine, 159

Halibut Salad, 92
Lemon Sole with
  Beurre Blanc and
  Raspberries, 160
Marinade for Barbecued
  Fish, 170
Mussels
  Cheesy, with Herbs,
  16
  chilled, with spinach
  and basil sauce,
  Verde, 17
  in cream sauce, Sailor
  Style, 166
Oysters, Chesapeake,
  Capellini with, 186
Perch, fried, Lake Hu-
  ron, 163
Salmon
  Grilled, with Pistachio
  Butter, 162
  steaks with brown
  sugar, lemon, and
  butter sauce, Ko-
  diak-Style, 163
  Salad, 185
Scallop(s)
  Bacon-Wrapped, 25
  Mousse, 168
  and Parsley Sauce,
  Green Fettuccine
  with, 187
  Seafood au Gratin,
  169
  in tomato sauce, Prov-
  ençal, 164
Seafood Sausage with
  Shrimp Beurre Blanc
  Sauce, 170
Shrimp
  and Avocado, with
  Carnival Sauce, 15
  Beurre Blanc Sauce,
  171
  or Clam Sauce, 181
  and Clam Sauce, 178
  and cream cheese,
  Summer Spread, 30
  and Cucumber
  Bisque, Cold, 46
  Curried, and Rice in
  Pita, 255
  Fettuccine, Cold
  with, 182
  Gumbo, Plantation
  Point, 174
  in madeira sauce, Gulf
  Coast, 164
  and Mushrooms au
  Gratin, 166
  Salad, Oriental, 93
  and Scallop Salad, 89
  and scallops, Seattle
  Seafood Melange, 16
  Stir-Fry Apricot, 165
  stir-fried, Chinatown,
  167
  stock, Court Bouillon,
  185

Snapper Stuffed with
  Crab, 160
Swordfish, Lemon, 162
Tuna Sauce, Pasta
  with, 186
Whole Grilled, 161
Florentine dishes, see
  Spinach
Flour Tortillas, 248
Flourless Chocolate
  Cake, 291
Fondue, Swiss, 76
French Bread, Faux, 227
French Onion Tart, 32
French Toast
  baked with syrup,
  Skiers, 79
  with Grand Marnier,
  Elegant, 80
  Stuffed with cream
  cheese and pecans,
  78
Fresh Apple Cookies,
  282
Fresh Cranberry Torte,
  299
Fresh Peach Tart, 269
Fresh Salsa Dip, 31
Fresh Strawberry Sher-
  bet, 277
Fresh Tomato Sauce for
  Vegetables, 219
Frozen Amaretto Soufflé,
  300
Fruit Stuffed Pork Loin
  Roast, 128
Fruit(s)
  see also individual
  names
  Apples, baked, with
  Cranberries, Bour-
  bon, 218
  Figs, Curried, 66
  with meringue and
  whipped cream,
  Pavlova, 294
  Pineapple, Baked, 218
  Rhubarb, Scalloped,
  219
  Sangria Compote, 65
  Sauce for Fresh, 304
  Strawberries Romanoff,
  66
  Strawberries, Sherried,
  65
Fruit Soups
  Papaya, Iced, 44
  Strawberry, 46

G
Game
  Elk, medaillons in red
  wine and brandy
  with mushrooms and
  hazelnuts, Silver
  Bow, 133
  Elk, Roasted with Lin-
  gonberry Sauce, 132
  Pheasant in Green Pep-

percorn Sauce, 154
Pheasant Stew, Fargo,
  154
Venison, stew, Paprika,
  132
Garlic
  about peeling, 48
  Cheese Dressing, 106
  Sticks, 231
Gazpacho Blanco, 45
German Apple Pancake,
  77
Gingerbread Muffins, 242
Ginger root, fresh, about,
  21
Glass baking pans, about,
  228
Glorious Grits, 74
Golden Cream Dressing,
  106
Good Life Rice, 215
Gorgonzola-Stuffed
  Mushrooms, 27
Goulash, Hungarian, 118
granola bars, Trail, 280
granola cookies, Power
  Balls, 281
Grapefruit Sherbet, 276
Greek Spinach Salad, 95
Green Beans Polonaise,
  202
Green Chile Aspic with
  Avocado, 102
Green Fettuccine with
  Scallop and Parsley
  Sauce, 187
Green Onion-Lemon
  Vinaigrette, 107
Green Pea, Cashew, and
  Jicama Salad, 101
Green Peppercorn Sauce,
  Pheasant in, 154
Green Salad with Walnut
  Vinaigrette, 94
Grilled Salmon with Pis-
  tachio Butter, 162
Grits, with cheese and
  garlic, Glorious, 74
Gulf Coast Shrimp, 164
Gunnison River Barbecue
  Sauce, 111

H
Halibut Salad, 92
Ham
  and Cabbage Soup, 51
  Chicken, and Shrimp
  Casserole, 153
  Crêpes, Asparagus and,
  82
  and Herbs, Spaghetti
  with, 198
  Jellied, Bennington,
  104
  Loaf, 123
  Mousse-Stuffed Eggs,
  28
  and Mushroom Las-
  agne, 194

and Pasta Salad, 184
  -Stuffed Manicotti with
  Cheese Sauce, 196
Harvey Wallbanger Souf-
  flé, 86
Hawaiian Salad, 97
Hazelnut Butter Sauce,
  Asparagus with, 201
Hearty Hodgepodge, 50
Heavy cream, about, 294
Herbed chicken with Co-
  gnac, 143
Herbs, used in barbecue,
  111
Hobo Bread, Sun Valley,
  236
Honey Oatmeal Bread,
  232
Horseradish Mousse, 114
Hot Chocolate Ring with
  Whipped Cream,
  303
Hot Fudge Sauce, Black-
  hawk, 303
Hungarian Goulash, 118

I
I Never Want to See An-
  other Zucchini
  Bread, 230
Iced Papaya Soup, 44
Italian Rice, 214
Italian Sausage Calzones,
  256
Italian Sausage Frittata,
  70
Italian-Style Steak, 118
Italian Tomato Sauce,
  179

J
Jack O'Lantern Bread,
  233
Jackson Hole Veal Ca-
  price, 121
Jambalaya, Chicken Sau-
  sage, 150
Jellied Ham Bennington,
  104

K
Kanapali Crab Bites, 26
Kielbasa Soup, 48
Kodiak-Style Salmon, 163

L
Lake Huron Perch, 163
Lamb
  about, 130
  Leg of, Butterflied
  (broiled), 129
  leg of, roasted, with
  currant jelly and port
  wine glaze,
  Espresso, 129
  Leg of, with Tomato
  Conserve, 130
  Shanks, braised, with
  Fruit, 131

Stew, 53
Lamb Shanks with Fruit, 131
Lasagne, Ham and Mushroom, 194
Lasagne, Terrific, 193
Leg of Lamb with Tomato Conserve, 130
Leek, Celery, and Potato Soup, 42
Leeks, about, 50
Lemon
  Cake Top Pudding, 298
  Chicken, 142
  Drop Ice Cream, 275
  Swordfish, 162
  zest, about, 92
Lemon Sole with Beurre Blanc and Raspberries, 160
Lentil Soup, 54
Lima Beans Fermière, 202
Linguine Carbonara, 191
Linguine with Spring Vegetables, 190

M

Manicotti, Ham-Stuffed, with Cheese Sauce, 196
Marinade(s)
  for Barbecued Fish, 170
  for Meat, 113
  Marinara Sauce, 180
  Marinara Sauce with Meatballs and Sausage, 180
Marinated Vegetables, 257
Maui Pineapple Bread, 234
Mayonnaise, 108
Meat(s)
  Marinades for, 113
  pastries filled with, Vermont Pasties, 251
  see individual names
  slicing, 119
Medaillons, definition, 121
Mediterranean Eggplant, 220
Mediterranean Rice Salad, 257
Melting Moments, 279
Meringue, Pavlova, 294
Meringue Torte, Red Oak, 284
Mexican Dishes
  Chicken, Monterey, 137
  Chicken and Spinach Enchiladas, 151
  Chili with Green Chilies, 49
  Chimichangas, 117
  Corn and Chili Quiche, Crustless, 260

Tortillas, Flour, 248
Mexican Eggs, Yampa Valley, 68
Mexican Layered Dip, 23
Miniature Sausage Loaves, 81
Minnesota Cranberry Pudding, 297
Minnestoa Wild Rice Soup, 37
Mississippi Spoon Bread, 247
Mocha Tortoni, 285
Molded Broccoli, 203
Monkey Bread, 229
Monterey Chicken, 137
Mostaccioli e Broccoli, 188
Mount Rainier Apple Cake, 266
Muffins
  Bran, Six Week, 243
  Gingerbread, 242
  Spice, 244
Mulligatawny Soup, 40
Mushroom(s)
  about, 41
  and Chive Bisque, 40
  Gorgonzola-Stuffed, 27
  Soufflé, 208
  Soup, 41
  Stuffed Pork Rolls, 127
Mussels
  about, 17
  Cheesy with Herbs, 16
  Sailor Style, 166
  Verde, 17
Mustard
  Dressing, Creamy, 106
  Sauce, Creamy, 112
  Sauce, 112
  Sweet Hot, 33

N

Never Fail Pie Crust, 283
Noodles, Cheesy, and Chives, 189
Nutmeg, about, 104

O

Oils, vegetable, about, 15
Oklahoma Barbecued Brisket, 115
Oklahoma Chili Dip, 21
Old Fashioned Buttermilk Biscuits, 242
Old Fashioned Potato Salad, 98
Olive oil, about, 70
Omelet
  Chocolate-Strawberry, 84
  Deluxe Vegetarian, 68
  fillings for, 68
One-Pot Dinner, 115
Onion(s)
  pie, Bermuda Tart, 262
  in casserole with

cheese, Thanksgiving, 207
  Sweet and Sour, 208
  tart, French, 32
Orange-Ginger Dressing for Fresh Fruit, 105
Orange Refrigerator Rolls, 240
Orange Soufflé, Harvey Wallbanger, 86
Oriental Shrimp Salad, 93
Oysters, Capellini with, 186

P

Palm Springs Salad Dressing, 105
Pancakes
  baked, German Apple, 77
  Cottage Cheese, 77
  Potato, with Sour Cream and Lingonberries, 78
Panhandle Pork Roast, 126
Papaya Soup, Iced, 44
Pasta
  about, 177
  Canelloni with Chicken, Cheese, and Mushroom Filling, 195
  Capellini in casserole with Chesapeake Oysters, 186
  and Chicken Primavera, Cold, 183
  curly, Antipasto Salad, 258
  Egg, 177
  Fettuccine
    à la Crème, 192
    Green, with Scallop and Parsley Sauce, 187
    with ham, peas, and new potatoes, Summer Pasta with Pesto, 188
    with Shrimp, Cold, 182
    with spinach, Florentine, 189
    with spinach and cheese, Gorgonzola, 191
  Lasagne, Ham and Mushroom, 194
  Lasagne, Terrific, 193
  leftover, Eggs alla Spaghetti, 190
  Linguine
    Brie and Bacon, 198
    with eggs and cheese, Carbonara, 191
    with Spring Vegetables, 190

Manicotti, Ham-Stuffed, with Cheese Sauce, 196
Mostaccioli e Broccoli, 188
Noodles, Cheesy, and Chives, 189
Salad, Ham and, 184
Salad, Pot-Luck, 182
Shells, Stuffed with ground beef and Italian sausage in casserole, 197
Spaghetti with anchovy sauce, alla Puttanesca, 188
Spaghetti with Ham and Herbs, 198
Spinach, 177
Tortellini, Cheese-Filled, 196
with Tuna Sauce, 186
Pasta, Sauces for
  anchovy, Puttanesca, 188
  basil and cheese, Pesto, 178
  Cheese, for Ham-Stuffed Manicotti, 196
  Clam, 181
  cream, Fettuccine à la Crème, 192
  Marinara, 180
  Marinara, with Meatballs and Sausage, 180
  Scallop and Parsley, 187
  Shrimp, 181
  Shrimp and Clam, 178
  Tomato-Basil, 179
  Tomato, Italian, 179
  Tuna, 186
Pasties, Vermont, 251
Pastry
  about, 251
  Anchovy Puffs, 32
  cheese and onion in phyllo, French Onion Tart, 32
  Danish Croissants with Lemon-Cream Cheese Filling, 238
  eggs, ham, and spinach in puff pastry shell, Tourte Milanaise, 72
  feta cheese with phyllo, Cheese Burek, 75
  meat-filled
    Atlantic City Puffs, 21
    Pepperoni Puff, 24
    Piroshki, 253
    Pork Dim Sum, 18
    Pot Stickers, 20
    Vermont Pasties, 251
    Wontons filled with Pork and Shrimp, 22
  Never Fail Pie Crust, 283

INDEX

Puff, Easy, 73
Sweet Short, 283
Pâté, anchovy, Quick Picnic, 260
Pavlova, 294
Peach Kuchen, 270
Peach Tart, Fresh, 269
Peachtree Pecan and Chicken Salad, 91
Peas in Cream, 209
Pecans, Candied, 33
Pepperoni Puff, 24
Perch, Lake Huron, 163
Pesto Sauce, 178
Pewaukee Pistachio Cake, 286
Pheasant in Green Peppercorn Sauce, 154
Pheasant Stew, Fargo, 154
Picnic Spinach Torte, 261
Pie Crust, Never Fail, 283
Pies
Apple Crumb, 273
Apple, Upside-Down, Tarte Tatin, 270
Apple, White Pass, 273
chocolate, The Best Mud, 300
pastry, Never Fail Pie Crust, 283
pastry, Sweet Short, 283
Peach Kuchen, 270
Peach Tart, Fresh, 269
Pumpkin Chiffon, 274
Rhubarb Meringue, 274
Pineapple
Baked, 218
Bread, Maui, 234
Cookies, 264
Sherbet, 276
Piroshki, 253
Pistachio Butter, Grilled Salmon with, 162
Pistachio Cake, Pewaukee, 286
Pita, Curried Shrimp and Rice in, 255
Pita Toasts, 248
Plantation Point Shrimp Gumbo, 174
Plum Sauce, 34
Popovers, Spectacular, 246
Poppy Seed Bread, 232
Poppy Seed Bacon Bread, 23
Poppy Seed Pound Cake, 265
Pork
chops, butterfly, Mushroom-Stuffed Rolls, 127
chops in casserole with potatoes, Amana Pork Chop Casserole, 123

chops in Orange Sauce, Quick, 124
Dim Sum, 18
in gyoza skins, Pot Stickers, 20
loin cutlets in sour cream and dill sauce, Schnitzel, 125
loin roast with apple and chili glaze, Panhandle Pork Roast, 126
Loin Roast, Fruit-Stuffed, 128
Ribs, Basic, 124
Schnitzel, 125
Potato(es)
and Bacon, 210
Bread, Monkey, 229
in casserole with sausage and cheese, Dutch Potatoes, 84
and Cream, 209
Leek, and Celery Soup, 42
New, Caviar-Stuffed, 17
Pancakes with Sour Cream and Lingonberries, 78
salad
about, 98
Dilled Apple, 99
Old-Fashioned, 98
Ranch, 98
Pot-Luck Salad, 182
Pot Stickers, 20
Poultry, see individual names
Power Balls, 281
Prairie City Barbecue Sauce, 111
Pudding
Cranberry, Minnesota, 297
Lemon Cake Top, 298
Rice, Shaker Heights, 85
Rum, 295
sour cream and vanilla, Swedish Cream, 295
Puff Pastry, about, 72
Puff Pastry, Easy, 73
Pumpkin Bread, Jack O'Lantern, 233
Pumpkin Chiffon Pie, 274

Q

Quiche, cheese and spinach, Copper Mountain, 74
Quiches, see also Pies
Quick Breads, see Breads
Quick Picnic Pâté, 260
Quick Pork Chops in Orange Sauce, 124
Quick Saucy Chicken, 139

R

Ranch Eggs, 69
Ranch Potato Salad, 98
Raspberry(ies)
with Lemon Sole and Beurre Blanc, 160
Sauce, Duck with, 155
Vinaigrette, 107
Vinegar, 155
Red Oak Meringue Torte, 284
Rhubarb Meringue Pie, 274
Rhubarb, Scalloped, 219
Rib Eye Sandwiches, 252
Rice
about, 150
Brown, in casserole, Confetti, 214
brown, with nuts and lentils, Good Life, 215
Brown, and Vegetable Stir-Fry, 222
Italian, 214
Mold, 139
Pudding, Shaker Heights, 85
Salad, Artichoke, 100
Salad Mediterranean, 257
Wild, Pilaf, 213
Wild, Soup, 37
Rio Grande Corn Bread, 245
Roast Chicken with Mushrooms and Cream, 148
Royal Rusks, 246
Rum Glaze, Yams with, 217
Rum Pudding, 295

S

Saffron, about, 47
Salad Dressings, see Salads, dressings for
Salads
Antipasto, 258
Artichoke-Rice, 100
Broccoli, Molded, 203
bulgur, Tabouli, 259
cabbage, Santa Fe Cole Slaw, 96
Cheese, nut and fruit Mold, Snow Cap, 103
Chicken, Peachtree Pecan and, 91
Chicken Salad Pie, 90
Crabmeat, Creamy, 92
Green Pea, Cashew, and Jicama, 101
green, with snow peas, peanuts, and sesame seeds, Hawaiian, 97
Green, with Walnut vinaigrette, 94

Halibut, 92
Jellied Ham Bennington, 104
Ham and Pasta, 184
Macadamia Nut and Chicken, 90
Pasta and Chicken Primavera, Cold, 183
pasta, Pot-Luck, 182
pasta, Salmon, 185
Potato
with beef stock and green onion, Ranch Potato Salad, 98
with green onions and capers, Old-Fashioned, 98
Dilled Apple, 99
Shrimp
Cold Fettuccine with, 182
Oriental, 93
and Scallop, 89
Spinach with Chutney Dressing, 94
Spinach, Greek, 95
Rice, Mediterranean, 257
Tomato(es)
aspic, Green Chile Aspic with Avocado, 102
Cobb, Cold, 212
marinated, Diablo, 101
Vegetables, Marinated, 257
Zucchini Slaw, 96
Salads, dressings for
Chutney, 94
cream, for fruit, Golden Cream Dressing, 106
Crème Fraîche, 108
Garlic-Cheese, 106
Honey, 103
Mayonnaise, 108
Mustard, Creamy, 106
Orange-Ginger, for Fresh Fruit, 105
Sesame Seed, 105
sour cream and fruit, Palm Springs, 105
Vinaigrette
Green Onion-Lemon, 107
Raspberry, 107
Tarragon-Mustard, 107
Walnut, 94
Salmon Salad, 185
Salsa Dip, Fresh, 31
Sandwich in the Round, 252
Sangria Compote, 65
San Francisco Egg Rolls, 18
Santa Fe Cole Slaw, 96

Sauces
  Barbecue, Gunnison River, 111
  Barbecue, Prairie City, 111
  basil and cheese, Pesto, 178
  Beurre Blanc, Lemon Sole with, 160
  Butter, Pistachio, Grilled Salmon with, 162
  Cheese, for Ham-Stuffed Manicotti, 196
  Clam, 181
  Crème Frâiche, 108
  Dijon for Broiled Fish, 159
  Egg Cream, for Vegetables, 219
  for Fresh Fruit, 304
  Green Peppercorn, Pheasant in, 154
  Hazelnut-Butter, for Asparagus, 201
  Hot Fudge, Blackhawk, 303
  Lingonberry, 133
  Mayonnaise, 108
  Mustard, 112
  Mustard, Creamy, 112
  Mustard, Sweet Hot, 33
  for Pasta, see Pasta, Sauces for
  Pesto, 178
  Salsa Dip, Fresh, 31
  Scallop and Parsley, 187
  Shrimp, 181
  Shrimp Beurre Blanc for Seafood Sausage, 171
  Shrimp and Clam, 178
  Sour Cream, for Fresh Fruit, 304
  sweet and sour, Plum, 34
  Tomato
    -Basil, 179
    Creamy, for Scallop Mousse, 168
    Italian, 179
    Marinara, 180
    Marinara Sauce with Meatballs and Sausage, 180
    for Vegetables, 219
  Vanilla, for Alta Chocolate Soufflé, 302
  Whiskey, for Chopped Steak, 112
Sauerkraut, 210
Sausage
  in casserole with chicken and ham, Chicken Sausage Jambalaya, 150
  in casserole, Picnic Spinach Torte, 261

in casserole with potatoes and cheese, Dutch Potatoes, 84
Italian
  Calzones, 256
  with chicken in tomato sauce, Chicken alla Roma, 149
  with potatoes and eggs, Italian Sausage Frittata, 70
  in soup, Zuppe Italiano, 54
  Kielbasa Soup, 48
  loaf, Apple Sausage Ring, 81
  Loaves, Miniature, 81
  Polish, in soup, Hearty Hodgepodge, 50
  Seafood, with Shrimp Beurre Blanc Sauce, 171
  Stuffed Whole-Wheat Buns, 254
Sauté, how to, 141
Sauternes, about, 26
Scallop(s)
  Bacon-Wrapped, 25
  Mousse, 168
  and Parsley Sauce, Green Fettuccine with, 187
  Provençal, 164
  Salad, Shrimp and, 89
  Seafood au Gratin, 169
  and shrimp, Seattle Seafood Melange, 16
Scalloped Cabbage, 204
Scalloped Rhubarb, 219
Seafood au Gratin, 169
Seafood Sausage with Shrimp Beurre Blanc Sauce, 170
Seattle Seafood Melange, 16
Sesame Chicken Breasts, 263
Sesame Chicken Wings, 26
Sesame Seed Salad Dressing, 105
Shaker Heights Rice Pudding, 85
Sherbet
  Cranberry, 275
  Grapefruit, 276
  Pineapple, 276
  Strawberry, Fresh, 277
Sherried Chicken, 142
Sherried Strawberries, 65
Shred, definition, 18
Shrimp, see also Fish and Seafood
  and Avocado with Carnival Sauce, 15
  and Clam Sauce, 178
  or Clam Sauce, Creole, 181

Curried, and Rice in Pita, 255
  Gumbo, Plantation Point, 174
  Ham, and Chicken Casserole, 153
  and Mushrooms au Gratin, 166
  and Scallop Salad, 89
  Salad, Oriental, 93
  stir-fried, Chinatown, 167
Silver Bow Elk, 133
Six Week Bran Muffins, 243
Skiers French Toast, 79
Snapper Stuffed with Crab, 160
Snow Cap Cheese Mold, 103
Snow Peas, Filled, 28
Soufflés
  Carrot, 205
  Cheese, in Tomatoes, 211
  Chocolate, with Vanilla Sauce, 302
  Harvey Wallbanger, 86
  Mushroom, 208
Soups
  Avocado, 44
  beef, ham, and sausage, Hearty Hodgepodge, 50
  Beef Stock, 56
  Black Bean, 52
  Bouillabaisse, West Coast, Cioppino, 173
  Celery, Leek, and Potato, 42
  Cheesy Chowder, 43
  Chicken, Curried, 39
  Chicken Stock, 56
  Chicken Walnut, 37
  Chili, Cowboy, 50
  Chili with Green Chilies, Spicy, 49
  Clam Chowder, 60
  Corn Chowder, 43
  Crab Chowder, 62
  Crab, Cuttyhunk, 61
  Cucumber, Chilled, 45
  cucumber, Gazpacho Blanco, 45
  curried vegetable, Mulligatawny, 40
  Fish Chowder, 60
  fish stock, Court Bouillon, 185
  Ham and Cabbage, 51
  Lentil, 54
  Mushroom, 41
  Mushroom and Chive Bisque, 40
  Papaya, Iced, 44
  Pea, Split-Second, 38
  sausage, Kielbasa, 48

sausage, Zuppe Italiano, 54
  Shrimp and Cucumber Bisque, Cold, 46
  Shrimp Gumbo, Plantation Point, 174
  Sour and Hot, 58
  Strawberry, 46
  Tomato Bisque, 38
  Tomato, Spiced, 57
  Wild Rice, Minnesota, 37
  Wonton, 59
Sour and Hot Soup, 58
Sour Cream Biscuits, 241
Sourdough Bread, 226
Sourdough Starter, 226
Southern Cream Biscuits, 241
Southern Fried Chicken and Gravy, 144
Soy Sauce, about, 58
Spaghetti with Ham and Herbs, 198
Spaghetti alla Puttanesca, 188
Spectacular Popovers, 246
Spice Muffins, 244
Spiced Tomato Soup, 57
Spices, about, 8
Spicy Chili with Green Chilies, 49
Spinach
  in casserole with sausage, Picnic Torte, 261
  and cheese pie, Copper Mountain Quiche, 74
  and Artichoke, à la Crème, 201
  Florentine Fettucine, 189
  Florentine, Fillet of Fish, 159
  Pasta, 177
  Salad with Chutney Dressing, 94
  Salad, Greek, 95
Split-Second Pea Soup, 38
Spoon Bread, Mississippi, 247
Springfield Dip, 30
Squash, acorn, Steamboat Springs Stuffed, 221
Star-Spangled Strawberry Shortcake, 272
Steamboat Springs Stuffed Squash, 221
Stew
  Chicken, 47
  beef with paprika and sour cream, Hungarian Goulash, 118
  Beef Provençal, 48
  Lamb, 53
  Pheasant, Fargo, 154

INDEX

Veal Ragout, 120
Venison Paprika, 132
Stir-Fry Dishes
Apricot Shrimp, 165
Beef and Tomato Sauté, 119
Brown Rice and Vegetable, 222
Chicken with Cashews in Chili Sauce, 146
Chicken, Orange, 147
Shrimp, Chinatown, 167
Strawberry(ies)
Bread, 236
Romanoff, 66
Sherbet, Fresh, 277
Sherried, 65
Shortcake, Star-Spangled, 272
Soup, 46
Stuffed French Toast, 78
Stuffed Pasta Shells, 197
submarine Sandwich, in the Round, 252
Summer Pasta with Pesto, 188
Summer Spread, 30
Sun Valley Hobo Bread, 236
Suprême de Volaille aux Tomates, 138
Swedish Cream, 295
Sweet Hot Mustard, 33
Sweet Short Pastry, 283
Sweet and Sour Onions, 208
Swiss Fondue, 76

T

Tabouli, 259
Tarragon-Mustard Vinaigrette, 107
Tarragon Vinegar, 89
Tarte Tatin (Upside-Down Apple Tart), 270
Tarts, see Pies
Terrific Lasagne, 193
Thanksgiving Onions, 207
The Best Mud Pie, 300
Tomato(es)
about, 168

-Basil Sauce, 179
Bisque, 38
Cheese Soufflé in, 211
Cobb, Cold, 212
Conserve, 130
Diablo, 101
Provençal, 211
Sauce, Italian, 179
Sauce, Marinara, 180
Sauce, Marinara, with Meatballs and Sausage, 180
Sauce for Vegetables, Fresh, 219
Soup, Spiced, 57
Tortellini, Cheese Filled, 196
Tortes, see Cakes
Tortillas, Cheese Filled, 28
Tortillas, Flour, 248
Tourte Milanaise, 72
Trail Bars, 280
Tuna Sauce, Pasta with, 186
turkey in casserole with tomatoes and rice, Turkey Risotto, 156

V

Vanilla Sugar, 270
Veal
chops in cream sauce, Sheboygan, 120
Ragout, 120
Scallops with Cream, Calvados, and Apple, 122
scallops with mushrooms in brandy and sherry, Jackson Hole Veal Caprice, 121
Vegetable Dip, 231
Vegetable Pudding, 216
Vegetable Soups, see Soups
Vegetables, see also individual names
Artichoke and Spinach à la Crème, 201
Asparagus with Hazelnut Butter Sauce, 201
Beans, Green, with

eggs and parsley, Polonaise, 202
Beans, Lima, in casserole with carrots and onion, Fermière, 202
Broccoli, Molded, 203
Broccoli, Mostaccioli e, 188
Cabbage, in casserole with bacon, ham, and green pepper, Scalloped, 204
cabbage, Sauerkraut, 210
Carrot Soufflé, 205
Carrots, Apricot, 204
Carrots, Dilled, 205
Celery Root with Cheese and Bread Crumbs, 206
Corn, whole ears grilled, Coal Creek Canyon, 206
Eggplant, in casserole with cheese and tomato, Romano, 207
Eggplant, Mediterranean, 220
Marinated, 257
Mushroom Soufflé, 208
Onions, in casserole with cheese, Thanksgiving, 207
Onions, Sweet and Sour, 208
Peas in Cream, 209
Peas, Snow, Filled, 28
Potato(es)
and Bacon, 210
in casserole, and Cream, 209
Dutch, 84
New, Caviar-Stuffed, 17
Salads, see Salads
Spinach Salads, see Salads
Squash, acorn, Steamboat Springs Stuffed, 221
Tomato(es)
Cobb, Cold, 212
Cheese Soufflé in, 211

cherry, Provençal, 211
Turnip Pudding, White, 215
Yams with Rum Glaze, 217
Zucchini Tomato Bake 212
Venison Paprika, 132
Vermont Pasties, 251
Vinaigrettes, see Salads, dressings for
Vinegar, Raspberry, 155
Vinegar, Tarragon, 89

W

Waffles, Whole-Wheat Oatmeal, 80
Walnut Torte, 286
Water chestnuts, about, 146
Whiskey Sauce for Chopped Steak, 112
White Pass Apple Pie, 273
White Turnip Pudding, 215
Whole Grilled Fish, 161
Whole-Wheat Oatmeal Waffles, 80
Wild Rice Pilaf, 213
Wild Rice Soup, Minnesota, 37
Wontons filled with Pork and Shrimp, 22
Wonton Soup, 59

Y

Yampa Valley Mexican Eggs, 68
Yams with Rum Glaze, 217
Yeast, about, 226
Yeast Breads, see Breads

Z

Zest, about, 92
Zucchini
Bread, I Never Want to See Another, 230
Casserole, Crab-, 172
Italiano, 116
Slaw, 96
Tomato Bake, 212
Zuppe Italiano, 54

U/S SKI TEAM

Ski Team Cookbook
W. Hampden, Suite 401
glewood, Colorado
10

ceeds from the sale of
book will be returned
he U.S. Ski Team. Thank
for your support.

Date:_____

Please send_____copies of <u>America's Best</u> at $13.95 plus
$1.30 postage and handling per copy to:

_____
Name   please print

_____
Address

_____
City/State   Zip

Make checks payable to U.S. Ski Team Cookbook. Enclosed is my
check or money order for_____.

_____   _____
Mastercard #   exp. date   American Express #   exp. date

_____   _____
Visa #   exp. date   Signature

U/S TEAM

Ski Team Cookbook
W. Hampden, Suite 401
lewood, Colorado
0

ceeds from the sale of
book will be returned
e U.S. Ski Team. Thank
for your support.

Date:_____

Please send_____copies of <u>America's Best</u> at $13.95 plus
$1.30 postage and handling per copy to:

_____
Name   please print

_____
Address

_____
City/State   Zip

Make checks payable to U.S. Ski Team Cookbook. Enclosed is my
check or money order for_____.

_____   _____
Mastercard #   exp. date   American Express #   exp. date

_____   _____
Visa #   exp. date   Signature

U/S TEAM

Ski Team Cookbook
W. Hampden, Suite 401
lewood, Colorado
0

ceeds from the sale of
book will be returned
e U.S. Ski Team. Thank
for your support.

Date:_____

Please send_____copies of <u>America's Best</u> at $13.95 plus
$1.30 postage and handling per copy to:

_____
Name   please print

_____
Address

_____
City/State   Zip

Make checks payable to U.S. Ski Team Cookbook. Enclosed is my
check or money order for_____.

_____   _____
Mastercard #   exp. date   American Express #   exp. date

_____   _____
Visa #   exp. date   Signature